UNDERDOGS II: DOG DAYS

MAN'S BEST FRIEND IS HIS DOG - ESPECIALLY DURING LOCKDOWN

Gray Freeman
with Brendan Freedog

ISBN-13: 9798386853785
ISBN-10: 1477123456

Cover design by: Art Painter
Library of Congress Control Number: 2018675309
Printed in the United States of America

CONTENTS

ABOUT THE AUTHORS

Gray Freeman is a writer and traveller – and often a travel writer. He lives in south Manchester with his dog, where he sits and writes stuff and then takes his dog for a walk. He is a reviewer, part-time carer, dog-lover and no stranger to tea. Or cake. A long time ago, he focused on writing walking and cycling books. More recently, he has penned a short play about Alzheimer's, which was staged twice in Manchester. People cried, shook his hand and told him how much they could relate to it. It is currently being recorded as a radio play.

He is the author of Underdogs, the story of how he and his dog, Brendan – he came with his name – met and went travelling, bonded and became inseparable friends.

Me with The Boy. We go everywhere together; if I go, my dog goes.
You invite me, you get my dog. If you don't want my dog, you don't get me.
(That could explain why we rarely ever get invites.)

2023 FOREWORD

Man's best friend is his dog; never more so than during lockdown. As much as anything, this is a book about celebrating quality time with your dog, but set against a backdrop of a world that's falling apart. This is a personal journey through an extraordinary time, a surreal time. For me – and many of the people I've spoken to – it's difficult to believe the pandemic happened. We were all but under martial law; you weren't allowed out of your home, you couldn't see your relatives, you couldn't drive anywhere or go anywhere, you had to queue to get into a shop, food was rationed but was still running out. At first it was frightening and no one knew where it was going to end... then it became a way of life.

This account was written at the time, on a daily basis, as events occurred and news was reported, it doesn't necessarily reflect current opinions about Covid and the effectiveness (or ineffectiveness) of lockdowns. We now know a lot more about Covid than we did then and it doesn't make very comfortable reading.

This diary was originally *so much* longer. You'll be pleased to know I've edited it considerably, to give the flavour of the days rather than all the tedious ins and outs. How do you fill a diary when you aren't doing anything and aren't going anywhere? On some days nothing happened at all - and I've tried to convey that. This diary is largely about the minutiae of life, the small, inconsequential things that we usually take for granted – that suddenly become so important in a situation like this. Sometimes the mundane, everyday things were so welcome – you cling onto them, simply because they are trivial and normal in a world that seems so un-normal.

The only person I saw every day was my dog, Brendan. He was there for me; he gave me a routine and forced me out of the house. We spent every second of every day together, hence the title Dog Days, plus the phrase means "a period of inactivity, stagnation or decline" which these days certainly were. I had the title before I put pen to paper on Day One. When the diary was finished, I was very unsure about whether to release this book, so it hung around gathering dust, but I was convinced by others that it was an important record of the times, a snapshot of a period when nothing made sense. So, here it is.

This is Dog Days…

Website: Home | mysite (wixsite.com)
Facebook: https://www.facebook.com/BrendanFreedog
Email: the2underdogs@outlook.com

PROLOGUE

This is the stuff of science-fiction. But it happened. At the time of writing, it's *still* happening. The coronavirus, Covid-19, gripped the world and changed our lives irreparably.

[Dog days (noun)
A period of inactivity, stagnation or decline.]

INTRODUCTION

What's This Diary For?

I like travel writing. I like reading it and I like writing it. And I *love* travelling. Yet – along with the rest of the country, and indeed the world – I've found myself in a situation where I'm trapped at home; I can't travel and so there's nothing to write about.

With that in mind – and with life currently on hold – I decided to keep a lockdown diary. For one thing, I thought the discipline of writing a short piece every day would keep me alert, interested, questioning and would help to flex my creative muscles. Also, I'm hoping that as a project it will give me a focus and stop me feeling like a caged animal. Finally, I'm very aware that this is a moment in history and I want to record it from the perspective of an ordinary(ish) person. And his dog. His (less than) ordinary dog. This diary is not about the coronavirus per se, it is more concerned with lockdown and the effects of that experience on the everyday person and on our society; it is about how an average person copes... or perhaps doesn't cope... during bizarre enforced circumstances.

I realise these are potentially dark and depressing times; I want to use my diary to document my attempts to keep busy and to improve myself and to try and find positivity in every day. I hope to use the time wisely and learn and grow. I want to be healthier, eat healthier and get more exercise. I want to read some classic books and watch some classic films. I want to spend quality time with my dog, Brendan. I spend virtually every minute of every day with him anyway, but I want us to share lots of *quality* time. Hopefully, he'll agree. I want to cultivate a positive outlook and remain so busy and so full of new experiences that I won't be aware of the dark side of this corona world. That's my plan; those are my goals. I also want to remain safe, well and alive.

What is coronavirus?
What is Covid-19?

If you didn't live through this pandemic, then it might seem quite confusing. However, if you *did* live through this pandemic, you might *also* find it all very confusing... because I think most of us do. Did. Are doing.

A coronavirus is a type of virus, obviously. There are many different coronaviruses. The specific virus causing the current global pandemic was first identified in 2019. The World Health Organisation (WHO) gave it the official name of Coronavirus Disease 2019, abbreviated to the punchy and headline-friendly Covid-19.

Covid-19 causes a respiratory illness, symptoms of which include coughing, headaches, shortness of breath, aching muscles, fever or chills, sore throat, loss of taste, fatigue, nausea, vomiting and diarrhoea. The disease can be mild, moderate or can cause death. It is spread via droplets released when an infected person sneezes or coughs. It can also be picked up from contact.

Covid-19 first appeared in the Chinese city of Wuhan in December 2019. It has been claimed that it was accidentally – or purposefully – released from the Institute of Virology in the same city. However, initial investigations suggested that the most likely explanation was cross contamination of foodstuffs at a so-called "wet market", where live animals are slaughtered on request.

According to the charity, Animal Equality: "These markets... have been the source of documented disease outbreaks in the past, including SARS... Not only do these markets pose an immediate danger to humans, they are also intensely cruel to animals."

Whatever the origin, Covid-19 spread around the world as people commuted. As the death toll increased, countries went into a state of lockdown to try and halt the spread of the virus.

*What exactly is "lockdown"
and what does it entail?*

Because the disease spreads from person to person by proximity, the aim is to keep people apart as far as possible. All shops, except essential food shops, are closed. All social places, such as pubs, restaurants, cinemas, libraries, hairdressers, gyms, even outside sports are closed. Playgrounds are closed. In many cases, beaches and some parklands are closed. Virtually everything is closed.

People have been instructed not to go to work, unless

their profession falls under one of the permitted "key worker" roles, providing essential services, such as police, NHS workers, carers, staff in food shops and food factories. Schools have been closed, apart from small classes for the children of key workers. People are required to work from home wherever possible. Many staff have been "furloughed", which means they have been laid off but still receive – from the government – 80% of their wage.

Non-essential travel has been made illegal. You must stay indoors apart from driving to local shops and providing essential services, such as caring for a relative. The police are randomly stopping cars to check why they are on the road. Fines are being issued for improper and illegal use. Going to the beach for a walk, when the beach is a hundred miles away is not a valid excuse. Everyone has to stay local. As, when or indeed *if* you do go out, people are required to maintain a distance of two metres and everyone is encouraged to wash their hands frequently, using soap and water, for at least 20 seconds and to use hand sanitiser regularly.

Elderly people and anyone with any sort of illness or vulnerability, especially a breathing-related condition such as asthma, are advised to "shield" by staying indoors at all times and avoid all contact for their own safety.

Likewise, if you feel unwell and start to display Covid-like symptoms, you are required to self-isolate in your own home and not come into contact with anyone.

People are only advised to seek medical assistance if symptoms persist and increase. For many people, after a couple of weeks at home with 'flu-like symptoms, they begin to recover without the need for medical intervention.

My life before lockdown

I am... or rather I *was*... a writer by trade. Amongst other things I wrote theatre and live music reviews, but there are currently no performing arts, as bizarre as that might sound to anyone reading this in the future. Or the past.

I live in a rented flat with my dog, Brendan: he came with his name. I met him at an animal sanctuary, where my partner and I were volunteering. Although I didn't want a dog, we had an instant rapport and I agreed to foster him for one night, but while my back was turned, he moved his things in permanently.

Brendan looks exactly like a dog should look. People often stop us and ask what make he is. I have no idea; as a former street dog he's a mixture of different breeds. In some ways he's a rather disparate collection of dog components thrown together, seemingly at random. He's medium-sized, has long legs and the slim waist of a racing dog, but a terrier-like face, with a scruffy, straggly beard and sideburns. He looks like he should probably wear a flat cap and perhaps drive a tractor. (He does neither.) He looks very athletic, which he's not, though he can run like a greyhound, when he wants to.

He just doesn't want to. He much prefers a sit down and a nap. (You can read about his story and how we met in our book "Underdogs".)

I don't live with my partner, Nicky – it's complicated – she lives a mile away. It's twenty minutes or so for me to walk there alone or nearly an hour with Brendan, because of all the sniffing and weeing. For the sake of coronavirus, technically we live together but have two properties.

As a writer, I worked mainly from home, when I wasn't away travelling. I had a camper van and had previously travelled around the coast with Brendan, exploring and writing about our mis-adventures. In February 2020, my van failed its MOT. That wasn't unexpected; it *always* failed its MOT. This time though, the garage refused to do the necessary repairs. Although the van looked good on the outside and was immaculate inside, the underside was the problem, in that it was badly corroded... in fact it was only held together by the carpet. In addition, everything that made the van roadworthy was failing. The life of my van had come to an end. I was devastated. I love travelling, I love exploring new places whilst also having my home with me at all times. I loved that van.

One day, on the south coast, we had met a couple and their dog. The woman had looked around the van in awe and remarked: "This is great! What a nice place to live and work! You're living the dream!" This was one of the proudest moments of my life! Although I don't like the expression much, it really struck a chord with me; we really *were* living the dream. But now, sadly, the dream is over.

It's funny how things work out, as I was grieving the loss of my van, the announcements about the impending lockdown began, when all travel would be suspended. If I had been paying a fortune to tax and insure my van but was unable to use it due to restrictions, I would have been very frustrated. In a way it was a blessing.

The other large part of my life, and another reason why travelling is no longer an option, is the care of my father. He's 86 and has a number of serious health issues. He has lived alone since my mum died six years ago. Amongst his list of illnesses and health problems, Dad has Alzheimer's and vascular dementia, a heart condition, a pacemaker, asbestosis, prostate cancer and three aneurisms. (There are other conditions, including chronic earwax, but we need to stop somewhere.) Dad has carers going in four times a day, in order to keep him living semi-independently as long as possible.

I visit most days, in-between the care calls. I thought long and hard about not visiting him during lockdown, but I figured I'm a lot more sanitary and Covid-aware than a good many of his care workers, so I don't see what harm it can do, except possibly to increase my own exposure.

And that was pretty much my life immediately before

lockdown. News about the virus that had started in China began to creep into UK news reports. But it didn't feel like Big News. It felt like something happening a long way away...

The coronavirus cometh

...But it was getting steadily nearer. Other countries were declaring a state of national emergency and closing their borders; their hospitals were being over-run and they were going into lockdown.

The Coronavirus officially arrived in the UK at the end of January 2020, when two Chinese nationals staying in York became ill. At the end of February 2020, the first British death from Covid-19 occurred. From there, the situation spiralled out of control and there was talk of Britain going into lockdown. It seemed unlikely, it seemed unreal, but then it happened. It was official and an announcement was made. From midnight on 23rd March 2020, Britain would be in lockdown.

PART I
THE FIRST NATIONAL LOCKDOWN
Attempting To Make The Most Of Lockdown

Tuesday 24th March 2020.

At first, this morning seemed very ordinary. My alarm rang at the usual time, 7am. It was still dark. I share the bed with my dog, Brendan, and I usually have considerably less room on the mattress than he does. He remained asleep beside me; he didn't stir. He's categorically *not* an early riser.

I got up. I put the kettle on. This is what I do every single day. This is routine. So far everything felt normal. But it *wasn't* normal. Today was the first *official* day of lockdown; the first day that our lives changed – and our *world* changed – possibly forever.

Breaking News: It is estimated that globally over 400,000 people have already been infected with the Coronavirus.

9am. It's a bright, sunny morning. We set off along the street. It's far too nice for this first day of incarceration. Apart from shopping, exercise or "essential business", we are effectively under house arrest. This thrills Brendan, as he's no fan of shopping, exercise or "essential business" and he *loves* being under house arrest. Actually, getting him *out* of the house is quite an issue usually; he tries every delaying tactic he can think of. Once he's out though, he will usually tolerate a short

1

walk.

Today, as we amble along, nothing is in any way *physically* different, yet everything seems unreal. No one knows how things will unfold, because this has never happened before in (almost) living memory. Lockdown is a foreign country: they do things differently there.

Then, unexpectedly, I get my very first taste of how the world has suddenly changed. It seems bizarre, like something out of a film, but people approaching us cross the road and hurry along with their heads turned away. There's a very strange atmosphere of mistrust; anyone could be a Covid carrier, so everyone is the enemy.

We cut through the park, which is eerily quiet. The children's playground is empty; the gate is locked. There is no movement and no sound. Brendan looks around anxiously for any other dogs to run up to and ignore at close quarters, but there aren't any. There's no one. No dogs, no people. There is no traffic; there is no vehicle noise. There are no planes! There are *always* planes! It's really unsettling and alien. Everything feels very hostile, threatening, ominous.

Breaking News: ONLY THE BEGINNING. So far over 18,000 have died worldwide of the coronavirus, Covid-19.

Our walk is becoming quite disturbing; everywhere is disconcertingly still. The streets are deserted. The town feels abandoned. There are probably people in every house we pass: the curtains are open, there are cars on the drive, but there are very few signs of life.

We arrive at my dad's flat. I almost expect it to be empty, Dad to be missing, but with his half-drunk cup of tea still warm and perhaps a record turning endlessly on the turntable... the turntable that he doesn't have. I'm getting carried away with the film images. Dad *is* there, sitting in his chair, cup of tea in his hand and everything again seems normal. Dad likes to talk; he likes to be with people. He's a people person. I'm much more of a dog person. Brendan's more of a dog. Dad and Brendan don't always get on; they antagonise each other. I'm the peace-keeper. We always start with a chat, then I do whatever small jobs need doing. Today's crisis: Dad's lost his keys. He doesn't know where or when or how, but they've gone. I search the flat thoroughly, but can't find them, so I have to go and get some replacements cut from my key. By the time I set off for home I'm feeling tired and stressed. It's not Dad's fault, he's got Alzheimer's, but this is just an average day at the moment. His condition is getting steadily worse.

Breaking News: UK death toll thought to be in excess of 400 and rising.

At 2pm my landlord phones. He's speaking to all tenants to make sure they're alright and can get their own shopping. This crisis really does seem to have unleashed a tide of community spirit. People are knocking on the doors of elderly neighbours they have barely ever spoken to, volunteering assistance. I have already left a note for John next door – he's 86, like my dad – offering to pick up any supplies from the local shops.

Britain is pulling together to get through the crisis; it's like the Blitz, but without the nightly bombings.

Breaking News: The police have been repeatedly called to various gatherings, parties and barbeques, with crowds of people attending illegally.

Somehow, Day One of Lockdown draws to an end. It hasn't made very much difference to my daily routine; I walked the dog, I went to my dad's, I did some work from home, I drank a lot of tea. I have pretty much gone about my business as usual. As has Brendan; he had a nap on the sofa, he had a nap on the bed, he stretched out on the floor. Just an average day really. All across the nation, dogs are thrilled and slightly incredulous, because instead of being left alone for eight hours, their humans have stayed at home with them all day. But cats are contemptuous and narrow-eyed, because their day of lazy slumber has been interrupted by a houseful of people, who would normally be at work, school or bingo.

Like the shellshocked animals, I think most people can't really believe this is happening. It hasn't sunk in yet. If I had to pick one word to describe these times, it would probably be *surreal*. The world seems to have closed its doors, rolled down its shutters and effectively ground to a halt.

Wednesday 25th March 2020.

10am. It's really hot today, much too hot for March.

I'm uncomfortably hot as we walk along, so is Brendan; he scampers by my side with his tongue out. There's very little traffic. It would normally be quite busy at this time. A lone bus goes past; it's close to empty. The pavements are deserted, but the sun is shining on the immaculate suburban gardens. Everywhere seems so oddly quiet.

At the Big Field, there are a few lone dog walkers, but they ensure they keep a good distance from anyone else. Without exception, every single dog ignores their human calling them. This is quite reassuring, because I always feel Brendan is the most badly behaved dog on the block, but he isn't really; they all are. When they're chasing a squirrel, or playing, they are completely lost in the moment and become oblivious to someone shouting their name with increasing annoyance. Brendan just loves seeing these acts of insubordination. He's on cloud nine.

On the way home, we pass a woman wearing a face mask; she's walking down the middle of the road to further segregate herself from anyone. It looks very odd seeing someone with their face covered in this way. The government have repeatedly said that there is no point wearing a mask, as it will not offer any protection. (UPDATE: Yes, there will be many U-turns in the future!)

Breaking News: PRINCE CHARLES, 71, TESTS POSITIVE FOR COVID. The Prince is said to be displaying mild symptoms, but is otherwise in good health.

Nicky has reluctantly decided not to visit her

mum, Rosie, because the over-seventies are the most vulnerable and are supposed to be "shielding", which means not going out, if at all possible. Every morning, Nicky is cycling down to the bus station in the centre of town to collect a free newspaper, then delivering it to Rosie, because she loves the cryptic crosswords. Nicky also takes shopping every day and is talking to her mum through the window of her flat; it's on the second floor, so it's mainly shouting and waving. It isn't ideal, but it gives them both some comfort, but not enough. It is devastating for Nicky; she is very upset.

Breaking News: MOURNERS LIMITED. Funerals can go ahead, but attendance is severely restricted. Numbers vary according to local councils, but most are allowing around 10 people.

In the lead up to lockdown, people went out panic-buying staple items, stockpiling bottled water and tinned goods, as though preparing for the nuclear winter, so now there is a shortage of food. As a result, many items are being rationed; for example, each shopper is allowed a maximum of three packets of microwave rice. Many more items are completely out of stock. Bizarrely, there is a nationwide shortage of toilet paper. Also, flour, as in wholemeal or self-raising, hasn't been seen in a shop for some time. People have snapped it up in a mad frenzy, presumably with a view to making scones for afternoon tea. We might be facing our doom, but we're still British.

In the evening, Nicky does an online supermarket

order for us both. It takes her ages. It has been very difficult to get a delivery slot; the spaces are going as soon as they're released. (Only half the order arrives, because so many items are out of stock. Many of the fruit and vegetables are way past their best, or the sell-by date is midnight today. Other products have been substituted: Maris Pipers instead of Jersey Royals, which is acceptable; Granny Smiths instead of Royal Gala, also understandable, but a cucumber arrives instead of an aubergine. These two are not in any way interchangeable. You wouldn't have aubergine in salad and you wouldn't get away with slicing a cucumber on top of a moussaka. It makes me think some spotty teenager who has never come into contact with a fruit or vegetable before has been responsible for the picking.)

So to recap, we're basically under house arrest, there is a food shortage and what food *is* available is being rationed; it really feels like a country under martial law during wartime.

Just before 10pm, I take Brendan out for his night walk. It's cool and still outside. There are no cars at all, no pedestrians, just empty darkness and pools of orange light. There is no sound of any traffic in the distance and not even anyone walking their dog. That kind of silence in a town is really unusual. It's one of those occasions, like in a film, when you feel some catastrophe has occurred that you're not aware of and – although you don't realise yet – you're the last person left alive. It actually feels like a horror movie. As they say, in lockdown no one can hear you scream. Except your neighbours.

Thursday 26th March 2020.

In the night I wake up short of breath, my whole body is shaking and I feel sick. I've no idea where this came from or why. Maybe the bizarre surrealness of this global situation has got to me subconsciously. Because it *is* bizarre and it *is* surreal. A few weeks ago, you couldn't imagine that this could ever actually happen. I turn over and put my arm around Brendan, feeling his sumptuous and reassuring fur. He sighs and reclines his head to look at me. The wisdom in those eyes: they say "Come back during office hours, I'm off duty. You're on your own." He stands up and walks away. I hear him jump onto the sofa and settle down. I know what he's doing; he's forcing me to deal with my problems myself, with the safety net of knowing he's only a few strides and an appointment away. It's tough love, obviously, and he's very good at it. He knows it's the best thing for me; he's a genius.

I'm not purposefully thinking about the Covid situation very much, as we have no control over it. I'm getting on with my own day-to-day routine. Dog walk/Dad's/working from home. Again, I'm struck that the whole lockdown scenario is like a film set in a dystopian future, *Soylent Green* or *1984* perhaps. Or the premise of a TV series, like *Day of the Triffids* or *Survivors*. I've always been quite morbidly drawn to that kind of desolate future premise, because I like the chilling warning.

Perhaps my subconscious mind is dwelling on all the negatives that my conscious mind is avoiding. That sounds like me. I always cope in a crisis, it's what I do. I get on with things in a practical way and get the job done. It's generally when the crisis is over that I can't function.

Breaking News: 100 PLUS COVID DEATHS OVERNIGHT: UK death toll leaps to 578.

On the way to Dad's, we pass several buildings surrounded by scaffolding, but there's no work underway. There's no banging or hammering, no slightly off-tune radio belting out and no men in hard-hats whistling off-key or swearing. It's quite eerie. The world itself might still be turning, but the wheels of industry have stopped dead.

Dad's fine today. He suggests – as he so often does – that we go to the pub for lunch. I explain again that all the pubs are shut due to the pandemic. "Oh, for God's sake!" he shouts. I patiently explain all the closures and all the dos and don'ts. He listens and nods, then says: "Alright, let's just go for a pint then."

I'm very stressed and anxious about him, and most likely my night sweats, nightmares, insomnia and panic attacks are caused by my concern for him. Dad has a social worker, and Social Services want him to stay in his own home as long as possible. I want that as well, but I'm concerned that his time for living alone *safely* is running out. And yet, I know from his past experiences in respite that when and if he goes into a home that will be the end, so I would rather he enjoyed his limited freedom in his own flat. Even if it does mean I'm permanently stressed and on edge.

Breaking News: STAY AWAY! Fleet of Police drones watching illegal walkers in countryside beauty spots.

Tonight at 8pm, the nation has been asked to come together to show thanks to the NHS workers who are on the frontline caring for Covid patients, and anyone who is a carer or keyworker. Just before 8 o'clock, I'm putting my shoes on when a premature ripple of clapping starts outside. As it's warm, I have the windows open, so the sound is very audible. Brendan immediately leaps up and starts barking ferociously. He's very nervous by nature – he's afraid of most things. Once the barking stops, he cowers on the bed trembling. So, we don't make it to our gatepost; I sit on the bed with him, talking to him in a calm voice. Sadly, we have music blasting out to cover up the noise: the sound of gratitude and solidarity. We're all in this together; we might all be segregated, but we're a kingdom united. (For once.) We might all be in our own homes, but we're only next door.

(Meanwhile, Nicky stood outside her flat with a handful of other residents. She said it was quite touching and she heard a wave of applause swelling over the rooftops as millions across the nation joined in.)

Friday 27th March 2020.

It's sunny again, but much colder today. Typically, I made the mistake of putting shorts on. I'm freezing!

Dad suggests the pub again. Brendan is also very keen

on this. Once more I go through the basics of lockdown with them both: everywhere is shut and Dad's supposed to be shielding. He gets quite tetchy.

I go to the supermarket with Nicky to get Dad's shopping. We have to queue for forty minutes to get in. They are allowing a few people in at a time, which keeps it very quiet inside. Shoppers are walking along avoiding contact, which is good. But eerie.

The pandemic isn't bringing out the good Samaritan in *everyone*. There have been several cases of profiteering in the form of "price hiking" reported, where retailers have charged outrageous prices for much-sought after products, as there are shortages. In some places toilet rolls have quadrupled in price and hand sanitiser is being sold for as much as £20.

Breaking News: Prime Minister, Boris Johnson, contracts coronavirus.

In the afternoon, I pick up Brendan's lead and say "Shall we go out, Boy?" He looks up from the bed, where he's stretched out luxuriating. He casts me a glance, as though to say "If we absolutely must. But not far. I'm quite busy."

So, we walk to the local field. Brendan doesn't *always* get his own way. Not always. If there's ever a health and safety issue, I overrule him. If there isn't, I don't. The field is his favourite place, apart from home. It's a square of green surrounded by houses. It was the first place I brought him on his very first day with me. It has trees around the outskirts; when they're in full leaf the houses are lost behind a curtain of foliage. It takes us five minutes to walk there and it's the nearest open space to our flat. I think that has a lot to do with why Brendan loves it: the proximity.

As soon as we arrive, Brendan always sits down and waits patiently for his public to arrive and come over to visit him. It used to be busy with people and dogs, but in lockdown we barely meet anyone here. He sits for a long time while I walk around the perimeter of the field. No one comes at all. Eventually, I put him on his lead and coax him away with the promise of a sit down at home. It never fails.

Saturday 28th March 2020.

People have taken to putting pictures of rainbows in their windows as a beacon of hope. It's a nice touch. It's supposed to give the kids – who are all at home as the schools are closed, allegedly being home educated – something positive to focus their creative talents on. It's also meant to be a symbol of gratitude for the NHS for doing such a sterling job looking after the Covid patients.

I pass a driveway which has rainbows chalked on it, along with the messages: SMILE and BE HAPPY. I *do* smile and I feel happy, so it's a success on their part.

Some complete walls and gateposts have been painstakingly decorated by children, with whole landscapes, rainbow-filled skies and messages of appreciation for the NHS. Brendan isn't an art lover and it's quite difficult trying to get him not to wee on them.

Breaking News: Health Secretary Matt Hancock also tests positive for Covid.

In the news there are photographs of various UK beaches, completely deserted, as visitors have been told to keep away. It brings a pang of longing. I love travelling. Last year, I travelled around the coast of Britain with Brendan. We really bonded over that experience. They were such happy times. Now it's difficult to imagine ever having that kind of freedom again.

Another photograph features a desolate Skegness. In the background is the hauntingly empty esplanade and motionless big wheel. It's quite chilling. Things made *for* people, just look so wrong *without* people. On a wall, someone has daubed the words: "IS THIS THE END?" You might think this is paranoid or overly dramatic, yet right at this moment the question doesn't seem all that far-fetched.

Breaking News: Up to now more than a thousand people are known to have died of Covid in the UK.

Sunday 29th March 2020.

The clocks have gone forward in the night and robbed us of an hour. This always annoys me and is completely pointless. But in real terms, will the loss of that hour actually make any difference to our lives? No. Not really. Not in lockdown, it won't. Except possibly to Brendan, who's mourning the loss of an hour of Big Sleep.

Breaking News: BRITAIN RUNNING SHORT OF RUBBER GLOVES AND APRONS - DESPERATELY NEEDED BY NHS.

Covid infections and the death toll are rising alarmingly. The Prime Minister has written to every household saying the crisis will get worse before it gets better. He's definitely half right; it's certainly getting worse.

This morning, I saw more chalked rainbows on a driveway, accompanying the message: MILLIE, I MISS YOU, which I thought was really sad.

Brendan has developed his own new lockdown hobby. "Yawning in different places." In the park, he ran up some steps, yawned and came down again. He looked very pleased with himself. I was actually quite impressed he went up the steps at all, rather than just sitting and looking at them and yawning from the bottom. He also yawned on the bowling green, in the playground and on the path.

We would normally go to Nicky's mum's for tea today, but as she's shielding we aren't able to do this. This is probably the first Sunday we have ever missed, except when we've been on holiday. Nicky is quite upset about it.

In the evening there is some snow, just a bit; the flakes are only small and it doesn't stick. An hour later there is no trace that it's been there at all.

<u>Monday 30th March 2020.</u>

I take Brendan to the field. We bump into a young woman I vaguely know, Sarah, who lives nearby. We stand several metres apart and shout at each other. She is generally annoyed and frustrated by lockdown and the limitations it imposes. She is also angry and depressed because there is now talk of an increase in the length of lockdown from a few weeks to a matter of months. She lives alone and feels isolated, as must so many people.

These days of solitude must be unsettling to some, frightening even. With my dog beside me, I never feel lonely or alone. But I'm very aware that not everyone's got a Brendan to keep them organised, give them purpose, to give them a routine and a reason to get up in the morning and to light up the room just by being there. (I should probably go into marketing.) For some people this lockdown experience will be a very difficult and lonely affair.

[UPDATE: I saw Sarah locally several times for the next few weeks, then didn't see her again. I haven't seen her for well over a year and I wonder what happened to her. I hope she's OK. The same has happened to a number of fellow dog walkers; they just stopped coming to the field and some will never be seen again.]

Breaking News: Lockdown having positive effect on Covid, though there are currently 9,000 people in hospital with Coronavirus and deaths have peaked at over 1400.

I leave Brendan having a nap at home and walk to the local shops. The majority are shuttered and in darkness, which really sells the dystopian atmosphere. There are few people about. There is very little traffic. The smaller food shops are limiting customers to two at a time, so there are a couple of people waiting outside. I go in the local health food shop. The staff are wearing face masks and rubber gloves. It's quite unsettling and alien at first.

I go into the Co-op next door. The shelves are virtually empty and several aisles have packets of food on the floor that appear to have been trampled underfoot. It looks like there's been a riot. I've never seen anything like it. The biscuit aisle is completely and utterly bare; there are no biscuits of any kind; none at all; absolutely no biscuits whatsoever. The McVitie's factory is only down the road, yet there isn't a Hobnob in sight, absolutely nothing to dunk in your tea. There's no washing-up liquid either. In a mad, frenzied stampede, people have panic bought anything that has a significant shelf-life. It really is like the population are preparing for some biblical End of Days.

I'm very pleased to get back home to my boy. Brendan gets up from the bed to greet me. He stretches, which exhausts him, so he flops back down again. I go to greet him instead; it's easier that way.

Tuesday 31st March 2020.

Today marks a week of lockdown. Already. Surprisingly, it's flown by. It's also the last day of March. We're a quarter through the year. It's quite shocking.

So, on this momentous and significant day, did anything actually happen? Not for me it didn't. And not really for Brendan. We went to the field. I did some work. Brendan had a snooze. Then we repeated it all until the evening, when Nicky came for tea. Brendan wafted over to say hello to her, before drifting off back to bed again. We had cans, we had curry, we chatted, we even laughed a bit. It was the highlight of an otherwise rather dull day.

Wednesday 1st April 2020.

It's April Fool's Day. Are we all being fools? Imagine if this was all one big hoax, as some people suspect it is. There is a lot of doubt, mistrust, distrust and suspicion surrounding the pandemic. Some people dispute that there is even a virus at all. With that in mind, I've been looking into some of the major Covid conspiracy theories.

- The 5G network is spreading the virus. 5G is the fifth-generation standard for broadband cellular networks. (I read that. I've no idea what it means.) Quite how it's allegedly spreading the coronavirus is anyone's guess.

- Bill Gates, business tycoon and founder of Microsoft, is somehow responsible. I'm not sure exactly why poor Bill is being targeted, or what he's hoping to get out of it.

- The virus leaked from the Wuhan Institute of Virology in China. This is so plausible; I can't actually believe people lump it together with the various outlandish theories. It is an undisputed fact that the Covid outbreak originated in Wuhan in China. It is a fact that there is a virology institute there. It is a fact that they were doing research into coronaviruses in bats. If it is a coincidence, it is surely one HELL of a coincidence!

- The virus is in fact a bio-weapon created in the aforementioned Wuhan laboratory and released into the world intentionally. Conversely, the Chinese have accused the Americans of inventing it and infecting *their* nation.

- The virus is a way of allowing the New World Order to take over. Depending on who you chat to, the NWO are either a human ruling elite or a race of invading alien lizards; the lizards are often shape-changing and usually they have cloned various key humanoids, including the British royal family.

- Finally, multi-national pharmaceutical companies (known collectively as "Big Pharma") have created the virus and have pushed the vaccination programme because they'll make a fortune from it. The huge pharmaceutical conglomerates are tasked with developing and manufacturing the vaccine on a worldwide scale, so – conspiracy theories aside – the pandemic has served them *incredibly* well.

Some of these theories are very plausible and hold a lot of weight. Some are clearly sheer lunacy.

Or perhaps that's just what they want you to believe...

DISCLAIMER: These are not *my* theories, I'm just reporting them, so don't be thinking of suing me, Bill Gates, Big Pharma plc or New World Order Ltd.

Breaking News: UK reports further 563 deaths, bringing total UK Covid deaths to 2,352.

In the evening, Nicky texts. She's just realised it's Brendan's birthday. It might be April Fool's Day, but Brendan's no fool. He might have had a rough start in life as a street dog in Bulgaria, but he's certainly landed on his feet. Because of his rough beginnings, he's determined to make sure he never goes without a bed, sofa or flat screen TV ever again.

He has some birthday biscuits, a birthday cuddle and a birthday nap. (Just inserting the word "birthday" in front of anything makes it celebratory.) I know that's a rubbish birthday party, but it's the best we could do in lockdown. Besides, I'm sure it's still his second-best birthday ever, after last year, which was his first in his new home. He's seven! In a few months he will be older than me, and then he'll be in charge. Watch out world!

Happy Birthday The Boy!

Breaking News: Brendan is seven today!

Thursday 2nd April 2020.

Today I'm really feeling that every day is the same. That's mainly because every day *is* the same. Exactly the same.

I walk with Brendan to Dad's flat. Dad shouts at Brendan; Brendan barks at Dad. Or the other way around. I wash his pots, clean the fridge and throw away some rotten food and all the other jobs that the carers have neglected to do.

I have a brew with Nicky on her lunch break. She's working from home, but isn't enjoying it, which surprises me. She used to cycle to work and she enjoyed the ride. She also enjoyed the delineation of her day, work was work, home was home; when she left her desk the working day was over. Now the office is at home and it's there 24 hours a day. It can be quite soul-destroying working from home, and you'd think it would be the opposite. On the plus side, she gets to spend all day, every day with her cats, Hector and Pixie.

I walk back to my home (and office) with Brendan; there are very few people about. I'm so glad I have my dog, not just for companionship, as he's not always such a good conversationalist, but for the routine he imposes on me. It would be very easy to give up and stay in all day.

At 8 o'clock, as it's a Thursday, I'm again sitting with my arm around Brendan, with Blondie on excessively loudly, while the nation claps for the NHS. Despite the music, he still hears the clapping and howls like a banshee, but I like to think it's in solidarity.

Breaking News: UK reports 569 deaths today,

bringing death toll to 2,921.

One of those deaths was comedian Eddie Large, who died today of coronavirus, contracted in hospital. He was best known as the larger half of the comedy duo Little and Large. He was 78.

> Eddie Large (Born Edward McGinnis)
> (25 June 1941 – 2 April 2020)

Friday 3rd April 2020.

Today is National Walk to Work Day, which falls on the first Friday in April, so I get out of bed and walk over to my desk. Alone. Brendan prefers to think of the bed as his place of work, so he stays put.

Some time later, when Brendan has finally stirred himself, we set off to the field. There are even more rainbows today. This time they don't make me smile. They're everywhere. They've become commonplace, a hackneyed cliché. Besides, a rainbow is actually a multicoloured frown, not a smile. Bah humbug.

I sit at the field for an hour with Brendan. It's unnaturally quiet. It starts to rain, so we walk home. We see no one at all. Not a soul. There's a really post-apocalyptic feel to some days. Once home it annoyingly goes sunny.

Breaking News: Birmingham man arrested for shoplifting coughs and spits in the faces of shop staff, shouting "I've got coronavirus!"

I walk to the shops. There are still many empty shelves.

Regardless of what the government keep saying, stocks are *not* getting through. There is a maxim: a society is only ever three meals away from revolution, meaning that if food is deprived (for three meals) then the population will riot and rebel in search of food. It feels very much like we're on the brink of that now.

Because we have elderly and vulnerable parents, we are hypersensitive about contracting or carrying the coronavirus. As a result, apart from being fastidious about social distancing and hand washing, we avoid touching door handles and so forth and either use a glove, or use hand sanitiser immediately afterwards. We also wash our shopping, or where possible leave it in quarantine for several days. This makes the whole shopping task into a mammoth time-consuming event, but we feel it is necessary.

There has been much controversy and disagreement about how long the coronavirus can survive on different materials. For paper the time varies from a few minutes to up to several days, depending on the particular strain of the virus. For aluminium it is between two and eight hours. Glass and ceramics are up to five days.

Breaking News: In holiday regions second home owners' cars sprayed with "Go home!"

Despite the no travel order, people have been stopped by police, driving repeatedly around town centres, not going anywhere in particular, just going for a drive because they're bored. Countryside beauty spots are still getting unwanted visitors. Police are randomly stopping vehicles and issuing fines for improper use.

* * * * * * * * * *

Nicky comes over in the evening. Brendan always gets so excited when she arrives. He loves having visitor. (Singular.) He will only let Nicky into his flat, no one else is allowed. But that's never been much of a problem. He brings all his toys to show her. He leaves them scattered around her and wafts off again for a lie down. He's exhausted. It's all been too much for him.

Despite this gorgeous welcome, Nicky is stressed and upset because she can't see her mum; it's really getting to her. I ask her if she would consider a socially distanced visit, but she thinks not being able to hug her mum would be worse and she doesn't want to take any risks at all.

We're both really tired... exhausted in fact. Doing virtually nothing is apparently very tiring.

Saturday 4th April 2020.

I find I'm thinking about the state of the world a lot, especially in the first hour of the day. On waking I find I'm incredibly pessimistic. I wonder where it's all heading and what's going to happen. It's frighteningly easy to believe that the virus will kill virtually everyone, and that for the few survivors the future will be one of destitution, poverty and famine. It's a generic sci-fi trope, of course. I've even unwittingly used the word "survivors", the title of the 'Seventies TV series by Terry Nation, about a band of people who survive a virus which wipes out most of the global population. Perhaps society will go feudal and feral and people will kill for food. I wonder whether we will ever go back to normal after lockdown. *Can* we ever go back? And do we really want to?

But none of these thoughts are helpful, so I stop them and focus on the present. We live in the moment; we have to deal with the here and now. So, I look at my dog, lying beside me, hogging most of the bed. He looks back at me. He has a way of looking at me, it's more like he's studying me, running his eyes over every feature of my face, searching, like an artist. I really doubt that he's about to paint a portrait of me – landscapes are more his thing – so I'm sure he's wondering how he can better manipulate me. The answer is, he couldn't; he's an expert.

* * * * * * * * * *

We walk over to Nicky's in the afternoon. It's a frustrating walk. The police have voiced concerns because they expect the good weather to bring the public out into open spaces and not respect social distancing. Lo and behold, the streets and park are busier than they have been since lockdown began, but people are not keeping their distance and are happily invading the space of others. This would be very annoying at the best of times, but these aren't the best of times.

Sunday 5th April 2020.

It's a lovely sunny day. I do my back exercises and yoga. It only takes five minutes or so, but it makes such a difference. I need to do it every day – at least once – or my back seizes up. That should be motivation enough, but I forget all the time. Today I did it properly, I did it mindfully and I felt energised afterwards. Brendan also does yoga. He does a leisurely dog-stretch every time he stands up. If I say "Walk!" He'll look at me as though to say "Fine. I'll be here when you get back." When I approach him to put his lead on he'll roll onto his back to make it difficult. After we've had a few words and he's conceded defeat, he'll start the stretching. He'll generally stretch three or four times before he's crossed the room to the door. He's either very into his yoga or it's a delaying tactic and he's hoping I'll forget the walk and give up. At the mention of the word "Walk" a normal dog would be bounding to the door and jumping up and down, whining in excitement. That's not Brendan at all.

Breaking News: Queen thanks NHS and key workers in public address.

We spend the day at Nicky's, as usual for a Sunday. It's very nice. Nicky has two sofas; I sit on one with Brendan, she sits on the other, usually with one or both of her cats. We talk for a while and then we usually watch something. It's nice to just relax and lose yourself in something fictional and forget for a while that out there the world is all going wrong.

Monday 6th April 2020.

The weather is all over the place. It's mainly mild, but there was a heavy shower in the morning. In the park, Brendan is busy sniffing a really interesting blade of grass. I sit down on a bench, but don't take my eyes off him. After a minute or so, he raises his head and looks around for me, spots me and comes charging over with puppy-like enthusiasm. He sits at my feet, leaning against my legs, looking up at me. This is probably the high point of my week.

Tuesday 7th April 2020.

It's another sunny day. Again, I'm feeling it's as though we're in a war, or a country in the eastern bloc, where they have to queue for food. Produce is still not getting to the shelves; it isn't serious yet, but it's troubling that it *might* get serious.

Breaking News: PRIME MINISTER IN INTENSIVE CARE. PM Boris Johnson moved to ICU with breathing difficulties.

I had juice today. My aim is to have fresh juice, either fruit or vegetable or mixed, on "most" days. The health benefits of real juice are astronomical. We used to have juice a lot, but it's expensive and time consuming and we got out of the habit. Today I had apple, pear and carrot. The carrot is barely detectable, but is a good, healthy carrier. This is probably my standard juice. It was very palatable.

I walked to the park with Brendan and we sat together enjoying the sunshine. Brendan loves sitting down; it's a huge part of his walk. And his life. So I sat beside him with my arm around him. It all felt very relaxed and peaceful. It's odd, but today I felt that I might be getting used to the mundane and limited lockdown way of life.

Wednesday 8th April 2020.

I slept very badly and awoke several times after nightmares, but can't remember what they were about.

We walk over to Dad's. Brendan yawns a lot and tries to sit down at every opportunity. I attempt to engage Dad in some of his favourite subjects and get his memory going. During his National Conscription he was stationed at Spandau jail, guarding Rudolph Hess. He was a very keen cyclist in his youth – Dad, not Rudolph Hess – which is something he really misses, as he's no longer capable of cycling. He was a plumber by trade – Dad, not Rudolph Hess – but at one time also drove heavy goods vehicles and coaches, which he loves to talk about. He's very proud of his HGV licence. Usually, a mention of any of these subjects will get him cycling happily down Memory Lane. Dad, not Rudolph Hess.

It's a really nice visit and I come away very happy... which I don't always.

Thursday 9th April 2020.

Of course – as you'll know – it's National Unicorn Day today. Can't say I've seen any in the area recently, so maybe they've died out. But we do have a lot of bright green parakeets living locally, which were presumably released from captivity at some point.

It's warm and sunny. Apparently, it's Easter tomorrow. I had no idea. Bank Holidays don't affect my daily operations, so I never really notice them. Especially this year, when there will be no Easter celebrations anyway.

Breaking News: Prime Minister still in intensive care, but his condition is "improving".

I have a growing feeling that we're trapped in aspic: we can see out, but we're not going anywhere. It seems foolish to make any plans for the future, because it feels like the future is hanging by a thread. People I speak to at the field appear to be stoically going about their daily business, being polite and friendly and very British, but if you scratch the surface and ask what they think about the situation, most people seem to be quite frightened and quite upset, because most people are unable to see their friends and family and they feel isolated and vulnerable. But they still smile, say hello and comment on the weather. During lockdown I have really come to value these exchanges at the field. Without Brendan I wouldn't go to the field and I wouldn't have these conversations; people wouldn't stop and start talking. Brendan is like a social passport, which is odd for a dog so unsociable.

Friday 10th April 2020.

So, it's Easter. A weird Easter. People are still having barbeques and having friends round and the coronavirus death rate has grown hugely.

I never used to be a fan of Bank Holidays. In my childhood they were just another day like a Sunday, when everything was lifeless and closed and stultifying. Of course, that's potentially every day in lockdown.

Breaking News: Police issue warnings for Easter revellers after breaking up 660 parties last weekend.

Today's juice was kiwi, pear and grapes. It was tangy but very nice. I added a carrot. It tasted like kiwi, pear and grapes with added carrot, rather than it bringing a new and exciting dimension, but it was still nice.

Saturday 11th April 2020.

It's National Pet Day. Although he finds the term "pet" somewhat patronising, Brendan is fully embracing the nature of the day and plans to exploit it in every way possible.

Breaking News: GPs switch to telephone appointments for most cases, seeing only an average of 7% of patients in person.

Nicky came over and we sat in the garden. It's a shared garden, but it's rarely used by anyone else, which is good news for Brendan, who doesn't like to share. He sits on the grass and watches the birds, enjoying every second.

Bird watch: wood pigeons, magpies, sparrows and a big, sinister, shiny black crow.

Breaking News: Huge numbers dying. 823 died in English hospitals today.

Sunday 12th April 2020.

Time is passing so quickly, which seems odd considering most days are a carbon copy of the day before. I get up in the morning and it seems five minutes since I was last brushing my teeth at the same time yesterday. There's nowhere to go and nothing to do... and yet I actually find that quite comforting. In a way. I think things will be very different afterwards... if there ever is an afterwards. I'm enjoying having an excuse to stay in with my dog, not that I need much of an excuse, as we spend virtually every hour of every day together.

Nicky says that working from home is making time move quicker for her as well. She mentioned today that being outside made her feel like she's in a zombie film. Whenever she sees a person approaching in the streets, looming towards her, she wants to run and get out of their way. I thought that was a very good analogy.

Breaking News: Looking good! The death rate for London has "levelled out" today.

Actor, comedian, broadcaster and former *Goodie* Tim Brooke-Taylor, died today of coronavirus. He was 79.

Timothy Julian Brooke-Taylor OBE
(17th June 1940 – 12th April 2020)

Monday 13th April 2020.

Apart from taking Brendan to the field, I stayed at home today. I had a sinus flare-up and was in a lot of pain. Not a good day. Most of the day I spent lying down with a hot water bottle over my face. Brendan spent most of the day lying down as well, minus the hot water bottle. He thought it was great.

Breaking News: UK facing 4th week of lockdown. Government to review social distancing measures.

Tuesday 14th April 2020.

It's difficult keeping a diary when nothing ever happens. What can I say about today? Well, it's Bin Day, that's about it.

Breaking News: Army veteran, Captain Tom, raises a staggering £2m for NHS.

Captain Sir Thomas Moore, better known to the nation as Captain Tom, was born in 1920. During the Second World War he served in India and Burma. On 6th April this year, he began fundraising for the NHS. His aim is to walk 100 lengths of his garden by his 100th birthday, on 30th April. His original goal was to raise £1000, though he has already far exceeded that. In the process Captain Tom has become a national hero.

Wednesday 15th April 2020.

Another OK day. But exactly the same OK day as all the other OK days. At this point though, an "OK day" is perhaps all we can hope for. OK?

Breaking News: A lucky 106 year old has been

discharged from hospital; after recovering from Covid-19.

I'm continuing to notice how the atmosphere of lockdown is changing. People in the street are walking closer and closer, whereas they used to cross over or step aside while you passed, but that's all starting to go. At first people were afraid and perhaps traumatised by something unknown and unprecedented happening in our ordered lives. But now, everyone's getting used to it and people are accepting this as the norm. They are increasingly letting their defences down and becoming lazy and careless in regards to the virus. This really can't be a good move.

Thursday 16th April 2020.

Breaking News: LOCKDOWN EXTENDED FOR "AT LEAST" 3 WEEKS.

It was inevitable: the government have announced there will be a three week extension to the lockdown. I have mixed feelings about this. I feel it is the best thing, especially if it helps to stop the virus in its tracks, however it will have a devastating impact on the economy, with many businesses surely likely to fold. I'm also grateful from the point of view of my dad, as it will keep him away from mixing with people for longer, so hopefully keep him safer.

I explained the lockdown extension to Brendan. He looked at me quizzically from a seated position. His eyes said "What's a lockdown?"

<u>Friday 17th April 2020.</u>

Today is a stay-at-home day. I do the washing, household jobs and walk to the field with Brendan. I make a real effort with my exercises and make apple, pear and grape juice, so it's quite a productive day. (I've just reread that sentence. THAT was a productive day? I really should get out more. Or ever.)

In the afternoon, we return to the field. It should really be called "Brendan's Field", because he clearly owns it. As one of the dog people, Irene, observes: "Look at Brendan. He rules this field doesn't he?"

I nod in agreement. "He does."

"I think he's in charge."

"He is."

He usually sits a short distance away from the other dogs, slightly aloof, looking casually around, with his paws crossed in front of him.

"He's the boss." Irene says, "Look at him surveying his kingdom."

Apart from his failure to master the royal wave, he's every inch regal. He will sit like this for hours now and will only move when I insist we go home.

* * * * * * * * * *

Nicky comes over after work. Brendan, as usual, brings

his toys to show her. He brings Pink Pig, Nelliephant #1, Nelliephant #2 and his rugby ball. After the toy display he has to go and have a lie down. He's emotionally exhausted. It's been quite a five minutes.

I have a small round table and chairs placed at the window, so it feels like we're in a bar or café. Sort of. We usually sit there with our drinks with a view over the garden. Our garden is just knee-high grass and dead apples, but the gardens on either side are well-tended and exotic. There is a eucalyptus tree where the doves and wood pigeons gather, which is beautiful.

We each keep a "chat list": a list of conversational things that have happened to us throughout our day. We've always done it, so we don't forget to tell each other some important – or even unimportant – detail from our lives, it's just that recently our lists are getting shorter and we're really scraping the barrel for news, as we don't go anywhere, we don't see anyone and not very much happens. As a result, there is probably more current affairs in our conversation than there used to be, but we're still talking about something.

We have both said we don't really miss going to the pub. We used to go a few times a week, but when lockdown came, we adjusted immediately. That's something I think we'll struggle to go back to, one of the things that's gone forever.

Saturday 18th April 2020.

I was chatting to people in the park. We've been in lockdown for nearly four weeks now and the UK death toll stands at 15,464 and the global toll exceeds 159,000, yet I don't know anyone who's actually had the coronavirus. Not even a friend of a friend. No one I speak to knows anyone who's had it. One of my neighbours is a paramedic. He's Polish and hasn't been able to go home to see his wife and little girl for months. He says he has seen no evidence of the coronavirus and none of his colleagues have succumbed to it. I'm in no way disputing that the virus is real, but it does seem very odd.

Breaking News: Captain Tom's fundraiser passes £19 million!

Captain Tom Moore really has become something of a legend and a folk hero. He is featured in the news a lot, because his is a rare positive story in a world that has so little positivity at the moment. He is being pro-active and doing something positive and selfless. To use a cliché, he has captured the nation's heart.

Sunday 19th April 2020.

I had lunch with Nicky, then in the afternoon we played Boggle and did quizzes with her mum, Rosie via Zoom. It was good old fashioned – yet futuristic – fun. And I won the Boggle. (I *always* win Boggle. I'm good with words, but less good with numbers. Ask me how many beans make five and I'd need to use a calculator.)

I walked home across the common with Brendan. A plane passed low overhead. He set off after it, barking furiously, but didn't catch it.

In the evening, we sat together and watched an episode of the TV series *Millennium*. I've been watching it in order and have reached the end of the second series. This was designed as being the end of the show for good. I have seen it twice before, but this time had an additional, disturbingly real quality to it, as it revolves around a virus which originated in China, that came about due to species crossover. That is eerily familiar. It conveys madness and hopelessness, with repeated, harsh and shocking imagery. The disease appears to be taking over the world and we hear, rather than see, the collapse of society. It is genuinely and terrifyingly realistic. The programme ends with bursts of sharp white noise and the sounds of panic and chaos. It's the end of the world as we know it...

In an interview, one of the *Millennium* writers explained that he looked into the most likely ways that the human race would come to an end and he found a list compiled by scientists, based on scientific reasoning. I Googled the same question and also came across the happy little list, which contains something for everyone, including nuclear annihilation (on purpose), nuclear annihilation (by accident), biological warfare, climate change and – the one we're currently experiencing – a global pandemic.

The *Millennium* episode is called The Time Is Now. It originally aired 22 years ago. It's not quite a perfect episode, but rather a slightly flawed masterpiece, but a masterpiece nevertheless. It is brave and stunningly effective. And it feels uncomfortably close to home.

Breaking News: UK reports 596 Covid deaths today, bringing the death toll to over 16,000.

Monday 20th April 2020.

Dad went missing for a while today. I got quite stressed and panicked, but as usual, he reappeared and acted as though nothing was wrong. When this happens, we never get to find out exactly what went on.

I couldn't get to sleep at night. When I finally did, I had nightmares revolving around Dad. I barely slept at all. I know Brendan was concerned about his granddad as well; he didn't say as much, but I can tell.

Tuesday 21st April 2020.

It's National Tea Day. I love tea. Tea brightens up my day and brings a feeling of warmth and joy, it relaxes and it soothes. I can also use all those adjectives to describe Brendan, but I'm talking about tea. I did try The Boy with a bowl of tea when I first got him, but he didn't like it, whereas my previous dog, Jake, absolutely loved a nice weak, milky cup of tea.

I don't binge drink tea; I have three or sometimes four cups a day, so each one is special. My usual tea times are 7am, 11am and 3am, with an optional one in the early evening. I never have a tea with a meal, that's just wrong. The tea is an event in its own right. There used to be a TV advert, the strapline of which was "Tea... Best drink of the day." I couldn't put it better myself.

Breaking News: Government "throwing everything" at developing coronavirus vaccine.

It was sunny earlier, but now it's clouded over as we set off on our walk. It's Bin Day again. How quickly it comes around. Bin Day seems to define the week. It's one of the major events of the week, because it's something different, as the pavements are lined with black wheelie bins. At one time this was a really big issue for Brendan, as he was terrified of them and had to snarl and bark at each one; getting to the field took us ages. Now he just strolls past without a care in the world, gives them a lazy sniff and wees on them.

Breaking News: Happy Birthday, ma'am. Queen is 94 today. HRH spends day at Windsor Castle with Prince Philip. No celebrations due to lockdown.

<u>Wednesday 22nd April 2020.</u>

It's a nice day again. At lunchtime we walk to the park to meet Nicky; she cycles over for some exercise. It feels a bit decadent and summery. I stay in working for the rest of the day. I'm quite used to staying in and seeing no one and not going to the pub or the cinema. Part of my job used to involve theatre reviews, but that has stopped completely, of course. At the moment I'm not missing it at all. But I do miss the simple act of going in a café and having a coffee, reading for a while and watching the world go by. I'm so like Brendan, because that fairly accurately describes his ideal day, sitting at the field watching life unfold around him.

Breaking News: It is believed that over 178,000 people have died globally due to Coronavirus.

Reading to my dog on World Book Day.Brendan is absolutely rivetted, because the book I'm reading is excellent. And about him.

Thursday 23rd April 2020.

It's World Book Day, so wherever you are in the world you are encouraged to read a lovely book. Read non-fiction to increase your knowledge, or fiction to help you relax, or have you on the edge of your seat. Or read *Underdogs* by Gray Freeman and Brendan Freedog. It's a great story and a gripping read. I've read it many times.

I take Brendan to the field. The air feels clean and people are commenting on the increase in birds, due to the noticeable lack of pollution. There is a continual background hum of birdsong. One bird in particular, in the nearest tree, is singing at the top of his voice. I wonder what he's actually trying to say, what he's hoping to convey, or whether he's singing simply because he can, because he's happy.

This is another of those perfect moments; it's beautifully sunny, I'm surrounded by nature, there's blossom everywhere and I'm sitting with my dog. The world might be going to hell in a handcart, but nature is getting the chance to shine.

Friday 24th April 2020.

Today marks a calendar month since lockdown began. A whole month. It's strange how we can hold two completely opposing viewpoints at the same time, but we can, because I'm used to lockdown now, I'm used to every day feeling exactly the same and I'm used to the nothingness… whilst simultaneously feeling that it's surreal, unbelievable and hard to accept.

Breaking News: Tomorrow will be PM Boris Johnson's first day back at work following Coronavirus.

Saturday 25th April 2020.

We're spending a lot of time sitting in the grass at an old sports club near Nicky's. It has been abandoned for years and is up for sale. It's almost like the countryside if you keep your view reined in. Brendan absolutely loves it and we sit under a tree for hours. He snuffles about or sunbathes and I read or take work to do. It's everything we need and it's made such a difference to our lockdown experience. From here we can see Nicky's flat. Sometimes she waves at us. Often, I don't notice and I get an irate text: I'M HANGING OUT OF THE WINDOW WAVING!

It's another warm and sunny day and there is a lot of blossom. There are a lot of birds and the air is clean and fresh. Nicky has just waved and I've waved back, so I've avoided an indignant message.

When I'm here - with my dog beside me - in the sunshine, being in lockdown doesn't seem so bad. And yet...

Breaking News: "Tragic and terrible milestone". More than 20,000 people have died of Covid in UK hospitals.

Sunday 26th April 2020.

In the evening, I got a call saying Dad had gone missing. My brother was driving around the neighbourhood trying to spot him. One of Dad's neighbours had seen him at the bus stop on the main road. Dad walks with two sticks; I'm surprised he could even get that far. When my brother arrived at the bus stop there was no sign of Dad, so he drove into town and searched around the bus station area, but couldn't see him.

Meanwhile, I was phoning anyone I could think of, including reporting him to the police as a missing person. As he's elderly and vulnerable they acted immediately and took all the details.

Although it seemed a lot longer, probably less than an hour had passed when my phone rang. I grabbed it and answered. It was Dad, calm and relaxed, phoning from home; he sounded like he was eating something and he kept pausing to take another bite.

In the space of a few minutes, he told me various different stories about what had happened and where he had been, which is what he does. It was later reported by the neighbours that he had been brought back in a police car, but we'll never know for sure exactly what had gone on. The main thing was that Dad was back safe and well. He had no concept of the worry he'd caused. This latest incident just hammers home how vulnerable Dad is. I'm very aware that we're at the point now that even with regular care, he's becoming a liability to himself. I'm really stressed about it.

Monday 27th April 2020.

7.15am. Right now I'm sitting up in bed with my laptop and a cup of tea. I can occasionally hear Brendan sigh deeply, probably because I'm typing too loudly. Sometimes the world and the situation seems overwhelming, but I narrow my view to the here and now and I try and pinpoint the things around me that I'm grateful for. Right here, right now, I'm grateful for my flat which is warm and secure. I'm grateful for my cup of tea. I'm grateful that I have no upstairs neighbours at the moment, after three years of terrible neighbours. I am very grateful for my view: from this position all I can see are trees, swinging slightly in the breeze. I'm grateful for all the comforts around me. And I'm always grateful for my ever-present companion, Brendan.

Breaking News: 3,000,000 Coronavirus cases globally.

9.35am. Today, I'm taking Brendan for a walk across the golf course. This is the local and still-functioning (lockdown-permitting) 18-hole golf course, as opposed to be derelict driving range near Nicky's. Neither Brendan or I play golf, so it's not somewhere we regularly frequent. During lockdown the club is very kindly allowing people to use the grounds for recreation, which is very community-spirited of them. The course is quite beautiful, essentially the former sculptured parkland of a stately home. The green, tree-fringed landscape is like a small slice of the countryside and I love it. Brendan also clearly loves it. The moment I let him off his lead, he gets golf madness, running around at full pelt, barking and snarling at the grass. After five or so frenzied minutes, he flops down in the sunshine and relaxes by watching the industrious squirrels.

Breaking News: 4 million jobs furloughed in UK.

12.15am. I'm working at my desk. Brendan has gone for a lie down after all the sniffing excitement and running around.

Breaking News: PM Boris Johnson returns to

work after recovering from Coronavirus.

11.40pm. We're in bed, side by side. This is the end to our lockdown day. This is how *every* day ends.

Tuesday 28th April 2020.

Breaking News: Figures show that a third of all coronavirus deaths in England and Wales are now occurring in care homes.

I rarely think about money. It just doesn't interest me. But today, for some reason, I found myself wondering how my life would change if I won the lottery. Firstly, I'd be quite amazed by my win, because I've never, ever bought a ticket.

I firmly believe money can't buy you happiness. If you look at the core ingredients of human happiness, they generally revolve around comfort, food, sex and companionship. As long as you've got a roof over your head, sufficient comforts, enough food, then you're doing alright. The amount of money you have really shouldn't affect your sex life. (Unless you're paying for it!) And it shouldn't affect genuine friendships, as real friends don't care how rich or how poor you are. And even when you move and leave no forwarding address real friends will still track you down.

One of my very favourite things ever is sitting somewhere nice with Brendan, preferably with a view. We have done this all over the country, perhaps most memorably on a clifftop in Cornwall, where we sat on a sunny day looking out over the most stunning, iridescent sea. But we can do this equally well locally, sitting in the park, the golf course, the common, watching the clouds, watching the flowers dancing in the grass, just being together. Everything I really need to be happy is already right here. I think lockdown has underlined that fact.

Wednesday 29th April 2020.

There have been many pandemics throughout history, for as long as there have been people, in fact. The Black Death (bubonic plague) is one of the most notorious, of course. It spread through Europe and the Near East, reaching England in 1348. Globally it claimed between 50 and 200 million lives. It ran from 1346 to 1353 and then stopped. No one knows why.

The Spanish Flu outbreak of 1918 left between 17 to 100 million dead, though many historians settle on "at least 50 million". Social distancing was used to try and hinder the spread of the virus, and mask-wearing and frequent hand-washing were promoted, along with quarantining and the isolating of patients, and the closure of non-essential public places. Basically, it was a lockdown. There was no vaccine, but due to these methods the virus ran for just over a year and then died out. Some academics believe that the population developed a collective immunity to the virus.

Covid-19, to date, has claimed over 3 million lives globally. Of course, at the moment Covid is still in its infancy, it's still in short pants in pandemic terms. Unfortunately, there is still a very long way to go.

Breaking News: 26,000 in UK have died of coronavirus. For the first time this figure includes deaths in the community, including care homes.

Thursday 30th April 2020.

Breaking News: Today is Captain Tom's 100th birthday. He has so far raised in excess of £30 million for the NHS.

The weather is very changeable, sunny one minute, then raining the next. I take Brendan out anyway, because I laugh in the face of bad weather. I laugh and I get quite wet.

My aim every day is to try and make each day matter, to try and make it memorable and slightly different, wherever possible. I very often fail, of course, but that's beside the point. I think it's especially important during lockdown, because it's so easy to stagnate, it's easy for every day to become the same, it's easy to be lazy. Options are very limited during lockdown, so today, even though it's only a very small difference, we make an effort by doing our regular walk in reverse. Brendan isn't keen on this, as he really is a creature of habit. We only need to do something once for him to accept it as an established routine, and that's not how life works. I explain my reasoning and he grudgingly accepts it. He trudges beside me as we do our backwards walk, until he's forgotten that he's supposed to be in a mood; his tail is aloft, he's sniffing frantically and weeing excitedly on every gatepost and every tree.

Breaking News: Prime Minister: "UK is past the peak of Covid pandemic".

<u>Friday 1st May 2020.</u>

I've noticed the roads are considerably busier. People seem to be starting to drift back to work. B&Q have opened, against a tide of opposition. The pub chain, Wetherspoons, have announced that they will be opening imminently. Everything feels like it's slowly returning to normal. Yet nothing actually feels very normal.

* * * * * * * * *

Brendan is sprawled across the bed. His last walk was nearly four hours ago, but he shows no signs of wanting to go out. Mind you, he very seldom shows any signs of wanting to go out. I put my coat on and get his lead. This would have most dogs leaping about in excitement. Brendan puts a paw over his face.

"Shall we go to the field?" I ask him. It's his favourite place, so how can he refuse?

He refuses. He looks at me but doesn't move.

"Come on, up you get. We're going to the field."

His eyes say: "What for? We went yesterday. "

"Come on. Get up. You love the field."

He rolls onto his back, which is his way of making it more difficult, if not impossible, to get his harness on. But in the end, I succeed and we set off along the road. Once out, he's quite perky and full of enthusiasm, but less so than for his morning walk, which is his favourite.

It's so difficult to get him to come out. I used to think perhaps he was in pain. The vet said no, there's nothing physically wrong with him. I had a canine psychologist to see him when he first arrived. He said some dogs are just lazy. Some breeds, such as greyhounds, are *notoriously* lazy, and Brendan does have a similar racing-type physique, which is somewhat wasted on him, as his most frequent urgent journey is between the bed and the sofa and the fastest he moves is when changing channels after *Midsomer Murders* to catch the start of *Ready Steady Cook*.

Nicky says Brendan is more like a cat; he likes lying in the sunshine, he likes comfort, he likes warmth, and he likes luxuriating. If he had a litter tray inside the flat, we could probably say goodbye to the outside world completely.

Saturday 2nd May 2020.

Our Saturdays are quite regimented, but in a good way. We go to the field and Brendan either has a vigorous play with Annie or Bruno, from next door either side, or he sits down and ignores them, depending on what mood he's in. Today, neither of them turn up, so he doesn't ignore anyone. That's not a good start.

In the afternoon we walk to Nicky's over the common and the field, which takes about an hour. Brendan loves this, because it's the busiest day of the week at the busiest time, so there are lots of dogs around to snub. He never used to do this; he used to run up gleefully and engage in rough play, now he runs up gleefully and ignores everyone, possibly followed by a sit down. I assume it's as we've bonded more, Brendan has become more human and less canine.

At Nicky's we have cans and chat, then Nicky makes tea. After ten, I walk home with Brendan. He drags and pulls to go back to Nicky's, until we hit the half way point in our journey, then he pulls to go forwards, because he realises we're now nearer to home. He loves getting home, where he has a big supper and then dashes excitedly off to bed. I think he's only ever truly happy at home and after many hours away from it, he's exhausted and always sleeps like a log.

Breaking News: the UK Coronavirus death toll reaches over 28,000.

Sunday 3rd May 2020.

I had another call from my brother. He told me Dad had gone out and tried to gain entry into his neighbour's flat, which caused an upset. He didn't understand the quarantine measures... again. The neighbour was apparently quite annoyed and started ranting that Dad should be in a care home. Bearing in mind the recent statistics about coronavirus deaths in care homes, that's the one place I think he definitely *shouldn't* be. We were supposed to be meeting with Social Services the day before lockdown to discuss Dad's ongoing care; now the meeting has been postponed indefinitely.

Breaking News: Two people have been arrested in an anti-lockdown protest in Glastonbury after violence broke out.

Brendan is very dogmatic. We walk past a house that's having some work done. There is a ladder leaning against the wall, where there isn't normally a ladder, so he barks violently at it. It isn't in his way, it isn't on the street, but there isn't normally a ladder there, so he's not happy at all. I have to drag him away while he howls hysterically.

Monday 4th May 2020

I wake up in the morning, Brendan is still asleep beside me. I watch him sleep for a while, as I often do; it really isn't difficult, because he does a lot of sleeping. He looks so handsome, with his teddy bear face and his straggly beard and his triangular ears, his big, oversized puppy-paws, his long legs and his thick, multi-coloured, luxuriant coat, lying there breathing steadily, or sometimes yelping with his paws twitching. He's a work of art. He opens his eyes suddenly and stares at me. He sighs in irritation. He turns his back on me and goes back to sleep.

* * * * * * * * *

Another day, another call about Dad. This morning he slipped in the shower and banged his head. Poor Dad.

One of his carers was there, as he isn't supposed to shower without support. The paramedics were called; they checked him over and deemed him fit and well. Usually, they insist on going back to the hospital for a head injury, but possibly they didn't due to the pandemic.

Tuesday 5th May 2020.

Today Brendan had a sit down at the park, at the field, in the garden, on the drive, in the porch, on the landing and in the flat. He's chalked it up as a very successful day. As if that wasn't enough, Nicky came for tea. As usual we each chatted about our day. She has adjusted to working from home and now loves it, especially being with her cats all day. She can get more work done and can't imagine ever going back to the office. We have (vegan) sausage and mash for tea. I'm a practical rather than inspired cook, but it's really nice.

Breaking News: Global death toll exceeds 250,000.

Wednesday 6th May 2020.

Life seems to be at a standstill... for me and everyone. As usual, my days are all exactly the same, a repetition of dog walks and visits to Dad. All things considered though, this isn't such a bad routine.

Today's big conundrum was whether to have malt loaf or banana bread with my tea at 11 o'clock. I made a strong argument for each of them and in the end I compromised and had both.

Thursday 7th May 2020.

I awoke early. Brendan didn't. He lay curled up beside me, intermittently snoring and sighing and whinnying like a very attractive small horse.

I'd had nightmares throughout the night and kept waking up in a cold sweat. I've no idea now what they were about, but when I finally got up in the morning, I felt hungover with tiredness and stifled by an overwhelming sense of dread and foreboding.

Breaking News: UK reports 539 new deaths. Toll now 30,615.

Friday 8th May 2020.

At lunchtime, I step into my trainers. Brendan's lying on the bed, looking up at me warily.

"It's V.E. Day." I tell him. "We're going to Nicky's for afternoon tea. And yes, we're walking."

Most dogs would be thinking: *"Another* walk? I'm so lucky!" But not Brendan. We have to negotiate and barter until we've arrived at a peace treaty, and only then do we set off.

So, it's V.E. Day. The 75th anniversary of the Victory in Europe. The end of the war is now an average lifetime ago, so every year there are fewer and fewer survivors left. The country is celebrating as best it can, with televised, socially-distanced tributes and performances. It's a strange affair though; a singer finishes her song and there is an eerie silence with no clapping or cheering. There are no live audiences, no crowds, no street parties. Perhaps red, white and blue bunting flaps in the breeze on deserted streets throughout the country. Despite these conditions, the world is doing its best to make this a memorable and touching day of remembrance and celebration.

Nicky loves pageantry and events, parades and occasions. She has prepared afternoon tea for us and has laid it out beautifully with teapots, cups and saucers and a cake stand. She's made cucumber sandwiches – with the crusts cut off – and a range of small cakes. It's a very fitting accompaniment to the V.E. Day songs and commentary on the TV. It's a strangely civilised, patriotic and touching day.

Saturday 9th May 2020.

There is such a contrast to the country today, compared to the first few days of lockdown. Technically, we're *still* in lockdown and the same rules apply now that applied then, but social distancing is largely being ignored and people are constantly infringing on the space of others. The police have become aware of an increase in car use and illegal visits to the countryside. It's hardly surprising, as we're repeatedly being told that things are getting better, but the UK reported 346 coronavirus deaths today, which doesn't sound to me like a country on the mend.

Breaking News: UK death toll now 31,587.

It's a Saturday, so we walk to Nicky's in the afternoon via the Big Field. Brendan gets so distracted by all the other dogs, that he completely ignores me when I call him when it's time to go. "Brendan! Come here! Here, boy! Come on!" But he won't come. He's so focused on what he's doing that I don't think he can even hear me. I try a new angle, inspired by my parents. "Brendan, do as you're told... or I'll be *disappointed* in you!" It always worked with me. I was mortified at the thought that Mum and Dad might be disappointed in me. Brendan isn't mortified though. In the end I have to use the angry voice and he comes meandering towards me, trying to look as though he was coming this way anyway.

At Nicky's, he has a nap while we drink lager and then Nicky makes our tea. We walk home later in the evening. The streets are deserted, but this is mainly due to the heavy rain. It's pounding the orange-lit pavements and forming rivulets along the sides of the roads. I'm happy walking in the rain; Brendan – who is technically *a dog* – is less happy about it. We get completely soaked to the skin. It's so nice to get home and get towelled down in Brendan's case, and showered in my case, and then sit together with the heating on, snuggling.

Sunday 10th May 2020.

While out walking with Brendan, I notice the phenomenon of "lockdown hair". Unless you see someone frequently, it can pass by unnoticed. I became aware that a number of the regular faces I see in the street have all got longer hair as they have, by now, missed at least one – in some cases *several* – hairdressing appointments due to everywhere being closed. Former neat cuts are getting collar-length, straight hair is going wavy, fringes are becoming a visual impairment, roots are showing and ends are splitting. It's a strange and interesting side-effect of lockdown. It doesn't affect me, as I have clippers, beard trimmer and a razor. It doesn't affect Brendan either. He has his daily morning brush and still looks as handsome as ever.

Breaking News: We're getting there! Prime Minister announces plan for lifting lockdown. People who cannot work from home should return to the workplace, but avoid public transport wherever possible.

We walk over to Nicky's in the afternoon. Brendan is dragging wearily. A plane passes low overhead and he duly growls at it, but it's a perfunctory growl; he can't really be bothered. He sits down in the middle of the field to have a rest. He watches in wonderment as people throw balls for their dogs and the dogs actually go and pick them up. Bizarre.

At Nicky's we play Boggle with her mum, Rosie, via Zoom. This is now part of our routine. I win Boggle. (This is also part of our routine. Wonder if I'll ever get sick of winning. Don't think so.)

In the evening, I walk home with Brendan. A man with a beard cycles past us and shouts "Aw, nice dog!" It makes Brendan's day, but then several fireworks go off;

the poor boy is terrified. We run the second half without stopping.

Breaking News: UK reports another 269 Covid deaths.

Monday 11th May 2020.

It's cold and windy and there is rain in the air. I walk to Dad's with Brendan. We arrive at 10.05 precisely. The door is unlocked but the chain is on. Dad's carer is nearly two hours late. This is an on-going and increasing problem. I have noticed a lot of sloppiness creeping into the care provided by the agency, including false records being kept, completely random times, failure to administer medication and some questionable attitudes by the staff. I have repeatedly complained about all the issues, but have largely been ignored. I appreciate that these are trying times, but I can't have my father being regularly incorrectly medicated and missing meals, so it's time to take some action.

Tuesday 12th May 2020 to Tuesday 19th May 2020.

I woke up unable to move. My back had gone; I was in agony. I could barely move at all and there was no way I could stand up. I had to crawl to the bathroom on all fours. I thought it might get better as I loosened up, but it didn't. I was virtually immobile and in a great deal of pain.

My dad has always had a bad back. He told me that when he was in the army, during a gym session, his sergeant asked what was wrong with his back. Dad said nothing. He probably said: "Nothing, sir!" The sergeant said "Well, it's not right." Dad was plagued in later life with back problems. I inherited that. Thanks Dad.

The pain went on for a week. Nicky very kindly came twice a day to take Brendan for his big walks. In between I had to take him into the garden. It took me ages to get downstairs, I was bent double and each step was agony, but it couldn't be avoided.

I couldn't get any respite from the pain. Even lying down was excruciating. The pain was too severe to allow me to focus on reading or watching anything. It never let up, night or day.

Brendan was very patient and understanding. He used this time to catch up on his sleep.

Breaking News: More than 11,000 Covid deaths in UK care homes.

Saturday 16th May 2020.

Nicky cycled down to her mum's to meet her in the park next to her flat. This was their first face to face visit after eight weeks of lockdown and shielding. They maintained social distancing throughout, which was difficult, as they both wanted to hug. They had a flask of tea and a vegan lemon cake. It was the first step back to some sort of normality.

Wednesday 20th May 2020 to Monday 25th May 2020.

My back is getting gradually better. I have managed

to take Brendan out for short walks and even to the field once. I had to go slowly and it was agonising, but I did it. One dog walker stopped me and said they'd seen Brendan with a woman. I said that was my girlfriend. He said: "Oh… she was quite pretty." I'm not sure whether that meant "She's too pretty *for you*." Or "Yeah…" Wink "*I would*." And I didn't ask.

I'm just taking it easy at the moment and focusing on walking to the field, which is five minutes at a normal pace, though it's taking three times that. I can't yet manage the walk to Dad's, but he's doing fine. He's phoned me several times to see how I am, which I find very touching. The fact that he has remembered I'm ill means a lot. We're having long phone conversations every day, which is nice. Dad seems more coherent by phone than he does face-to-face. He sounds and seems like the old Dad. I think he makes more effort on the phone and seems less confused, so it's working well at the moment.

Breaking News: UK unemployment increases by 50,000 due to lockdown

Tuesday 26th May 2020.

It's Nicky's mum's birthday today. Nicky cycled down to meet her in the park next to her flat. They sat on opposite ends of a bench and kept a safe distance. Unfortunately, Rosie is spending the rest of her birthday alone, which is very sad. This is the first year in decades we haven't spent the day with her and taken her out. In the evening we communicate with her via Zoom, and she seems really quite chirpy considering her isolation.

Wednesday 27th May 2020.

Breaking News: American Covid death toll passes 100,000, equivalent to service personnel killed in Korea, Vietnam, Iraq and Afghanistan put together.

It's a sunny morning, so I sit in the garden with Brendan. Annie, the dog from next door, comes through the hedge and has a long play with the Boy. After a bit of energetic wrestling, they sit on the grass and relax; she gazes at him with love, while he looks around at the trees and the sky, in a completely disinterested and preoccupied manner. She seems to have been won over by his good looks, but I'm afraid it clearly isn't mutual, Annie, no matter how beautiful you are. He's a player and he won't be tied down.

Nicky came in the evening and all in all it was a good day. At least it was for us:

Breaking News: Locust swarms storm India, worst since 1993.

If I was religious (which I'm not) or pessimistic (which I'm also not. Honestly!) I might believe this was some sort of prophesized biblical plague signifying we really are on the road to the End of Days. So, it's a good job I'm neither. Amen.

Thursday 28th May 2020.

The final clap... "Clap for Carers" began in the UK on Thursday 26th March as a way of showing gratitude for the NHS and keyworkers in general: all the people doing essential jobs to keep the country rolling on throughout the pandemic. After two full months it is coming to an end, as lockdown restrictions are gradually easing. Tonight, at eight o'clock the nation will clap for the final time.

Of course, because of Brendan we won't be able to take part and, as usual, will be inside with the windows closed and loud music on.

Friday 29th May 2020.

Nothing really happened today. At least that's how it seemed. Of course, in reality a lot *did* happen today, people were born, people died, people had sex and people had arguments, people broke up and people broke down, but in the news and in my own life it all seemed a repetition of what had gone before: nothing was new and nothing had changed and everything was exactly the same.

Oh, it was National Biscuit Day. Unfortunately, I didn't have any biscuits. There has been a shortage of biscuits, so even that didn't happen.

Sunday 31st May 2020.

Nice lazy Sunday. We didn't do a lot and we *enjoyed* not doing a lot.

Breaking News: Risk of Covid resurgence if lockdown eases too soon, Scientists warn.

Monday 1st June 2020.

Breaking News: School kids return to school!

The streets are quiet until 3.15pm, when the schoolchildren are back, they're everywhere, swarming along the pavements, the field, the park, the shops, like the locusts in India. This is like a biblical plague... in uniform.

Wednesday 3rd June 2020.

I take Brendan into the garden in the afternoon. I sit under the apple tree, while he sits on the lawn engaged in Pigeon Patrol. He watches the birds with the interest of an avid twitcher, as they fly between Annie's eucalyptus tree on one side, over his airspace to Bruno's laburnum tree on the other. He isn't generally bothered about birds, but he absolutely won't let them touch down in his garden without a landing permit and he will enforce this rigorously; he's a stickler for rules, unless he's the one doing the breaking thereof. He really is a strange case; I've never met a dog quite like him.

A woodpigeon dares to land at the rear of the garden, probably thinking Brendan's too lazy to bother, but he's across the lawn like lightning. The poor pigeon makes a hasty retreat in a frenzied flurry of feathers. Brendan paces around the perimeter of the garden and then returns to his vantage point in the middle of the lawn.

No birds will get away with breaking the rules. Not on his watch.

Friday 5th June 2020.

Not a great deal happened today. How could it? Does it ever? I did my yoga and back exercises this morning. Today's session was good and I felt enlivened and motivated afterwards. Then I had pineapple, apple and blueberry juice. It was sweet and luxurious.

We walked to the park. Brendan had a manly wrestle with his new best friend, Storm. Storm looks like a Labrador, but he isn't apparently; he's got a more whiskery face. He's less than a year old, so he's got the advantage of youth, but Brendan knows the ways of the street. As a result, poor Storm repeatedly got battered. But – respect to him – he kept happily bounding back for more. And he never once stopped wagging his tail. Meanwhile, a gaggle of people stood in the middle of the field in a tight huddle, chatting and laughing and happily spreading disease.

Sunday 7th June 2020.

Breaking News: Global Covid death toll passes 400,000.

We walk to the golf course again. Brendan runs around the green in sheer joy, barking and snapping at the grass as usual. I don't do this; I just admire the views. The golf course really adds something to our lockdown lives. You aren't supposed to drive anywhere, though I find the logic of this rather tenuous. You're supposed to stay at home and exercise locally. The golf course has opened up a new world for us. Even so, it could become predictable, so in keeping with my policy of trying to do different things, we're planning to explore different parts of it each time, do the walks in reverse and shake things up wherever possible. It's hardly rock 'n' roll, but we're adding spice wherever we can. That's a metaphor, obviously; Brendan would never add spice. He hates all spices.

Monday 8th June 2020.

Today is National Best Friend Day, when we celebrate our best friend. Or friends, plural. Because I have two, one human and one canine.

Breaking News: It is estimated that lockdowns in European countries have saved 3 million lives.

My human best friend is coming round later for curry and lager, meanwhile, with my canine best friend, I crossed the beautiful golf course. We both had a spring in our step, until I realised there was an unmistakeable smell of burning in the air. We were approaching the clubhouse at the centre of the course, which was shuttered and dark. The burning was getting stronger. I was on the point of phoning the emergency services when I realised it wasn't coming from the clubhouse at all, but from the nearby McVitie's factory, which is a very short distance away as the crow flies. It wasn't an arson attack; it was the smell of slightly singeing chocolate Hobnobs.

Wednesday 10th June 2020.

I saw no one at all, all day, not a soul. I only had Brendan to talk to. And chatting to Brendan is never a bad thing. Apart from walking round the empty field several times, I did a lot of work on my book. It was actually a busy and productive day and I achieved a lot.

Breaking News: Earlier lockdown would have halved coronavirus death toll: Prime Minister's delay cost lives.

Thursday 11th June 2020.

As we're walking back from the field, two men, obviously two friends, meet in the street in front of us. They do the "elbow bump" that's apparently become quite common now, because of social distancing; it replaces the formal handshake, which they say has probably gone for good and will never come back.

I don't have a problem with this. I've never been very comfortable with shaking hands. Its excruciating if you proffer your hand first and get ignored. I'm also very self-conscious because I often have very sweaty palms, so in the event of a potential handshake looming on the horizon, I start frantically rubbing my hands on my trousers. Then there is the awkwardness of the strength of grip: do you go in hard to show you're a strong and assertive individual, or do you do a weak handshake to reassure the other person that you aren't overbearing and can be easily subjugated? There's no right answer and people will interpret your handshake differently, whilst also subtly trying to wipe your sweat from their palm. It's a minefield. But my main issue is actually that I don't really like touching strangers. It's awkward and embarrassing. I don't like interacting with strangers at all really, so to suddenly grab part of them is quite alien. Being British though, I am compelled to conform to the social niceties when expected and always politely say hello and comment on the weather. Some things go deeper than blood.

Breaking News: New data reveals that deprived areas have been hit by Covid-19 far worse than affluent areas.

Saturday 13th June 2020.

On the common, Brendan gets jumped on by three blondes. Golden Retrievers can be quite shameless when it comes to romance and hunting the male in a pack isn't nice. Rather than being flattered by the attention, Brendan is overwhelmed and keeps scooting away with his tail literally between his legs. One of the girls in particular, Izzy, won't be put off and pursues him mercilessly. Izzy's mum apologises. "I'm sorry... she's not like this with any other dog. I don't know what it is. She goes mad... Izzy! Stop that! ...as soon as she sees him. Izzy! Come on, you slut!"

Brendan can't evade his stalker. Izzy is eventually dragged off on her lead, but she turns to stare at Brendan, occasionally barking the equivalent of "Call me!"

But Brendan won't call.

* * * * * * * * * *

On the way home from Nicky's that evening, there are fireworks and a raging storm. Brendan is terrified. Of both. The weather is very odd and severe at the moment. The trees are thrashing, the clouds are streaming past and the sky cracks open with lightning. It feels like more dangerously prophetic End of Days stuff.

Monday 15th June 2020.

Today non-essential shops re-open in England. Not that I often go to any non-essential shops. I only go in shops when shopping is essential. I stay local today, shuttling between the field and home. I don't see Nicky today at all. It is a very quiet day. Just me and my dog. It thunders again in the afternoon and Brendan works himself up into a state and then goes almost catatonic, which is what he does when he gets over-stressed. It's terrible to see him like this. He comes round eventually, but it takes hours. Despite it being – I suppose – a landmark day in the easing of lockdown, it's actually a bad day.

Wednesday 17th June 2020.

There was more thunder, but this time Brendan was very brave and managed to rise above his fear, for which he probably deserves a medal.

Breaking News: HEALTH SECRETARY'S SOCIAL DISTANCING SLIP CAUGHT ON CAM! Matt Hancock slaps colleague on back in House of Commons, despite repeatedly warning the public about proximity.

I did my (supposedly) daily yoga and it was good. I'm also trying to do daily meditation to aid my relaxation. Today's session was very effective and I felt good afterwards.

Thursday 18th June 2020.

It was another of those days when we saw no one at all. They're very frequent now, but they aren't a problem. I've got my flat, I've got my dog, I'm good to go. (Nowhere.)

Breaking News: Global Covid death toll exceeds 450,000.

It rained all day. It never stopped. Not for a moment. I don't mind it, but Brendan *hates* rain. If he got into power, he would ban rain. If he ever comes to your door canvassing for your vote, don't be swayed by his silver tongue, just think about some of his ludicrous policies, like no rain. We wouldn't last very long without it.

We walked to the field several times – in the rain – and we got wet a lot.

Saturday 20th June 2020.

It's such a hot day! Unbelievably hot! And just in case you were wondering, today the highest *ever* temperature was recorded in the Arctic circle. It was 38C in Siberia. So now you know.

We walk to Nicky's via the common, trying our best to keep to the most shaded routes to avoid the blazing sunshine as far as possible. We have a nice afternoon and evening with Nicky and then we walk home again in the balmy summer's night. It's very warm and the sky is still light over the rooftops towards the west. It feels a bit like we're in a film. And maybe we are, because nothing feels very real any more.

Monday 22nd June 2020.

Today was a practical job day. I'm not keen on housework; I tend to do what *needs* to be done rather than what *ought* to be done. This is ironic, because cleaning things is very satisfying; it can actually be like a form of meditation. Cleaning, like exercise, is akin to a drug which can change your mood; I keep hoping I'll get addicted to both, but it doesn't seem to be happening.

Possibly due to the positive effects of cleaning... or strong tea... I had a really nice and productive day, and Brendan had a productive nap, on the bed and then on the sofa, because he's also trying to vary his routine. To cap it all we walked to the park in the early evening to meet Nicky, who cycled over after work. We sat on the grass, as far away as possible from the hundreds of other people who also sat on the grass. Groups sat in extended circles. People now bring deckchairs, windbreaks, barbeques and even pop-up tents. It's like Glastonbury on a hot day. But without the overspill of sewage and over-priced merchandise.

Tuesday 23rd June 2020.

Breaking News: Boris Johnson confirms the relaxing of the 2 metre social distancing rule. He says the UK's "national hibernation" is coming to an end.

The end is drawing near. The end of the 2020 English Covid lockdown. Perhaps I should be happy, but I have misgivings, because I don't think a lot of people are acting responsibly and I think social distancing should be maintained. I'm used to existing in a bubble now and only seeing a very small number of people. Certainly, for the safety of my dad and Nicky's mum, we'd rather it stayed that way until the danger has definitely gone.

I went for a long walk with Brendan. I can't say I noticed any difference in the world, to be honest. And neither did Brendan. After all, a smell's a smell, a wee's a wee. There were no street parties or banners. Lockdown is just fading away. It isn't news to most people, because they stopped abiding by the rules ages ago.

Sunday 28th June 2020.

Today is my birthday. I haven't been looking forward to it very much, because we usually go away for our summer holiday at this time, so that I have my birthday away. The last time we went to a cottage in Betws-ycoed in North Wales. On my actual birthday we drove to the coast, to the Llyn Peninsula and spent the day there. It was sunny and warm and beautiful. It was a perfect day, a perfect memory. That was our last holiday together. It seems a very long time ago. It seems another world. Of course, it was another world. No one had heard of Covid-19; no one knew what a lockdown was. It seems so implausible now.

Breaking News: "Swarmageddon!" Locusts continue to plague India.

I love going away, I love holidays and being on holiday is a *huge* part of my birthday, so staying at home is a disappointment, but it can't be helped. Nicky makes a real effort to ensure that the day is as special as possible and she has bought me lovely presents. She is a very thoughtful and ingenious gift buyer. I get lovely presents from Brendan and the cats as well; it seems they're also very thoughtful present buyers.

Breaking News: UK records 901 new Covid cases and 36 deaths.

In the evening we get a Chinese takeaway. We have a huge feast, which includes salt and pepper beancurd, which is our favourite. It's gorgeous. Despite not being on holiday, I've still had a really nice day.

Breaking News: The global Covid death toll passes 500,000, having doubled in under two months.

<u>Monday 29th June 2020.</u>

It's the day after my birthday and it's something of an anti-climax. It's raining and I feel miserable. I have no transport, no van and very little money. Though the country is in the process of re-opening, it still feels exactly the same as it did during the middle of lockdown.

In the afternoon, it's still raining. I decide to try and salvage my day. I sit on the sofa with my dog and open a can of Guinness (Brendan doesn't have any) and we start watching *Hinterland*, a Welsh neo-noir police drama, which I love, mainly because of the stunning photography and dark, foreboding scenery. It's brilliant. This feels rather decadent and turns my day around.

In the evening it's *still* raining. It's rained solidly all day... and it's June. I take Brendan out for a lovely walk in the rain. Everywhere feels cool and fresh... and wet... and we both enjoy it.

Breaking News: Matt Hancock announces Leicester will be UK's first local lockdown.

The government are now operating a "tier system" so that towns can lockdown separately if they get a Covid spike. There seems to be general confusion from the public about this. And no one seems to know what Tier their town is in and what they are permitted to do and what they're not. It's a very practical idea, but it's not really working. It has been announced that Leicester will go into full lockdown on 4th July.

<u>Wednesday 1st July 2020.</u>

Awful day. Saw no one, did nothing. The best part was sitting at the field with Brendan in the evening for an hour, which was lovely. (We're easily satisfied.)

<u>Saturday 4th July 2020.</u>

Breaking News: More restrictions eased in England. Pubs, restaurants and hairdressers reopen. But not in Leicester.

"Most" restrictions have been lifted in England today. Pubs, restaurants and hairdressers are now fully open for business, so people can get tanked up after having got their lockdown hair dealt with.

We have no intention of going in pubs or restaurants for the time being, even though they are supposedly being strictly run along social distancing guidelines, with queuing systems, separated tables and reduced occupancy. Judging by footage on the news, these guidelines are not being stringently adhered to. We are happy for now to stay in with cans. Brendan, however, would be back in the pub like a shot; inexplicably, he *loves* going to the pub. But not the hairdressers.

Breaking News: UK to hold minute's silence to remember those who have died of the coronavirus.

I didn't hear about this. It wasn't main news and I didn't see any evidence of it at all.

Sunday 5th July 2020.

Breaking News: Nation to clap to mark the 72nd anniversary of NHS.

The whole NHS thing seems to have worn off with the public. No one seemed to do this at all. It fell flat.

17th July 2020

Breaking News: Coronavirus no longer biggest UK killer for first time since March.

The old classic causes of death have bumped Covid from the top spot. Dementia and Alzheimer's are in the lead, followed by heart disease, then Covid, but it hardly seems a cause for celebration.

Wednesday 22nd July 2020.

Dad has been taken to hospital with a chest infection. It was quite unexpected and even though he has asbestosis, he generally has no problem with his chest. He wasn't allowed to have anyone accompanying him in the ambulance and he isn't allowed visitors, which makes everything so much worse.

Thursday 23rd July 2020.

It took ages to get through to the hospital, but when I did I was told Dad was doing fine. He's a fighter and usually has a fairly positive outlook. He quite enjoys trips to hospital, because he likes being surrounded by people – especially nurses – so as long as his health is stable I don't worry about him too much when he's in, which has been a lot in recent years. Actually, it's been a lot in not so recent years as well. He had a triple heart by-pass in his forties, which was supposed to give him ten years of life. Everyone else on his ward died within the given time frame, but Dad just kept on going. I hope this remains the case.

I make an effort with my yoga and exercises and I do a meditation session. I even do some cleaning, but it doesn't lift my spirits and I feel very down. I chat to Brendan, but his listening skills aren't really up to par today and nothing really helps.

Friday 24th July 2020.

Dad is still in hospital. It's terrible not being able to visit. It's near-impossible to get through to the hospital for updates and so far I have been unable to speak to Dad himself.

Breaking News: Government U-turn on masks.

From today, it became mandatory to wear a mask or similar face covering in shops and other public places. This is contrary to government guidance when the virus first reached our shores. It is now known that the coronavirus spreads primarily through droplets in a cough or sneeze, so masks are essential in the fight to prevent the spread. It is more about protecting other people from *your* germs, than protecting yourself.

I left Brendan having a nap and listening to The Smiths, while I walked to the local shops. It looked very odd with people out and about wearing masks, with half their faces covered. I can well believe some people might find it quite threatening and sinister. I felt quite self-conscious when I pulled my own mask on. I'd gone for plain black, though they come in all colours and patterns. The fact that everyone else was masked-up really helped. I found out straight away that one huge plus of wearing a mask is that you can rant and rave about people and the world in general and no one is aware. This really is an unexpected bonus.

Saturday 25th July 2020.

Dad is now out of hospital and back in his flat. I'm so glad he's home, though of course, that brings a host of Dad-related problems. But nevertheless, right at this moment I'm overjoyed!

Breaking News: Easing of lockdown continues with gyms, indoor swimming pools and leisure centres reopening.

Brendan visits his granddad and gives him the healing gift of tolerance, in that he walks into the flat, looks at Dad and then lies down on the carpet, turning his back on him. This is as good as it gets, so we all decide to see it as a step forward.

Thursday 30th July 2020.

Breaking News: Greater Manchester back into lockdown... with just 3 hours' notice, along with parts of East Lancashire and Yorkshire.

9.15pm. As of tomorrow, Greater Manchester will be in lockdown. This is an attempt to halt the rising number of coronavirus cases within the area.

Was it really worth coming out of lockdown? The Mayor of Greater Manchester, Andy Burnham, has been critical of the government's lack of warning, which he says has caused "confusion and distress" and "complete chaos".

The only restriction seems to be that people can no longer visit other households, either inside or outside, yet bizarrely, they can still meet in beer gardens. There has been much criticism of the seemingly random and "made up on the spot" rules and regulations.

While Brendan had a sit down at the field, I asked people how they felt about being thrown back into local lockdown and how it would affect them. Nobody seemed particularly aware of exactly what was going on or what they could or couldn't do, and no one seemed particularly bothered. I don't think it's a case of the British "stiff upper lip", I think most people are confused, bemused and fed up.

Breaking News: Boris Johnson warns: "We're not out of the woods!". Real chance of Covid resurgence.

Sunday 2nd August 2020.

It's Dad's birthday. It's not the greatest birthday, because we're in local lockdown, so everywhere's closed, but we make an effort. Happy birthday, Dad.

Breaking News: Major incident declared in Greater Manchester, as Covid infection rates soar.

Monday 3rd August 2020.

Breaking News: Lockdown restrictions are eased in Leicester: restaurants and pubs allowed to re-open.

Despite various places still being in lockdown, the government are encouraging people to "eat out to help out", a scheme to try and jump start the ailing hospitality industry. There is a 50% reduction on the price of meals on certain days and the government will pay the venue the remaining cost.

Let me spell this out... The number of Covid-19 infections is *increasing*: it's going up, not down, yet people are being encouraged to eat out and the students are returning to universities. Does anyone else see a problem here?

Thursday 6th August 2020.

I had a nice visit to Dad's. We watched a match in the snooker championships. Dad kept a commentary going and explained all the rules. I know as much about snooker as I do about nuclear fission, possibly less. It was really nice though, sharing in one of Dad's passions and spending some quality time together, rather than the visit being predominantly about practical things, like sorting out food and cleaning the toilet.

Brendan was indifferent towards the snooker; he's generally even less interested in sport than I am. So, unless sitting down becomes an Olympic event he's never going to be an eager competitor. During the match, he lay stretched out on the carpet and he didn't bark once at his granddad.

Breaking News: Covid infection rate STILL rising.

We walk to the Little Park, which is a formal Victorian park, complete with a bowling green, tennis courts and floral borders. It tries to cater for everyone and it feels very safe. You can come here and sit and read a book; in some parks you can only go in if you're intending to buy drugs or mug someone. Or sometimes combine the two.

Brendan's friend Storm arrives and the boys do a bit of alpha-male exertion. They have the weirdest way of fighting, both standing on their hind legs and locked in an embrace. Brendan doesn't do this with any other dog. It's very much like human wrestling. If they both had masks and leotards and were perhaps called *Desert Storm* and *The Bulgarian*, they could appear on Gladiators. (This is just a guess, as I've never, ever seen Gladiators.)

Saturday 8th August 2020.

This is the first time that either Nicky or I haven't had transport; the first time neither of us have had a car. Both our vehicles failed their MOTs towards the start of lockdown. It hasn't been a huge problem, as we haven't really needed one. But this week we've bought a car between us. A Ford Focus. It's blue. Today I drove it for the first time. I really like it. Brendan's travelling basket has been installed on the back seat and we're good to go.

Brendan gets very, *very* travel sick, so after not travelling at all for months we need to try and build up his tolerance gradually, so we won't be going on any huge trips for a while. But just to have a car and the potential to travel further than the field is amazing.

Sunday 9th August 2020.

Dad's fine today. He says hello to Brendan, but it's so loud it sounds like a threat. Brendan leans against my legs, suspiciously eyeing his granddad. We sit and have a chat. Dad's watching another programme on Alaska. Every time I go he seems to be watching a programme on Alaska. He's not particularly interested in Alaska and I didn't realise it was such a popular subject with programme makers. This is the third one this week. Unless it's the same one being repeated, but Dad thinks he's watching it for the first time.

Breaking News: Covid-19 daily infection rate exceeds 1,000 for the first time since June.

Today is National Lazy Day, which encourages laziness, obviously. In part, it allows people to take a break and manage stress levels. Apparently, people who are lazy are more resourceful, though I find that a bit unlikely. An unofficial ambassador for Lazy Day, Brendan Freedog, was asked to comment, but he was too tired.

<u>Friday 14th August 2020.</u>

Breaking News: More unlocking. UK eases restrictions.

Despite Covid infection rates increasing and despite restrictions remaining in Greater Manchester and parts of Lancashire and Yorkshire, the rest of the country saw a further move towards easing restrictions today, as most other businesses, including theatres and bowling alleys, are now permitted to open. However, nightclubs and "sexual entertainment venues" must remain closed. I'm not sure exactly what a "sexual entertainment venue" is, only that it's not currently allowed to open.

* * * * * * * * *

Today is National Tell A Joke Day. So, here goes...

My dog's a blacksmith. The first time I took him home, he made a bolt for the door.

A man lost his dog. His wife suggested he put an advert in the local paper. "Don't be stupid." he said, "He can't read!"

How do you stop your dog digging up your garden? Confiscate his spade.

(I didn't say they had to be good jokes.)

<u>Monday 17th August 2020.</u>

Breaking News: The number of global coronavirus cases has far exceeded 20 million.

I watched a short film about Doctor James Niven, a Scottish doctor who became the Medical Officer of Health for Manchester during the Spanish Flu pandemic of 1918. Amongst his many – at the time – quite revolutionary measures to fight the disease, he recommended an end to public gathering, promoted the need for people to keep distant from each other to prevent the spread, and encouraged those displaying symptoms to isolate themselves. Of course, we can see that this was a rudimentary form of optional social distancing. His influence and teachings saved *thousands* of lives, especially amongst the poor living in cramped conditions in the backstreets of Manchester.

I find it tragic that a man who worked tirelessly for the benefit of others and saved so many, suffered from depression and killed himself in 1925.

James Niven. Physician.
(1851 – 1925)

Thursday 20th August 2020.

It was a pleasant day and a pleasant evening, warm and sunny. Nicky cycled to the park to meet us. We sat on the grass chatting, Brendan lay beside us, watching the world go by. There was a nice, lazy, summer atmosphere. Everything seemed quite perfect in a small and local way. But you should never think that, because at 6.30pm Nicky got a call. It was her mum, Rosie. She was feeling very ill and had called an ambulance. Nicky went racing off to intercept her. Although it stayed sunny, it was like a dark cloud had moved above us and everything went sour.

<u>Saturday 22nd August 2020.</u>

Dad's managed to stay out of hospital at the moment, but Nicky's mum is still in. She has been diagnosed with an aortic ulcer. She has stabilised, is coping well and is due home in a couple of days. There is no visiting, of course, which is very difficult for Nicky.

Breaking News: New Covid cases rising daily.

I take Brendan to the common. I'm very much trying to focus on the moment and the things around me right now. As a result, I'm much more aware of nature and all of the beautiful plants and flowers at this time of year, including the so-called weeds: ground elder, rosebay willowherb, nettles, red campion and ivy on a gatepost. Brendan wees on them all.

Magpie count: two for joy. Well, there are two magpies, the joy part remains to be seen. If any joy happens, I'll get back to you.

<u>Wednesday 26th August 2021.</u>

It's National Dog Day. Though to be honest, it seems like every day is National Dog Day. But I love my dog. I am grateful for the difference he's made to my life. I love his revolutionary ways. He's introduced the concept of "the walk as a spectator sport". I love his philosophy, "if I can't do it from a seated position, it's someone else's responsibility". I love the fact that he's shamelessly handsome and doesn't even realise it.

I love The Boy. He's kept me slightly sane in an insane world.

Sunday 30th August 2020.

Many people have gone back to their normal lives. They are going to the pub and for meals and to parties. They're going on holiday. They're even going abroad. We're not doing any of those things. Our parents are ill and vulnerable and we're not doing anything to put them or ourselves at risk. We're not going anywhere; we're not doing anything or seeing anyone. So, our lives haven't changed at all since lockdown ended.

Breaking News: 850,000 deaths from coronavirus have been reported globally.

Nicky's mum is out of hospital and back home. My dad is still at home. It's starting to feel like these are the sort of events you should commit to paper. So I have done.

Wednesday 1st September 2020.

I'm a free spirit. At heart, I am. Or that's what I want to be, but I've never actually felt very free. Not really. I've always felt constrained. Not physically, but you don't need four walls to be imprisoned. We're all prisoners of our circumstances. I want to travel, but – pandemic aside – I can't just go and leave my Dad, who needs constant care. I could never just go travelling, because it wouldn't be right, so I'm not in any way free. I have never felt less free. And it has nothing to do with Covid or lockdown.

So, while I'm feeling trapped and far from liberated, I've decided to spend this month re-watching perhaps the ultimate treatise on freedom within popular culture, the 'Sixties classic, The Prisoner. Because after all, I'm not a number, I'm a Freeman.

Brendan used to be a prisoner; he was an inmate in a Bulgarian kill shelter. He had a number on a tag through his ear. Brendan is now not remotely a prisoner. He is free. He is Brendan Freedog.

Thursday 3rd September 2020.

I see Dad in the morning and we go to Nicky's mum's in the evening. Both are as well as they can be with their health conditions. Trying to be constantly cheerful and optimistic all the time for the benefit of other people is really exhausting, but it's essential.

* * * * * * * * *

Things that make Brendan cheerful: sitting down at a field or park; getting home and leaping on the bed; when Nicky arrives; going to the field; having his morning brush; going in pubs and cafes. Actually, it's anything that involves sitting down, lying down or sleeping.

Friday 4th September 2020.

It's Eat An Extra Dessert Day. I'm not making it up, it

really is. Though, it *is* the kind of national day I *would* make up. But I didn't. So, guess what I did today!

Saturday 5th September 2020.

Today is World Beard Day. I've already got that covered.

World Beard Day has been recognised for over a thousand years. It is always celebrated on the first Saturday in September. It is customary for the bearded ones to relax and do nothing; Brendan is already doing just that. Well, he does have a beard. One of the suggested activities – for some reason – is to change a tyre with some bearded friends, but we'll probably just go to the field.

* * * * * * * * * *

Things that make Brendan less than cheerful: going for his late night walk, around 10pm; people coming and going and making a noise or even being quiet, or existing really; travelling by car; walking to places other than the field; crowds; not having all his own way, all of the time.

Sunday 6th September 2020.

Brendan has a very impressive poker face. Strangers can never tell whether he's genuinely pleased to see them or whether he's lulling them into a false sense of security before mugging them. (It's *always* the latter.) They said at the sanctuary that he was unpredictable and had behavioural issues, but they just didn't understand him. We know each other well and I can read him like an open book. Coincidentally, it's Read A Book Day today. We read this one, Dog Days by Gray Freeman.

Breaking News: Health Secretary Matt Hancock is "concerned" about the rising Covid cases "predominantly among young people".

So, I've started watching the cult classic, *The Prisoner*, now, during lockdown, to try and establish a sense of what freedom is. I only watched it a year ago, but it was a different world then. ("We're all pawns, m'dear.")

Filming began in 1966, starring former *Danger Man* actor, Patrick McGoohan, who had a hand in every aspect of *The Prisoner*'s conception and realisation.

The first episode, Arrival, perfectly sets the premise for the series. It is undoubtedly one of the most important, influential and indeed *perfect* television instalments of all time. It is peppered with memorable action scenes and thought-provoking cerebral content, quotable dialogue and stunning location filming at the Italianate village of Portmeirion, in North Wales. I love every iconic second of it. Sadly, in my humble opinion, the series will never be quite this good again.

What I've learned about freedom: If I was a top secret agent and was kidnapped and imprisoned in somewhere as stunning as Portmeirion, I'd like to think I'd be a happy prisoner. But I wouldn't be. Sadly, the fact that someone else was saying I had to stay there would mean I'd have to do everything in my power to escape. However, seeing as I'm not *technically* a secret agent, if anyone kidnapped me and took me to Portmeirion, I think it would be acceptable for me to sit back and enjoy my incarceration.

Despite not being at all free, I feel a little bit more liberated for having watched *The Prisoner*.

Be seeing you.

Wednesday 9th September 2020.

Breaking News: Trials for a Covid vaccine being developed by AstraZeneca and the University of Oxford paused after UK participant suffers adverse reaction.

Despite vicariously discovering a sense of freedom via *The Prisoner*, I'm really missing going on holiday. One of my favourite places in the world is Portmeirion in North Wales, where *The Prisoner* was filmed. I discovered it before I discovered *The Prisoner* and not the other way round. It was built as a project by a local "errant architect" Sir Clough Williams-Ellis, who developed the faux Mediterranean village in this wooded site, to show that with "architectural good manners" a natural site could be enhanced rather than defiled. I think Portmeirion is a testament to his theory.

I'd love to wander along its beaches in the late summer sunshine. Or even in the rain. I've been many times with Nicky, but I'd like to introduce Brendan to the special, secret places on the tree-shrouded headland. Unfortunately, I believe they no longer allow dogs, so it doesn't look like we'll be re-visiting. My policy is very straightforward: no dog: no me.

<u>Thursday 10th September 2020.</u>

Today is World Suicide Prevention Day. In my time as a support worker, and volunteering as a Samaritan and on soup runs, I have encountered several suicides. They have always been tragic and unspeakably sad. I had assumed that during lockdown, the suicide rate would have increased. Strangely, figures so far show that lockdown has had no adverse effect on the suicide rate, though it has affected mental health in general.

I would posit that the suicide rate hasn't increased during these difficult times, because it has felt like real life is suspended, everyone has been stressed and imprisoned, so there has been that "wartime" feeling of good will and community. Possibly the rate will increase when and if we are ever back to a state of normality and people are expected to try and return to their former lives.

It's well known that mental health is aided hugely by talking about and sharing your problems. We're encouraged to talk to a friend, or your doctor or your priest or your village shaman, or to phone the Samaritans. Even talking to your dog has been shown to be very therapeutic. Apart from his rather steep hourly rate, Brendan is an excellent counsellor.

Breaking News: Coronavirus deaths have globally exceeded 900,000.

The coronavirus hasn't gone away at all.

Friday 11th September 2020.

At the Big Field, Brendan starts playing with a black and white spaniel called Oreo, who's out with his professional dog walker, who is calling him from the other side of the field: "Oreo, come on! Oreo! Oreo, come on! Oreo! Come on, Oreo! Oreo! Oreo! *Oreo!*" This went on for fifteen minutes, until he laughingly tried some reverse psychology: "Oreo… stay!"

It was a great idea, but that didn't work either. Oreo stayed put. He carried on playing until he was good and ready to head home. I could tell Brendan was completely in awe of him.

Breaking News: Infection rate increases: worst since March.

I watched another episode of *The Prisoner;* it was entertaining and thought-provoking.

Saturday 12th September 2020.

Breaking News: Expert warns: UK on verge of losing control. Recorded Covid cases exceed 3,000.

Nothing much happened today, but just watching Brendan in the park, sniffing and snuffling and scampering along with his tail in the air, is like the best therapy ever. No matter how bad the world is – and let's face it, it's quite bad – he never fails to lift my spirits.

Monday 14th September 2020.

Hell, it's a Monday, but I'm wearing my "Friday" socks. Is this the true meaning of freedom? (Probably not.)

Breaking News: Government's new "Rule of Six" comes into play. Social gatherings of more than six are banned in England.

A quick stroll around the park will prove to you that no one is adhering to the new social gathering regulations, partly because they don't understand the complex rules that surround them, but mainly because they just don't care. No matter how many times I see it, I never fail to be shocked by the flagrant disregard for social distancing.

Wednesday 16th September 2020.

Today's juice: apple, kiwi and pear. I thought it was going to be awful, because the pears were hard and unripe, the kiwis were soft and going brown and the apple was quite bitter. However, it was sweet and very nice, even though it did rather resemble an ostentatious sneeze.

Breaking News: As Covid infection rate continues to rise, UK warned "far worse things to come". PM says a second Covid wave is coming and further restrictions may be necessary.

When I was a child, I had a big picture book called something like "A Child's Encyclopaedia of Knowledge". It was very colourful and had features on many things to do with science. I think about this book a lot. I loved it. I especially loved a section on life in the future. The book had probably been written and illustrated decades before, as it seemed to convey the "future" as it might appear in the 1950s. There were open-plan living spaces, sliding doors and spindle-legged furniture. The people shown were like the cartoon *Jetsons*. It was already an anachronism. I read and re-read these sections with excitement, looking forward to the time when we indeed lived like this. But we never did. We still don't. We never will. That future never came.

Apart from those images, I don't know what I expected

the future to be like, because it seems to be tempting fate to imagine such things, and really, by the time I was in my teens I didn't think there would be a future, other than nuclear annihilation. I never expected to get beyond my teenage years. I certainly didn't envisage a future like this. I was convinced the world would end, but I was possibly only wrong about the timing and the methodology.

Monday 21st September 2020.

Breaking News: Wearing glasses can reduce the risk of contracting Covid, due to them creating a protective barrier and discouraging eye-touching.

At the park, we meet Brendan's friend, Storm, who we haven't seen for weeks. His dad tells me they haven't been coming here very often, because a couple of other dogs have been bullying him. I assume he means bullying Storm. Storm is so happy and boisterous I can't imagine him being bullied. He never stops and he never gives up. He seems to have grown considerably since we last saw him. He looks like he's been working out and he's learnt a few new moves, but Brendan will still come out on top.

Breaking News: Government's chief scientific advisor: by mid-October expect 200 deaths a day.

Today's juice: apple, kiwi and pear again. I thought it was going to be awful. This time I was right: it was.

Breaking News: UK coronavirus alert upgraded to level 4: "transmission is high or rising exponentially".

I finished watching The Prisoner. For me, the series loses its way somewhat over the course of its 17-episode run. Some of the later stories come across as obligational fillers rather than crucial thrillers with something to say. The final episode is a visual spectacle, but when unleashed on an unsuspecting public in 1968 it caused an outcry and McGoohan claims he had to flee the country, switchboards were jammed and reviewers spat venom. The basic cry was "What the hell did it mean?" It's actually packed with meaning, but it's only with repeated viewings that I understand it. Whilst certainly not everyone's cup of tea, The Prisoner remains one of the most important and ground-breaking television experiences of all time.

Tuesday 22nd September 2020.

We walk to the park. Brendan sits down on the grass and patiently, silently, watches everything that's going on, clocking every movement, but not reacting, just observing. I've never known a dog to be such an avid watcher, rather than participant. He remains still and silent all the time. He'd make a great Cold War spy. But he'd probably be working for the Russians.

Breaking News: PM ANNOUNCES NEW RESTRICTIONS. Boris Johnson: UK has reached "a perilous turning point".

In a televised address to the nation, the Prime Minister announced a new set of flimsy half-measures and ineffectual restrictions, including that all retail staff must wear masks (Why are they not already?), a limit to the numbers attending weddings, fines for Covid rule breaking, a return to working from home and a much-derided 10pm curfew for the hospitality trade.

On graphs, the red line showing coronavirus deaths has been climbing gradually, not steadily like Brazil, or massively like India, but climbing nevertheless, rather than going down.

Breaking News: UK records 37 deaths in just 24 hours, the highest number of fatalities in a single day in over two months.

Friday 25th September 2020.

Breaking News: 1,700 students in Manchester told to isolate for 14 days after glut of positive Covid tests.

Brendan had a dream in the early morning, whining and spasming. It always makes me sad, because I'm sure he's reliving past traumas from his life on the streets. Of course, being Brendan he could well be having a nightmare about missing the start of *Bergerac*. We'll never know.

Breaking News: British Transport Police reveal that nearly 15,000 people were tackled for not

wearing face coverings on trains for a four week period.

<u>Saturday 26th September 2020.</u>

We walk back from the park, passing a little pub I used to frequent in my teens and twenties. It's currently empty, perhaps undergoing refurbishment, or possibly closed for good due to this year's financial strain. I have always lived within the same square mile or so; it wasn't planned, I didn't intend to stay in this area, but things don't always work out how we imagine. As a result, there are a lot of memories around here. For me, not Brendan. I hope Brendan has very few memories of his past life on the streets of Bulgaria and is busily storing happy memories of his new life as a British citizen.

Breaking News: Thousands of anti-lockdown protestors gather in Trafalgar Square. The demo is broken up by the police as it contravenes social-distancing regulations.

<u>Sunday 27th September 2020.</u>

Breaking News: The global coronavirus death toll tops 1 million.

I feel resigned and hopeless. It seems like this is never going to end. Is this our lives now?

<u>Thursday 1st October 2020.</u>

Today is International Coffee Day, during which we

naturally enough celebrate that intoxicatingly aromatic queen of beverages. (Tea is the King. Get over it.) I love coffee, but I rarely have it. I want to savour it and I want a complete coffee experience from it, so I only drink it in a café, I never have it at home. Coffee must be freshly made. Some foul-tasting tar poured from a glass pot that's been stewing since Easter is not acceptable.

Johann Sebastian Bach said: "Without my morning coffee, I'm just like a dried-up piece of a goat." Yes, quite. Producer David Lynch said "Even a bad cup of coffee is better than no coffee at all." Well, I sat through the entirety of Twin Peaks Season 3 (2017) and as a result, David, I'm not sure your opinion counts. And I completely disagree with you. I would *much* rather have no coffee than an imperfect cup. Because I have black coffee, without sugar – because anything else is a criminal act – I have very exacting standards. I have an Americano, which is espresso topped up with hot water. I like it strong, but smoothly roasted; I don't want a bitter aftertaste.

I love independent coffee shops, the quirkier the better. My favourite mainstream coffee shop is Nero for its décor and ambience, but for the all-important coffee, it's Costa.

Today, however, whether it's International Coffee Day or not, due to circumstances beyond my control, I won't be going into a café for a perfectly brewed Americano, because I'll be spending most of the day at Dad's.

I set off with Brendan, through the crisp morning. I'm very aware that it's the first day of October, which –

to me – signifies the end of summer and the start of autumn, and also the slippery slope towards Christmas. Most significantly, October represents the winding down of another year. I love autumn. I love the colours, but I hate the end of summer. I hate the transition. We walk to Dad's, and although it's a nice enough day, there is a definite autumnal chill in the air and the trees are showing their autumn colours and Brendan's over-sized paws are padding through fallen leaves.

I leave Brendan with Nicky; he sits on the sofa looking very miserable and refusing to eat the treats he's been given. I walk up to Dad's flat alone.

After continual trouble from Dad's carers, Social Services have intervened and fired them. They have found a new agency to be responsible for my dad's care. I meet the new carers and talk them through Dad's needs and routine. Within an hour I feel we are out of the frying pan, into the fire. The new carers are even worse. *Considerably* worse. Dad's main carer is wearing a mask, but it's not covering his nose, so it is completely useless. He tells me he doesn't believe in the coronavirus and doesn't believe in masks and says: "I never thought I'd be doing *this* for a living." (UPDATE: Very soon, he won't be.) We don't get off to a good start.

Friday 2nd October 2020.

Dad went missing again. There was a fair amount of panic and tension, but he turned up, fit and well, with no explanation about where he'd been.

I was sitting at the field with Brendan, when Nicky

texted. She has a "track and trace" app on her phone. You check in wherever you go and you are alerted if there is a Covid outbreak. This morning, Nicky had an alert saying she had come into close contact with someone who had tested positive and that she should self-isolate. She was very upset; her main concern was how it would affect her mum, whether she had passed the virus to her mum and the upset of not being able to see her mum. She back-tracked where she had been and when, and was convinced it was inaccurate. It was on the news later that day that it was a frequent fault with the system, that people were erroneously targeted and told to self-isolate. At that point, Nicky – and a good proportion of the nation – removed the app from her phone.

My phone isn't capable of supporting the app. It's barely capable of making a telephonic communication or sending a text. However, I have my own defence system. Because of my bad-tempered dog, I don't tend to come into close proximity with anyone. Ever. People tend to look at him and give us a wide berth, and I'm more than happy with that. Brendan meanwhile is convinced people give us a wide berth because of me.

Breaking News: President Trump and wife test positive for Covid-19, amid outbreak amongst Whitehouse senior staff.

Saturday 3rd October 2020.

Dad's had a fall just outside his flat and has cut his head badly. An ambulance is on the way. Dad looks terrible.

He has blood down his face and all over his shirt. One arm of his glasses has snapped and is lost. Despite this, Dad is philosophical and quite good natured.

The paramedics arrive and examine him thoroughly. As usual, they're brilliant and have a great attitude. Dad's injuries appear to be superficial, but as he's banged his head quite badly, he needs to go in for observation. He's taken to a hospital in central Manchester. As before, no one can accompany him in the ambulance and no one is allowed into the hospital with him, which just feels awful. It feels like he's being abandoned. However, he goes off quite happily in the ambulance, having a laugh and joke with the two young paramedics.

* * * * * * * * * *

It's Buy British Day. I generally try to buy British fruit and vegetables wherever possible. Today, however, I bought nothing at all, so at least I bought nothing that *wasn't* British. I hope that counts, Britain.

Sunday 4th October 2020.

I've been so stressed today. Dad's in hospital. Allegedly. He's actually been missing within the system for nearly 24 hours. They knew he'd arrived; they had a record of him being admitted, but they couldn't locate which ward he'd been sent to. I kept getting put through to different people and going in a circle, until I started to shout at them. That didn't help either. My brother phoned later and managed to locate him. Dad was seemingly doing well and showing no signs of concussion.

Breaking News: UK reports nearly 23,000 new Covid cases. This was due to a backlog created by a technical error.

I'm so stressed. It really does feel like one thing after another. Everything seems to be going wrong. I just try to keep going and deal with one thing at a time in an attempt not to get overwhelmed. I take Brendan for a walk and try and focus on him, watching his tail and his urgent movements as he stops at a scent. This is about as relaxed as things get.

Monday 5th October 2020.

Nicky has taken her mum to a hospital appointment at the Haematology Clinic. The outcome isn't good. Rosie has been given a diagnosis of MDS, which can develop into leukaemia. This is an unexpected and terrible diagnosis. There are no words to describe how Nicky is feeling. It's like the world has ended. Everything is black; everything is sour. The meaning of everything has changed. What mattered yesterday doesn't matter today. Time has stopped and there is a deadness in everything. She is completely devastated.

Monday 12th October 2020.

A week of cold, dead hell has passed. I don't know how, but it did.

Breaking News: Yesterday India topped 7 million Covid cases.

I take Brendan to the Little Park. He has a play with his friend, Storm. It's a joy to watch. Our walks are probably the happiest part of the day. Actually, the *only* happy part of the day.

There is a steady breeze and leaves float slowly down like confetti. A beech tree has been daubed with the white painted slogan: I WANT TO BE HUMAN. That's not very wise at the moment. You're probably better off being a tree. It's not a great time to be human.

Wednesday 14th October 2020.

Brendan isn't a morning person at all, but once we're out of the flat and heading towards the field or the park, he scampers along with his tail held high, very excited to get there and see what's going on. Today, nothing is going on. Absolutely nothing. So, he sits patiently scanning all gates for any four-legs who might happen to come this way. But none do.

Breaking News: Government's new three-tier system of Covid restrictions starts in England.

The new three-tier system is confusing and pointless and no one takes any notice.

Breaking News: America exceeds 8 million Covid cases.

Tuesday 20th October 2020.

Nicky has taken her mum, Rosie, to hospital for a blood

transfusion. She phones to let me know they've arrived safely. She's very upset and despairing. I used to take my mum to the same ward every week for chemotherapy. It wasn't a nice experience, it was quite heart-breaking, though generally most of the patients were full of fight. I stayed with my mum and we did crosswords and chatted, but Nicky isn't allowed to stay, so she's had to leave Rosie, but you don't want to leave the person, because they seem so small and fragile and vulnerable. It's very upsetting.

Breaking News: Manchester to go into Tier 3 lockdown due to number of Covid cases.

At 5pm today, the Prime Minister announced that after much negotiation and mud-slinging with Manchester's mayor, Andy Burnham, Manchester will go into Tier 3 lockdown.

Andy Burnham said: "In summary, at no point today were we offered enough to protect the poorest people in our communities through the punishing reality of the winter to come."

Breaking News: The number of global coronavirus cases has surged to over 40 million.

By the time Nicky's back from the hospital, she's exhausted and just wants to go home alone. I don't see her in the evening, despite it being our anniversary. In the circumstances, no one acknowledges it or mentions it at all.

<u>Thursday 29th October 2020.</u>

Everything is terrible. I can't get to speak to Dad. Most days I just can't get through to the ward, when I do, I don't get any answers or reassurance, because they don't actually know what's wrong with him. Nicky's mum is quite ill and Nicky cries most of the time. The pandemic is passing us by, largely unnoticed; we've got bigger things going on in our lives.

Actor and comedian Bobby Ball, died in hospital today of coronavirus. He was 76.

Bobby Ball (Born Robert Harper)
(28th January 1944 – 28th October 2020)

<u>30th October 2020.</u>

I took Brendan to the park. He had a snuffle while I collected leaves, which I do periodically. It gets you out of your head and brings you into the present, makes you focus on the here and now. It makes you look and see. It's a very useful tool. I'm just trying to find some positives and at the moment it's not easy.

Breaking News: UK Covid deaths this week: 1,379. Global Covid death toll stands at 1.2 million.

<u>Saturday 31st October 2020.</u>

Breaking News: Research shows that Vitamin D can have a positive effect on Covid-19.

Vitamin D sources: sunshine.

It's Hallowe'en tonight. Dad's still in hospital and it's virtually impossible to get through to his ward; it's as though he's just disappeared. Nicky's mum, Rosie, isn't very well at all. Nicky is being strong and positive and is, I know, a tower of strength to her mum. Everything is so awful and so depressing and so stressful.

Breaking News: Prime Minister announces imminent lockdown, to prevent a "medical and moral disaster".

In the afternoon, the Prime Minister reveals that the whole of England will be going into a second lockdown in order to prevent a "medical and moral disaster" for the NHS. The three-tier system didn't work, as predicted by the government's own scientific advisors. No one understood it or paid it even the slightest bit of attention.

The second national lockdown will commence on 5th November 2020. Well, the freedom was good while it lasted. Except it didn't last. Greater Manchester was moved to Tier 3 lockdown early on, so in reality there was no freedom.

Breaking News: The planned 4 week National Lockdown will apply to everyone. Stay at home wherever possible. All non-essential retail will close.

Unexpectedly, Dad is released from hospital and brought back to his flat, so we head over immediately.

While any normal dog would relish the additional walk, Brendan begrudges the unscheduled change to his nap and relaxation itinerary.

When we get there, he's in excellent spirits; Dad that is, not Brendan. Brendan isn't. Dad's hair, which he usually keeps quite short, is longer and needs cutting. It makes him look a bit like a woodland animal. He's really funny and great company. Instead of his carers – the new carers have also been fired – Dad is currently having nurses several times a day to do his medication, food and check on him generally, as he's technically rehabilitating and getting used to his own home again, so they can assess his capabilities. The first nurse arrives. I go through all Dad's needs and so forth, then get out of their way.

I phone later and Dad is just going to bed and seems very cheerful and very well. It was so nice seeing him again. It has made my day.

Sunday 1st November 2020.

We walked over to Dad's in the early morning. Brendan dragged at first, when he realised we were going in the opposite direction to the field. He only really likes going to the field. Once he'd given up trying to persuade me to turn back, he sauntered along at a fairly brisk pace, stopping to sniff every few yards and yawning frequently. Just how much sleep does a dog need?

Dad was still in bed when we arrived. He said he wasn't feeling too good. He had stomach ache, but he very often had stomach ache, so it wasn't out of the ordinary.

I made him a cup of tea and we chatted for a while, but he wanted to be left in peace to get some sleep before the next nurse arrived, so we left him to it.

An hour later, I had a call from the nurse, to say she had sent Dad to hospital, as she suspected he had kidney stones. Less than 24 hours at home and he was back in hospital again.

Breaking News: PM warns the Covid situation will be "twice as bad" as spring.

I was awoken just before midnight, by my phone ringing. It was a withheld number. I answered, with a sense of foreboding. It was a doctor in A&E. He asked if I had discussed a "do not resuscitate" policy with my father. He was currently on oxygen, possibly had a bleed on the brain, pneumonia, was deathly pale and I was told he wasn't expected to survive until morning, but still he wasn't allowed visitors. The doctor said he'd phone back later for my definitive answer about resuscitation.

I didn't know what my answer was. My answer for me personally would be no, do not resuscitate, but Dad's such a fighter and is only alive now after a catalogue of serious illnesses, because of that fighting spirit. I was uncertain and didn't feel I could make the decision alone. I phoned my brother and between us we agreed on "do not resuscitate".

I had no number to phone the doctor back, so I could only wait for his call. I didn't sleep again that night, obviously. I thought about Dad constantly. I'd had a lovely time with him yesterday and I was very grateful for that. If that was the last time I saw him, then it was a lovely memory and a nice way to remember him.

I managed to convince myself that if he was unconscious now and slipped away without coming round, that wasn't such a bad way to go, all things considered. He'd been very ill for some time and his Alzheimer's was getting steadily worse. I found a sort of peace and some acceptance and I effectively said goodbye to my dad.

Monday 2nd November 2020.

I was awake all night, full of adrenaline. I couldn't catch my breath and my chest was burning. I was just waiting for the call from the doctor. He said he'd call back. He didn't. Eight hours passed and there was no call. I phoned the hospital and – because it was so early – actually managed to get through. I expected to be told, "Oh yes, your father died in the night, but we were too busy to phone you. There is a pandemic on, you know." Instead, I spoke to a very friendly nurse, who laughed when I mentioned Dad's name. "He's having toast and marmalade and asking for seconds."

"Pardon?"

"He's being cheeky. He's a right character, isn't he?"

"Dad? *My* dad? My dad's having toast?"

"Yeah."

A few hours ago my dad *was* toast, now he's laughing

and flirting and seemingly has the appetite of a ravenous toast-eating horse.

"Are you sure you've got the right person? I was told he wouldn't survive the night."

"Yes." the happy nurse said, "He looked *awful* last night when I came on shift, but he's fine now."

I was confused – and *really* surprised – but very happy. Dad was eating toast and being cheeky. That's so Dad. The nurse couldn't tell me what was wrong with him and there were no doctors available, but Dad was currently doing very well.

* * * * * * * * *

A District Nurse visited Rosie, Nicky's mum, for the first of her regular visits. She said Rosie had a temperature and needed to have a coronavirus test. Nicky took a test kit over. Thankfully, she didn't have Covid. She was just hot. At least this was a false alarm. But it does make you think "What exactly is going to be thrown at us next?"

Tuesday 3rd November 2020.

Today is International Stress Awareness Day. I'm only too aware of my stress; Nicky is only too aware of her stress. Brendan sleeps off his stress. We're trying to combat our stress as best we can, but we're not having much success.

* * * * * * * * *

I missed a call while I was in the shower. It was from

the hospital, so I was immediately on red alert. And stressed. When I finally got through to his ward, Dad was happy and chirpy and having his breakfast. He seems to have breakfast an awful lot. We had a lovely chat. He liked the ward, he liked the nurses, he liked the food and he said he was "enjoying the rest." Presumably from sitting down at home in front of the television. It was really nice to chat to him and to hear him sounding so well. It was nice to hear his voice, because I never thought I'd hear it again. I was aware that I felt a little bit less stressed.

Wednesday 4th November 2020.

Dad's still in hospital. Every time I speak to a doctor, Dad's diagnosis has changed, but gallstones gets mentioned a lot, so that seems to be where we're up to. He's expected to be in hospital for some weeks.

So, this is the last day before additional, bonus lockdown. The pubs are expected to be busy tonight with people making the most of the last night of drinking. As a result, by going out and drinking and inevitably being irresponsible, some will contract coronavirus and some will die, whilst some people won't contract it, but they'll carry it and pass it on to others, some of whom will die.

Tomorrow we'll be in full lockdown. It will also be Bonfire Night, the night we celebrate a 17th Century man in a funny hat who tried to blow up the government.

Brendan never misses a chance to use his hangdog expression.

PART II
THE SECOND NATIONAL LOCKDOWN
Dark Days

<u>Thursday 5th November 2020.</u>

Well, it's here. Day One of the Second National Lockdown. One of the tasks I've set myself for this lockdown is to try and improve Brendan's recall and to try and get him more active, especially with dog games, which will help to stimulate his mind. As a street dog he presumably didn't have much time for playing.

We walk to the park. I spot a suitable stick. I pick up the stick. I throw the stick. "Go and fetch the stick, boy!"

Brendan sits down and looks at me.

"Go on! Where's the stick?"

He tilts his head very slightly to one side, but he isn't going anywhere. Of course, we've been through this routine many times, always with similar results. I collect the stick, I throw it several times, while he remains seated and watching curiously, until he gets bored, stands up and walks off.

It's Day One; I won't be disheartened. It's early days.

Breaking News: PM says: Stay at home! 492 deaths reported yesterday.

I leave Brendan at home having his post-walk nap and

listening to the Smiths (he loves the Smiths), while I walk to the local shops. As in the first lockdown, instead of the warm lights of the shops, there are cold, grey, steel shutters or dark, unlit windows. Only the food shops are open.

There is a mulch of rotting leaves in the gutters and the air is grey. There is very little traffic and very few people about, but it feels like a carnival atmosphere compared to the last lockdown, when there was panic on the streets of London, Dublin, Dundee, Humberside. Local businesses were finding it difficult enough *before* Coronavirus, so I can't imagine how they will survive 2020.

In the Co-op, all but one woman is wearing a mask. When a member of staff confronts her, she impatiently holds up a hand and snaps *"Exempt!"*, then continues into the shop. People with certain medical conditions are exempt from having to wear a mask, but as you don't need to prove your exemption, absolutely anyone can yell "Exempt!" when they aren't, just as this woman did.

People jostle up and down the aisles and frequently invade each other's space, until the queue for the tills, when everyone duly positions themselves two metres apart, in accordance with the lines on the floor.

Back out in the street, the masks are quickly removed and no one seems to be carrying out any form of social distancing. And that could be why we're back in lockdown and the death rate keeps climbing.

Breaking News: Anti-lockdown protest leads

to 104 arrests in central London. Police say the gathering "is unlawful and putting others at risk."

Nicky comes to us in the evening. It's Bonfire Night, so there are fireworks and Brendan gets into a state. I spend all night trying to calm him down.

Day One of the all-new lockdown is coming to an end. I lie in bed with Brendan at my side. It hasn't felt remotely like the previous lockdown. Because it isn't *remotely* like the previous lockdown, because it *isn't* a lockdown. From what I've seen around me, most people just aren't taking it at all seriously, which could have disastrous consequences.

Friday 6th November 2020.

Lockdown really isn't the worst thing that's currently going on in our lives. Nor is coronavirus. My dad is in hospital and I can't see him, but he's being looked after and seems to be enjoying himself, enjoying being surrounded by people and that's a positive that I'm latching onto.

Poor Rosie, Nicky's mum, is having regular blood transfusions and is bouncing back and forth from the doctor's, having frequent spells in hospital. She is feeling ill most of the time.

With all this going on, it's very difficult not to be negative, but I'm purposely trying to not dwell on those negatives. This diary is categorically *not* about the negatives; in part, it's about actively seeking the positives. I'm a very negative optimist. There are positives in every day; they might be small and very difficult to find, they might be hidden behind a big pile of steaming negatives, but they're there. Somewhere. Probably. It's just that it often feels like they're not.

* * * * * * * * * *

We head to the Little Park. Not the Big Park, which is actually about the same size. On the tennis courts, a lone man is playing tennis by himself. He's having trouble getting a volley going, for obvious reasons. Is this the future? Tennis in isolation? Brendan watches for a moment through the chain link fence, then yawns and walks away, baffled by the pointlessness of the man's expended energy. Presumably he puts it on a par with fetching sticks.

Today Brendan meets a new friend, a seven-month-old collie called Junior. The pup goes from bench to bench looking for dropped food, he knows where the people sit and where the tasty morsels will be. Dogs are so intelligent; they learn really quickly. I don't know how he'd do sniffing out Class A drugs at an airport, but if you need a dog to sniff out pasty crumbs or dropped Hoola-Hoops, then Junior's your man.

As it's a Friday and the day after Bonfire Night, we're expecting a lot of fireworks. Nicky normally comes to ours on Fridays, but she's had a bad day, so we end up staying in with the curtains securely closed and loud music on. Brendan reacts very well. I take him out for his late-night walk at 10.45pm and surprisingly, not a single fire work goes off while we're out.

All things considered; Day Two of New Lockdown wasn't all that bad. By which I mean, everything was absolutely terrible, but I coped well with it, in that I made an effort to find small things to be grateful for and I kept moving forward. That's all I can say really.

Saturday 7th November 2020.

This is the first year *of my life* that I haven't been on holiday. Prior to the first lockdown this year, I had my camper van and was away all the time, including travelling around the coast with Brendan. I love travelling and I love holidays, so this year being forbidden and unable to travel has been very difficult. In order to combat this, we're trying to cultivate the feeling that we're missing from days out and holidays.

I've come to realise that being on holiday isn't just about the location, it's partly about *the feeling* of being on holiday. You undoubtedly *feel* differently; you might operate in a slower and more chilled fashion. That's what I'm trying to cultivate. With this in mind, I stroll very sedately around the park while Brendan has a sniff and a sit down. The trees and bushes are at their best; there are yellows, russets, coppers, reds. The paths are coloured with fallen leaves and the place is washed with sunlight. It's actually as beautiful as any holiday destination and I should be grateful to live here. And I am.

Breaking News: Government announce shocking statistics: one in 90 have coronavirus.

In the afternoon, my landlord phones to tell me that Old John in the neighbouring flat has been taken into hospital and has tested positive for Covid. He asks me if I'll sanitise the doors and hallway. Because of my dad and Nicky's mum being very vulnerable, I'm already incredibly careful. This is the first person I've actually known who has contracted coronavirus.

This second lockdown doesn't feel at all threatening like the first one did, yet this time there is evidence of coronavirus around us, drawing nearer, though no one seems to be taking it seriously.

Breaking News: Queen wears Covid mask in public for first time.

After lunch we walk to Nicky's, cutting through the Big Park. It's packed out. Absolutely packed; it's like the beach on a sunny day in the high season. It's actually quite shocking. There are people everywhere. The children's playground was closed throughout the last lockdown, but is currently open. It's full of people, it's packed with groups of parents talking while their children are playing. There is no social distancing whatsoever. You can call this a lockdown, but it isn't in any way a lockdown. Yet my father is in hospital and I'm not allowed to visit him.

Sunday 8th November 2020.

Breaking News: Over 1.25 million coronavirus deaths globally.

It's Remembrance Sunday... as far as it goes. This year

it's a very low-key affair. While there is no parade or gathering in London, nature seems to be doing its best to make a sombre atmosphere. At 7 am when I get up, alone – Brendan doesn't get up at this time, he doesn't even raise his head – it's still dark and I have to put the kitchen light on to brew up. This hasn't happened so far this year, it's usually light enough to see by.

Two hours later when Brendan's finally up and dressed, it's still very grey and dull. There won't be any sun today. It's rained, the pavements are wet. It's a miserable grey day, but there are still bronze and gold leaves on the beech trees at the field, beneath a thick blanket of low clouds. This is the kind of miserable Sunday when you should stay in and watch an old film.

Groups of people are standing far too close chatting while their dogs play. The main subject of conversation today seems to be the American presidential election. Donald Trump has lost, though he doesn't seem to be accepting it. I repeatedly hear: "Trump lost!"

"Thank god!"

"We might actually survive!"

"I know!"

Well, it's not at all a certainty, but you've got to admire their optimism.

Breaking News: Over 50 million coronavirus cases globally.

By 4.30pm, by sunset, we're inside – as usual – with the

curtains closed and loud music playing.

Monday 9th November 2020.

Breaking News: Upcoming Covid vaccines reported to protect 90% of recipients in initial tests.

I'm sitting up in bed with my morning tea, Brendan is curled up beside me while I read him some of the headlines from a world in chaos.

"Apparently, Donald Trump is still maintaining he *won* the American election! And 60 people were arrested at a house party in Manchester. *Sixty* people! In *Manchester*!"

Brendan doesn't care too much for current affairs, so we head out for a walk. It's pleasantly sunny and warm: the kind of day that makes you feel happy to be alive. But then it starts raining and we feel a little less happy.

Breaking News: PM: vaccine is coming, but it's still "very, very early days".

In the afternoon, the hospital phone about Dad. "He's good today, but he *is* a bit confused."

"Well, yes... He's got Alzheimer's and vascular dementia. "Confused" is normal for him."

"Oh! Right! That explains that then."

We have this same conversation every time I speak to them, not that I manage to get through very often, and every time I find it very disconcerting that they don't already *know* he's got Alzheimer's and vascular dementia. But – keeping things positive – Dad is doing very well and that's the main thing.

Tuesday 10th November 2020.

I lie awake in the early morning, before my alarm goes off. I keep thinking about the state of the world, people dying, businesses folding, and I keep asking myself: can things actually get any worse? And I know that yes, they can. They really can. And they probably will. With uncanny timing, things suddenly *do* get even worse. My phone rings. It's Nicky. Her mum, Rosie, is waiting for an ambulance to take her to hospital, as she's feeling ill and breathless. Nicky is understandably very anxious; the conversation is snatched sentences, she is awaiting a call from the doctor and looking out for the ambulance and she can't talk now, so I don't get the full picture. (The ambulance takes over five hours to arrive.) Then they're gone and at the hospital, with phones switched off and I can't get through to them and I don't know what's happening. Hours and hours go past without a word.

Breaking News: Health secretary Matt Hancock announces that Covid vaccine is ready to be administered "as soon as safely possible".

Because there's nothing I can do, I try to get on and do something, but I'm agitated, unsettled and anxious. Brendan refuses a walk in the afternoon. We have a play in the garden... meaning he sits on the grass and stares at the sky and I throw a squeaky toy and then go and collect it.

Rosie is kept in hospital overnight, the same hospital as Dad. Unlike Dad, she *does* have a mobile phone, but ironically there is no signal on her ward. Nicky can't get through, but then unexpectedly she gets a hysterical call from her mum in the evening, when the intermittent signal is stronger. Rosie has seemingly been forgotten and hasn't been given any food. She says one nurse in particular is very aggressive and she's frightened of her. In normal circumstances, this would be bad enough, but in lockdown it really is like your relatives have been taken away and imprisoned. You quite literally can't see them and can't get access to them and can't even speak to them. It is quite a terrifying situation. And if you want them to remain in hospital, hopefully getting the treatment they need, there is virtually nothing you can do about it.

Wednesday 11th November 2020

I'm having regular phone calls with my dad's partner, Val. She's in her early eighties, but her mother is still alive. Her mum is 102 years old, but has fallen ill and tested positive for Covid. She isn't expected to survive. Unlike the first lockdown, Covid seems to be getting very local now.

Breaking News: Northern England hit worse by coronavirus pandemic.

It's a dull and miserable day. At the Big Field, a squadron of dazzlingly white seagulls settle down on the vacant football pitch. Brendan runs towards them, expecting them to scatter. They don't, so he stops running and abruptly has a sit down instead. Above, there is a vast, open, empty grey sky. In the distance, the dark towers of Manchester city centre rise ominously towards the low clouds. Manchester, in the past few years, has adopted a policy of building upwards to create a dramatic skyline. All those new skyscrapers are unfinished and likely to remain so for some time, if not indefinitely. From here, Manchester is rapidly starting to resemble an American city.

We continue on to Nicky's and have a tea and a chat. There is a lot of talk about the supposed Covid vaccine. Nicky wisely points out that this news will probably mean people will think: "We don't need to do social distancing, there's a cure now." The vaccine is reportedly only 90% effective, which could mean anything depending on how you choose to present the statistics. Is it 90% effective on each person? Or effective on 90% of the population?

Breaking News: UK becomes fifth country to exceed 50,000 coronavirus deaths, after USA, Brazil, India and Mexico.

We spend the rest of the afternoon watching disposable, but comforting TV, the kind of thing you only normally do when you've got a sick day off work. Being in lockdown pretty much amounts to the same thing. It feels like a cosy oasis in a world of unrest and upset.

Thursday 12th November 2020.

It's considerably colder today and quite cloudy. We're

doing the same old walk but in a different direction. Brendan puts a paw on my foot to alert me that we've gone the wrong way, but I won't be deterred, as doing the same old walk but in a different direction is the best thing we've got on offer today.

We end up at the Little Park where Brendan sits on the bank on his own, staring at the other dogs and looking annoyed. But underneath that gruff exterior there beats a heart of absolute... well, gruffness really.

Breaking News: UK charts a record 33,470 new Covid cases, the highest daily increase so far.

Today's juice: two kiwis and one pear. One of the kiwis is soft and over-ripe, the other is hard and under-ripe. The juice wasn't very nice. It actually tasted like blue cheese, Stilton or something. Odd. Not recommended. Except as a way to round off a high-class meal, before serving port. (Always pass the juice to the left!)

Friday 13th November 2020.

It's raining heavily. It's quite dark and foreboding. Well, it *is* Friday the 13th after all. I think about this for a moment. Every day is currently like Friday the 13th. Things have been so bad lately. Again, I make the mistake of thinking "At least it can't get any worse!" which I need to stop doing, because it's like throwing a challenge down to the universe. With its customary acute timing, my phone rings. Withheld number. It's obviously the hospital. I try to answer, but my phone won't let me. I hate touch screens. I keep swiping at it, but nothing happens and then the ringing stops and the call is lost.

By now I'm anxious and agitated. All I can do is phone Dad's ward. It takes some time to get through and longer for anyone to answer. They're busy with breakfasts, so are quite rude. I'm told it wasn't them that phoned, but they very unhelpfully won't divulge any information about how Dad is, which might allay my fears and they adamantly won't let me speak to him. I'll phone again after lunch, when they're generally less busy and sometimes less rude.

Breaking News: UK Covid cases are seen to be falling.

Today is World Kindness Day. I aim to be a good and considerate person at all times, though I'm not feeling particularly kind today, I'm feeling stressed, anxious and angry. But I will endeavour to be kind to anyone and everyone I meet.

We set off on our walk. I'm partly hoping we won't meet anyone, so I don't have to be kind to them. The rain has stopped and it's now sunny. Brendan has been ambling along and sniffing in a soporific fashion until his paws touch the luscious green of the golf course, at which point he gets golf madness and runs around in wide circles, having the time of his life. It's so gorgeous to watch. We walk through the attractive parkland; most of the trees stand bare now, but it's still very pleasant.

We walk home along deserted streets and arrive back having met no one, so I can honestly say I've been duly kind to everyone I've met. Job done.

<u>Saturday 14th November 2020.</u>

It rained a lot in the night. There are puddles everywhere. There's damp in the air and a solid grey sky.

Things are not good with Nicky's mum. It's really quite a bad day.

<u>Sunday 15th November 2020.</u>

I had a dream last night, a nightmare rather, about Brendan getting lost. We were on the South Downs, near Beachy Head. I couldn't find him, couldn't see him anywhere. I was worried about calling him in case he came running across the road. I suddenly woke up, sweating and agitated.

Because of this dream, I get his treat pouch out of mothballs and we set off on our walk with it clipped to my belt, filled with tempting rewards. I have great plans and am filled with determination, but he just ignores me... and the treats.

Breaking News: PM Boris Johnson is self-isolating after coming into contact with Covid-infected person.

Nicky's mum is not doing well. She's currently in hospital, is struggling to get any food, feels she is being bullied and with Nicky not allowed to visit, she is hysterically upset.

Yet again, I can get no word from the hospital about Dad.

Try as I might to cling on to positivity, it's another awful day, made only slightly less awful because of the proximity of my dog.

Monday 16th November 2020.

I wake up at 6.30, before my alarm. I can barely move my neck and shoulders, and there is a crippling sinus pain across my head and face; it feels like I'm being repeatedly stabbed with a needle. Also, I have a pressure in my chest and it's difficult to breathe, which is presumably stress-related.

Between short walks with Brendan, I spend much of the day in bed with a hot water bottle over my face. As the day wears on, it doesn't look like taking it easy is having any positive effect. I decide that some exercise and some fresh air might be just what I need.

We head to the golf course; the daylight is fading fast. At the pond, Brendan watches in fascination as moorhens skitter across the surface like someone skimming stones. It's raining, but the cool droplets are very welcome. There are eerie calls from the crows in the naked trees. All colour fades and it goes completely dark. It's all very atmospheric and strange. Brendan runs between the boughs of the trees trying in vain to befriend the squirrels. This is the best part of an otherwise bad day.

<u>Tuesday 17th November 2020.</u>

Breaking News: Lab tests reveal mouthwash can kill Covid in 30 seconds.

It's a fine, sunny morning, but everywhere is wet. The grass is like a sponge.

Brendan sits at the field looking thoughtful. Does a dog have enough thoughts to occupy this much time? Brendan does. I know he has big plans for his field. Ideally, he would have it slightly extended, by demolishing the houses on Acrefield Road. He would also ideally have it moved slightly closer to home, for his own convenience.

I try an exercise I've seen others do. Brendan is standing, tail aloft. I scatter some treats on the grass in front of him. The idea is that the dog has to search them out, using their senses, their eyes and their nose; it's good brain exercise. Brendan looks at the grass and then looks at me. "Butterfingers!"

"Come on, find the treats! Come on, boy. Where are the treats?"

Brendan has a better idea. He wanders a few feet away and sits down. "I'll wait here while you find them."

This isn't going according to plan.

Breaking News: PM tests negative for Covid.

I finally hear from the hospital. Dad is supposed to be

moving to a care home tomorrow, but I'm told we still won't be able to visit him. Then Nicky texts to say her mum is supposed to be coming home from hospital this afternoon, which has made her day.

Throughout the evening, I receive a string of increasingly stressed texts from her. She's phoned the hospital repeatedly and they've told her a number of different things: "She's just waiting for her medication, then she'll be coming home in an ambulance." "She's in the discharge lounge now." "She'll be on her way shortly." "Yes, any time now." And then they completely stop answering. Nicky gets more and more agitated and upset. She continues to phone the hospital; she phones repeatedly. The next time they eventually answer, she's told her mum is no longer coming out today, but no valid explanation is given. The whole thing has been a fiasco.

Wednesday 18th November 2020.

It's a grey day, promising rain, but currently dry. It's cool but not cold, breezy but not windy. A few leaves remain on the otherwise bare trees. At the Big Field, we have a view of the sun shining on the city. It should be largely deserted at the moment, probably looking like a scene from a film, *Zombie Thursday* or something like that. The cranes hanging over Manchester are moving in slow arcs. They're still building those skyscrapers, up and up, building those offices that probably no one's ever going to use.

Breaking News: England due to come out of lockdown on 2nd December. This will depend

on the infection rate nearer the time.

My dad has been transferred from hospital to a respite home. Nicky's mum finally arrives home from hospital, so today feels like a good day for both of us, for all of us.

<u>Thursday 19th November 2020.</u>

It's World Philosophy Day today. I'm not sure how to celebrate it, so I'll have a think about it.

It's quite a cold start; it's probably the sort of day when you should stay in and think about the meaning of life, but we're heading out with some existential zeal.

We set off to the park. Brendan barks furiously at a parked car. There is a little girl standing on the driving seat pretending to drive, with her dad in the passenger seat. Brendan must have realised she was an underage driver and seems to be attempting a citizen's arrest.

I've brought the treat pouch out again. Brendan sits when asked and gives me his paw and then gently takes his treat, but only when he wants to; when he doesn't want to, he completely ignores me. He will not be bought. Unless he wants to be bought. That's *his* philosophy.

Breaking News: UK Coronavirus death toll increases by 529 in 24 hours. UK fatalities currently stand at 53,274.

Despite the grim Covid death toll figures, the government are talking of a five-day festive "amnesty", which will allow families to meet up over the Christmas period. Health officials are already stressing the lunacy of this madcap scheme.

It's two weeks today since this current lockdown began. Doesn't time fly when you're having fun? Apparently, it does when you're not having fun as well.

I don't feel we've fully made the most of World Philosophy Day. It's also World Toilet Day, which we could have celebrated, but that's taking the piss.

Friday 20th November 2020.

I can't believe it's a full week since I was writing about Friday the 13th. Time is going nowhere, but then, I'm going nowhere as well; I'm not really doing anything out of the ordinary, not really seeing new places and not meeting up with friends. I'm doing as well as can be expected, I suppose. I don't feel I'm achieving much with Brendan's training, but then there is so much else going on here.

Breaking News: Coronavirus cases starting to plateau in England and Scotland, but still on the rise in Wales and Northern Ireland.

It's quite cold today, quite breezy with low grey clouds. We go to the field, the local field, the Little Field, Brendan's Field; his favourite outdoor place, where he feels most comfortable and secure, because he's Top Dog.

But today there is a new visitor. We meet Remus, a handsome charcoal grey lurcher. He has a whitening muzzle (Who doesn't?) and deeply wise eyes. He and Brendan hit it off immediately and have an energetic roll around. This is a very timely arrival; with Storm seldom appearing now, Brendan has been contemplating holding auditions for the position of his new best friend.

Remus has just moved into the area with his mum, Sandra, who's come up from Bath to be near her daughters after her husband died. She charmingly calls the field "the green", which I really like. Brendan is very taken with her, as she has a pocketful of treats and a gentle Welsh accent.

It starts to rain, light at first, but getting heavier by the second, but I don't mind. For once, Brendan – still playing with his new best friend – doesn't seem to mind either.

Saturday 21st November 2020.

In these dark times, my dog has been like a beacon of hope. Sort of. Selfish hope, perhaps. Lazy hope, definitely, but still hope of some sort. In a way. Slightly. But not really at all. But at least he keeps me to a routine and even just looking at him fills me with joy.

I had a bad night. I had nightmares, but I can't remember what about. Brendan didn't have nightmares; he slept well beside me and didn't seem to wake up at all.

He skips and bounds along the street towards his favourite field and I trudge behind him in a grey haze of blurry-eyed sleep-deprivation. Once at the field, I let him off the lead and he scampers enthusiastically for a full ten or fifteen yards and then sits down.

The sky is getting darker by the second and it's rapidly getting breezier and colder. It's obviously going to rain again. I said yesterday that I liked rain, but I didn't mean *permanently*. Yesterday's clothes still haven't dried out. I decide we won't be doing the full golf course walk today; these are the exciting decisions I get to make at the moment.

Brendan comes cantering over to me, tail wagging, all excited as though we haven't met for a while. He leans against my legs and does a big yawn, because sometimes twelve-plus hours of Big Sleep just aren't enough.

Sunday 22nd November 2020.

It's a sunny morning and there is a bright blue sky filled with tufty white clouds, but it's absolutely freezing.

Today we're going for a walk along the river, the Mersey, which we haven't done for a long time. The great river begins its journey ignominiously in Stockport and terminates its winding voyage in a more celebrated fashion in Liverpool.

Here, the Mersey is almost pastoral, flowing through green fields, between grassy banks. It's a narrow green corridor and many of the apparent fields are sports pitches and golf courses, but it still looks unspoilt and bucolic.

As children, we used to come for walks here with Dad, especially on Christmas Eve, when it was his job to try and get us tired so we'd sleep that night. In those days the Mersey was filthy and polluted. Dad impressed upon us how dirty and potentially fatal it was. To this day I'm really nervous about coming into contact with it and when Brendan finds a shallow spot to paddle, it horrifies me, though the Mersey is now considerably cleaner and there are apparently octopuses in its estuary, though I've never seen one.

The riverside path is full of people jogging and people cycling too fast, without consideration for other path users, especially the dogs. The important thing to remember about a multi-user path is that there is no exclusivity and all the other users have as much right to be there as you do. The joggers make me very stressed, because they are often dressed in black, they appear out of nowhere, they're upon you before you know it and they come far too close. Brendan used to hate joggers. For a start, joggers run towards you. Brendan hates people running towards him. He reasons that if you're running, it's probably not good. He's generally much better these days and tends to ignore them, though he suddenly barks at a huge man wearing Lycra who comes far too close. For a man in Lycra, any distance is far too close.

Breaking News: Government pledges extra £3 billion for NHS.

As it's a Sunday, we go to Nicky's mum's for tea. Rosie isn't well enough to cook, so we take microwave meals.

Brendan is very well behaved and sits in his usual place on the settee between me and Nicky. We watch back-to-back episodes of Frasier and despite everything we have a few laughs and a really nice time.

Monday 23rd November 2020.

We go for a walk to the golf course. Brendan is quite badly behaved and ignorant, doing what he wants to, going where he wants to and completely ignoring my calls.

"For god's sake! Will you act your age! You're seven now, not six!"

The only time he listens and responds is when I use "Angry Voice". This is reserved for times of immediate danger, such as if he's running towards a hazard, like the M60. I will shout: "Brendan! Stop!" and he usually will do. But the problem is, you can't feign, fake or force Angry Voice; it is charged with genuine emotion, which Brendan picks up. If there is no immediate danger, it is just shouting-while-pretending-to-be-angry, which doesn't work and the dog laughs at you.

So much else is going on in life that his training is taking a back seat, though I actually think he's as trained as he ever will be.

In the afternoon I get really stressed speaking to the hospital about my dad. It's so difficult to get any information about him. It's virtually impossible to get through. They often hang up. Every time I speak to a member of staff I get completely different reports about how Dad is and what's going on with him. While I'm constantly trying to find the positives in everything, I feel very stressed. It's yet another bad day.

Tuesday 24th November 2020.

Breaking News: The Christmas Armistice: government reveals the holiday rules.

The leaders of all four nations within the UK have agreed on plans for Christmas, allowing three households to meet indoors, for five days in December, but they must wear something blue, stand on one leg at all times and not collect £200 when passing go. It's to be hoped that the coronavirus has read and fully understands these rules, because the human population haven't got a clue.

Breaking News: Scientists urge caution over Christmas, as the relaxing of rules is akin to "throwing fuel on the Covid fire".

I'm feeling very stressed about my dad and Nicky's mum, as does Nicky. As a result, I slept very badly and now feel exhausted.

It's a grey day with no trace of sun at all. There is very little colour left in the trees and there's a chilling wind.

At the Big Field we meet several dogs. Brendan does the usual: runs up wagging his tail, sniffs them, walks away, ignores them. He also ignores me when I call him, but then every other dog also ignores their human when called, so it seems like standard practise now. Times are changing and so are our dogs.

It starts to rain and the sky is getting darker. It's another of those afternoons when you should really stay in and watch a film, so we watch an old black and white Carry On film. This is ruined by Brendan chasing a fly. (Look for the positives! At least it gives him some exercise.) After a stressful hour, I manage to get it out of the window, at which point Brendan immediately falls into a deep sleep. He's exhausted. Unfortunately, he starts snoring and emitting a very similar wheezing noise to the buzzing fly.

Wednesday 25th November 2020.

It's a grey, dull, static day. It has rained in the night. There are puddles everywhere, droplets on the remaining leaves and the air is damp. The field is empty, but two minutes later, the grey lurcher, Remus arrives and charges across the grass like a grey bullet to greet his friend. Brendan stands impassively. It looks like there's going to be a collision, but Brendan doesn't move and doesn't flinch. Remus does a handbrake turn at the last minute, spins round and the two are standing side by side.

They do some wrestling, but when Brendan's had enough, he snaps at Remus in no uncertain terms to let him know it's now siesta time and the two sit side by side in perfect companionship.

In the early afternoon, I get a phone call from an unknown number. Dad's had a slight fall in the respite home, which wasn't serious in itself, but he was sick and complaining of stomach pains, so he's been taken back into hospital.

While I was on the phone, Brendan started barking. He was sitting on the sofa, staring into space, just barking continually. There was nothing to see, no noise from anywhere that might be upsetting him, no birds or squirrels in the trees. He sounded distressed and inconsolable. I tried to reassure him, but he wasn't paying any attention and the barking continued.

He barked and growled for fifteen minutes, I started to think he was having some sort of fit. I closed the curtains, sat next to him and chatted to him in a calm voice. He eventually settled down and went quiet, but I was still worried about him. I offered him a chew but he wouldn't eat it.

I was very concerned about my dad. I felt ill, stressed, anxious, and found it difficult to breathe. I wondered if Brendan had picked up on this. Dogs can smell the changes in our chemicals as we react to things, so it's not unlikely. Perhaps he too was worried about his granddad. He ought to be.

I couldn't get any word about how Dad was doing. No one was answering the phone. He couldn't have any visitors, no one could see him and he might as well be in a different country. It was like he was being spirited away in the night.

Breaking News: Another 696 UK Covid deaths reported, the highest daily toll in 7 months.

<u>Thursday 26th November 2020.</u>

Today is Buy Nothing Day. That won't be a problem. I rarely buy anything anyway, but during lockdown there's nowhere open, so this year should be one of the most successful ever. Buy Nothing Day is aimed at making people aware of consumerism, which has literally consumed our world. I always shop in charity shops for clothes – I rarely find any, as I'm too tall, plus there are seldom any men's clothes; men tend to wear their clothes forever, until they're only fit for dusters. (I've got lots of fashionable dusters.)

I shop locally wherever possible and I have a phobia about buying things I don't need. I hate the thought that we fill our homes and our lives up with clutter we'll never use, then we die and someone else throws it all in a skip. I regularly have a purge and send bags of things to the charity shop, but I've still got cupboards that need sorting out and de-cluttering. It would make a good lockdown project. But I'll probably ignore it and have a cup of tea instead.

So, it's Buy Nothing Day, so buy nothing. Except books. Keep buying books.

Breaking News: Tiers before bedtime. England's new tier system announced. Most of the country will be Tier 2. Much of Northeast and Northwest will be Tier 3.

I barely slept last night. I was on high alert, waiting for the hospital to phone, whilst also knowing they wouldn't. And they didn't. (Look for the positive! I was right!) I dozed fitfully and managed to have a dream. It was a nightmare and seemed to go on for ages, but the only thing I can remember was being stuck in a corridor of people, all coming towards me. I was battling to get through them, but got carried along with them. It was really stressful. Brendan slept beside me all night and didn't move.

In the morning, I looked the dream up. It's a variation on a fairly classic theme. There were many different interpretations, none of which struck a chord with me. My own interpretation is that I was battling against the crowd, trying to get to the room at the far end of the corridor, which housed my dad. The crowd were impassable and I was carried along against my will, further away from that room. I had a terrible night thinking about him. The fact that he is in hospital is made so much worse because I am not allowed to visit him due to the coronavirus.

I keep phoning the hospital all afternoon. It's either engaged or they pick up and hang up again. After several hours someone eventually answers. It's a bored nurse. I ask how Dad's doing. I can't see her shrug, but I'm sure she does.

"He's fine."

He's not fine or he wouldn't be in hospital. "Can you be more specific? How is he feeling? What's his medical condition?"

"Well... he's fine, fine... As far as I can tell."

"*As far as you can tell?*"

"Yes… as far as I can tell, he's fine."

"Has he seen a doctor?"

"A doctor? No. Not yet. Not here. He'll probably see one tomorrow."

"*Probably?*"

"Yes. I would've thought so."

She couldn't care less.

* * * * * * * * * *

We go to Nicky's mum's. We're supposed to be having Classic Film Afternoon, but Nicky and Rosie have chosen Toy Story, not quite what I'd had in mind, but it was enjoyable.

I walk Brendan home afterwards in the dark. There are some Christmas decorations starting to appear, but not very many, considering Christmas Day is now less than a month away. We are not looking forward to Christmas.

Friday 27th November 2020.

Breaking News: Government scientists warn the public to avoid board games and sleepovers over Christmas.

We walk to the Big Field. There is a greyness to the air.

If it tried a little harder you could classify it as slightly foggy.

In the distance I can see a woman with three female retrievers. One of the dogs is pulling towards Brendan. The woman's voice drifts across the empty field: "No, Izzy. I know you like him but we're going home."

Brendan sits in the middle of the field, making no effort to engage with anyone

We wander around the little pond. Brendan sniffs at the grasses, reeds and rushes for ages. Floating across the water there are a few mallards, coots and moorhens. Brendan watches them curiously. Even on a rather grey day like this, in a cold and dull month like November, there are still things to see in nature.

In the distance I can hear one of the professional dog walkers shouting: "Oreo! Come on! Oreo! Come here. Oreo! Oreo! *Oreo!* Oh, for... Oreo! Oreo! Here! Come on! *Oreo! Oreo! Oreo!*" Then: "It's *always* Oreo!"

Saturday 28th November 2020

It starts off as a dull day and gets worse. It begins raining. At the field we meet Archie, a French bulldog. Brendan ignores him. Mrs Archie starts talking about hospitals. Her uncle died and they weren't allowed to attend the funeral, so she got no closure. She gets quite upset. A lot of people are losing relatives to the coronavirus now and it's very real.

Remus appears out of nowhere and charges towards

Brendan. They embark on a bit of wrestling. On the surface, the boys seem easily matched in size and shape, but I think Remus is holding back a lot for Brendan's benefit and not going at full throttle. I'm sure Remus could beat Brendan on speed and agility, but then again, Brendan would definitely have the edge on use of the remote control and ordering takeaways online.

After ten minutes of tussling, Brendan disengages and has a sit down. Remus lies beside him. Sandra tells me lurchers don't sit, they don't have the joints for it, so they lie down. Brendan never needs any encouragement to lie down, so the boys lie together, like two of the lions in Trafalgar Square. They are so contented in each other's company. They are the best of friends.

* * * * * * * * * *

The actor, Dave Prowse, died in hospital today from Coronavirus. He was best known for being Green Cross Man in the UK and Darth Vader in the rest of the world and the remainder of the galaxy. He was 85.

David Prowse MBE

(1st July 1935 – 28th November 2020)

* * * * * * * * * *

We come out of the house in the afternoon to the sound of Christmas carols drifting from Bruno's house next door. They seem to be having a carol service with a real piano. They say people are starting Christmas early this year to try and counter the general gloom, but apart from this carolling, I'm not seeing much evidence of it. As we walk to Nicky's we do a survey. Three houses out of 20 have Christmas decorations up. One house still has Halloween paraphernalia in situ. I don't think three out of 20 is much when you consider it's nearly December.

In the evening, a nice man phones from the hospital. Dad now has E.coli in his blood. The man is just a liaison, not medically trained, so can't tell me what that actually means or what the implications are. I phone the ward repeatedly in the hope of speaking to Dad, but no one answers. It's really frustrating and something needs to be done about it. I Google "E.coli in the blood" and glean that it can be very serious or not very serious at all. That's really not very helpful.

Whilst Dad has taken a turn for the worst, Nicky's mum has improved and Nicky is deliriously happy.

Sunday 29th November 2020.

There is a dull, uniform greyness to the day, with still, damp air. It looks and feels like Sundays always seemed to be when I was a child, when everywhere was closed and nothing ever seemed to happen. I hated Sundays.

As we walk to the field it's eerily quiet. We pass no one, but at the field Remus is already there and waiting. We see him nearly every day now. As Sandra has moved into the area during lockdown, the only people she's met have been dog people. Again, it has been a dog that has opened up her world.

Breaking News: UK government now has 7 million doses of Covid vaccine, sourced from 7

different suppliers.

Tuesday 1st December 2020.

Breaking News: HAPPY ANNIVERSARY! Today marks one year since the pandemic started in Wuhan, China.

Today is officially the last day of lockdown. It's sunny and frosty. It's also the last day of the golf course being available to us, as it opens for business tomorrow, so we go for a sad last walk through the perfectly maintained formal parkland. There are groundsmen everywhere preparing the green for business. Another dog walker approaches me, a middle-aged man with horn-rimmed glasses. He is aghast. "I've been told to get off! By the gardeners!"

"Oh… they've not said anything to me."

"No…" He bats his eyelids. "You're over six foot tall… I'm not." He puts a hand to his chest, as though in deep shock, then walks quickly away.

Nicky is taking her mum for another transfusion today. She's very sad. It's heart-breaking for her.

Wednesday 2nd December 2020.

Breaking News: BUSINESS AS USUAL! England's second lockdown ends after 4 weeks!

It's raining quite heavily. The paths are flooded, the

ground is sodden. Brendan is soaked and very gloomy. It's the first proper day after lockdown has ended. I thought it would be busy, but it's very quiet. Eerily quiet actually. There's no one about at all. The weather doesn't help, of course, but all the houses look dark as well, as though everyone who was working from home has now gone back. There is a strange and oppressive atmosphere.

My trainers are already soaked. They're failing and need to be thrown away; as do my wellies, but I know I'm getting some new wellies for Christmas, because I mentioned to Nicky that they'd split and were leaking. She snapped back: "Yes, I'm aware of that! And I've already taken care of things, thank you!"

In the park, Brendan stands for five minutes under the trees just staring into space. The playground is deserted; the swings move in circles and the slide is a silver cascade of rainwater. Brendan suggests we get a taxi home, but we continue on foot.

Breaking News: England returns to a stricter Tier system.

Thursday 3rd December 2020.

I was cold in the small hours and didn't sleep very well, mainly due to Brendan; he fidgeted all night, but when my alarm went off at 7am he slipped into a deep sleep.

It's raining again. There's a uniform grey sky. Many people would find it a drab day, but I like it. This kind of weather makes you enjoy being inside more. The rain hammers against the windows. Outside the trees are bare, but the windfall apples give some colour to the lawn.

I really enjoy watching the rain. I think I should probably get out more. But it's raining.

Breaking News: America exceeds 14 million Covid cases.

Perhaps for the first time in my life I'm doing a fairly good job of living in the moment. It's not really by design; it's just happened, because of the situation. I'm not making plans for the future, there's no point, because I don't know what the future will be like after all this, if it ever ends... and besides, there is no future. There is only now. So, I'm seizing the day and trying to enjoy the small things life has to offer, without thinking of the future and trying not to think of the past, because neither really exist.

Friday 4th December 2020.

It's National Cookie Day. Well, I'll be having some plain chocolate digestives with my tea, not technically covering all the parameters for a cookie (typically round and flat, with a crisp or chewy texture) but that's what I'm having.

It's another cold, damp morning. Days like this make me think of Dad, not that he's ever very far from my thoughts. I haven't seen him for weeks and have only managed to speak to him by phone a few times. It's easier to get in touch with people in prison. Dad hates bad weather; he only likes sunshine. I like all weather.

In moderation. I think all weather and all seasons have their place. On dull days like today there are still colours and things of beauty, you just have to look harder for them. There are berries, red and orange, and still a few solitary leaves about and even some confused blossom. Today, Brendan barked at a plane for the first time in ages, but I'm not surprised, I nearly barked at it as well. It appeared suddenly out of the ether of clouds, mist swirling around it. It was really low and looked massive. He barked at it once, stared at it for a moment and then trotted off.

In the early afternoon, as forecast, it started snowing, quite heavily and they were big flakes. But it was too wet for it to stick.

Breaking News: The first batch of Covid vaccines arrive in UK.

Saturday 5th December 2020.

We set off walking to Nicky's. We cut through the park, which is packed out. The playground is open and full of children and parents. A weak sun starts to shine. This sounds like a metaphor, but it isn't, it's just the sun shining. Weakly.

Sunday 6th December 2020

It was freezing in the night, despite having my dog next to me. I had to get up and get an extra blanket. And I was still cold. We had a fairly good night though.

It's still very cold when I get up:14 degrees inside, colder in the kitchen. There's no sun and it's a grey morning. A dove is sitting in the eucalyptus tree next door and several magpies strut across the lawn. Everywhere is dull and it looks like it might rain.

I call at Dad's to collect the post – there's only junk mail – then I take Brendan for a short walk. We cut through the nearby churchyard, and encounter a small group of people standing solemnly, silently around a grave. It's not a burial as there are no burials here now, but presumably some sort of memorial gathering, perhaps an anniversary. They all have their heads bowed, are wearing black and have masks on. There is a slight fog in the air, so it all looks very filmic and ghostly. Thankfully – but very strangely – Brendan doesn't bark, but trots on silently with an unusual canine reverence.

We spend the afternoon with Nicky, then all go to her mum's in the evening. Rosie is very funny and upbeat and chirpy. She seems remarkably well and we have a really nice evening. There's just something so joyful; we're all in great spirits. Later, I walk home with Brendan. The pavements are glistening and it's really cold, but in a nice, frosty, Christmassy way.

Monday 7th December 2020

We were out walking when Nicky phoned. She was very upset. Her mum had just called her, she had sounded slurred, as though she'd had a stroke, so Nicky had raced over in the car. Her mum seemed very ill, barely able to speak and barely conscious.

We walked to Rosie's flat. Our car was outside, where Nicky had parked. I installed Brendan in his basket on the back seat and went up to the flat.

Rosie was lying in her chair with her eyes closed. It was quite shocking, because she looked so pale and weak, but she had been so well the night before. Nicky said: "Mum, Gray's here."

Rosie stirred and without opening her eyes she mumbled: "Hello, Brendan."

It made me so sad, because Brendan wasn't there, but she'd assumed he would be because we're *always* together.

Nicky held her hand, stroking it, and talked to her mum, though Rosie had stopped responding. It was as though she'd slipped into a coma.

The rest of the day is a bit of a blur. We were there for hours, but I can only remember the key points. The doctor came and said they would begin end of life care. Nicky and Rosie had specified they didn't want her to go back into hospital, so the doctor arranged for the district nurses to call.

I went home in the evening to feed and look after the cats, while Nicky stayed with her mum. Nicky was so brave and supportive. She kept her emotions in check. Apart from shifting her position occasionally, Rosie had become non-responsive, but Nicky talked to her constantly nevertheless. She maintained a watchful vigil; a perfect and loving daughter.

Tuesday 8th December 2020.

Nicky's mum, Rosie, died peacefully at home at 2.30 in the afternoon. Her daughter, brother and sister-in-law were with her.

Brenda "Rosie" Lambert

(26th May 1937 – 8th December 2020)

Her last words remained: "Hello Brendan." It breaks my heart.

Wednesday 9th December 2020.

We've been staying at Nicky's for the past couple of days and will remain there as long as we're needed. Brendan is exhausted; he misses being in his own, beloved flat. He seems completely drained. I take him for a walk along the river. As always, I'm trying to find positive things to latch onto, but it's fairly impossible at this point.

Thursday 10th December 2020.

Breaking News: Vitamin D has been shown to be effective for the prevention and treatment of Covid-19.

We're still at Nicky's. None of us had a good night. At some point, both cats were sick, then Brendan got up and started wandering about. We hardly got any sleep.

Today, we're going to the funeral parlour with Nicky's uncle and aunt. Brendan stays in alone, listening to the Smiths. We also viewed two cemeteries and chose the nearest one to Nicky. It was an awful day, but I suppose it's good for Nicky to be doing something and making the best arrangements she can for her mum.

Friday 11th December 2020.

Breaking News: Over 70 million coronavirus cases globally, with 1.5 million reported deaths.

The hospital phones. Dad is scheduled to have an operation on Tuesday. He needs the procedure to keep him alive, though it is complicated and may well kill him. Basically, it's a life or death situation. They are asking for my permission as they feel Dad no longer has capacity to make that choice. To me, there is no choice; he needs the operation. I ask if I can speak to him and they actually arrange it. Dad sounds well; he's tired, but happy enough. We discuss the operation and his opinion is the same as mine, so I give the go ahead.

Saturday 12th December 2020.

My brother tells me the hospital have phoned him and Dad is in a "critical state". I immediately phone the hospital back, but they deny all knowledge and say Dad is fine. I try to question why there has been conflicting information, but no one is remotely interested. I write a letter of complaint to the hospital and also to various MPs and counsellors, about the terrible condition regarding contacting relatives and the flow of information.

Breaking News: American surpasses 16 million Covid cases.

We're back at our own flat. Brendan's very glad to be home. Six out of ten houses have now got their Christmas decorations up. Obviously, for us, Christmas isn't really on our radar. It really can be a terrible time of year.

Sunday 13th December 2020.

It's Sunday I think, but it's difficult to say, as all the days are the same at the moment. It's raining nearly every day. Nicky is unable to work. I'm very worried she's going to get very ill with the stress and upset. At least, at the moment, she's got the practical aspects of a bereavement to keep her busy, like arranging the funeral, as awful as that sounds, at least it's something to focus on.

Monday 14th December 2020.

It's cool and breezy, but not raining. Really, it might as well be raining.

Breaking News: Anti-vaccine and anti-lockdown protestors clash with police. A dozen arrested. Many protestors not wearing masks.

We're spending a lot of time clearing out Rosie's flat. As it's rented, we only have ten days to sort it and hand the keys over. I thought Nicky would find this task very difficult, but she gets some comfort from being at the flat, though every object holds so many memories; she is rarely dry-eyed.

Tuesday 15th December 2020.

Breaking News: London to move into Tier 3 as infections continue to rise.

It's a mild, sunny day. Brendan pulls frantically to get to the golf course, but it's open now, so we can't use it for walking. He must be wondering why his membership has been suspended. He loves the golf course.

Breaking News: "Rash Christmas Rules will cost many lives" health officials claim.

Dad's operation has been cancelled and rescheduled for Thursday. No reason was given.

Breaking News: PM Boris Johnson urges the public to keep Christmas celebrations "short" and "small".

Wednesday 16th December 2020.

The sky is full of dark clouds and seagulls. We walk to the Little Park in the rain. The wind is raging and sounds like screaming. Brendan finds a sheltered spot under the overhang of a holly bush. He sits there beneath the shifting canopy looking from one gate of the park to another, clocking everything that's going on, looking for anyone of interest.

The noise all around increases, it's like a hurricane. There is an ominous, electricity in the air. Brendan looks at the sky then looks at me to make sure I'm aware of the rising atmospheric disturbance and am on hand to save him. It's windy and wild, bare branches are thrashing and there's banshee-like screeching from all around us. Brendan's not happy, so we head for home.

Breaking News: The US reports 3,656 deaths in one day, the world's highest Covid death tally to date.

My brother phones to tell me he's had heated words with the hospital. They are currently not answering calls and on the odd time we do get through it's as though they have a policy of not disclosing any information. He wanted to know how Dad was and ended up shouting at them until he was put through to a medically qualified person, who told him that Dad had been wrongly medicated, given meds that weren't meant for him and as a result his life-saving operation has been delayed while he's under observation.

I phone the hospital immediately to get some confirmation on this. When I eventually get through, they deny all knowledge. I complain again in writing to the hospital and the various counsellors and the local

MP.

<u>Thursday 17th December 2020.</u>

I've been assured that Dad's having his procedure today, but I'm afraid I don't believe a word of it.

It's cold and wet and windy. We go for our walk; the field is flooded. We don't meet anyone at all.

I leave Brendan at home, drying out, and go into town shopping with Nicky. It reminds her of her mum and she cries all the way round Tesco; because of her mask no one notices. With a mask everyone's a stranger.

* * * * * * * * * *

In the afternoon, I phone the hospital for an update on Dad. It takes two dozen calls to get through, but when I do their attitude is markedly different, they're courteous, they know my name and they immediately get Dad's records and give me a detailed report on his progress. It looks like my complaints have hit home. However, Dad has – yet again – not had the procedure. The reason being, and I quote: "He was taken to the operating theatre, then they discovered he had a pace-maker, so they couldn't go ahead." His pace-maker wasn't a secret. It's presumably written in bold felt tip in his medical records. Any last trace of faith I had in that hospital has gone.

Dad's operation has been rescheduled for Monday.

Friday 18th December 2020.

We've finish clearing Nicky's mum's flat. The rooms are like empty shells now. Everything that's going has gone. It's very sad. It's unimaginable really. All the objects, possessions and mementoes gathered over a full lifetime that make a house a home have gone. It's just four walls now. It's soulless, without a soul. It could be anywhere.

Nicky drops me back at home. A new neighbour, Lee, is moving in above. He seems very nice. I take Brendan down to meet him in the hallway. We've had no one living in the flat upstairs for nearly a year, so I want Brendan to get used to him. Brendan goes cautiously up to him and sniffs him. Lee holds his hand out, Brendan sniffs it tentatively and then barks. I'm chalking this up as an acceptable first meeting; a dog that barks or growls isn't a dog that wants to bite you; they're issuing a warning because they feel threatened. We go into our own flat and sit on the settee together. Brendan looks relaxed and happy. He loves his home; it would just suit him better if all the other flats were left vacant.

Saturday 19th December 2020.

Breaking News: Three becomes Four. A new level added to the "3-tier system".

Adding a fourth tier won't make much difference. No one understood 3 tiers, so adding another really won't help.

Breaking News: UK surpasses 2 million Covid cases.

We didn't have a good night. I didn't sleep well and neither did Brendan, though new neighbour Lee was completely silent, unlike the previous tenants.

We walk to the field. Seagulls circle overhead. I love their cries. I love seagulls; I love the sea. And I miss it.

Brendan lies down on the sponge-like grass. A woman with a black spaniel appears. Brendan watches them with interest, but makes no attempt to go over and introduce himself.

The woman looks at him and smiles. "Ah... is he old?"

"No, he's seven. He's just bone idle."

"He's lovely though...

Brendan stands up and walks over towards her and gives her a cursory look over, walking around her and looking her up and down.

"He's very good looking... in fact, he's got very good energy about him."

I gasp. "*Good* energy? He hasn't got *any* energy!"

She laughs. She asks about his past and I give her the potted history. He was a street dog in Bulgaria, he was captured, rescued, travelled overland, crept onto my lap and fell asleep... and landed on his feet. Now we're inseparable, except when we're not together.

"Well, he's a credit to you, you've done a marvellous job with him. Well done."

I haven't really, I've just loved him and spoiled him. I've been patient with him, tolerant and understanding, I've comforted him and reassured him, but as far as training goes I've completely failed... and am still failing on a daily basis. I could have said all this but I just beamed and said "Oh, thank you." Because I hate to be rude.

Perhaps I talk too long, like a proud parent, because I glance away momentarily and when I look back she has completely gone; there is no sign of her at all and with no foliage left, there is nowhere for her to hide, so it's very odd.

<u>Sunday 20th December 2020.</u>

When it gets light there is a strange, surreal yellow hue to the sky, which makes me think it might snow. And it's *really* cold.

The moment we step out of the door it starts raining. This seems to happen a lot. As we walk along the street towards the field, a line of five horses silently pass us, being ridden along the road at a dignified and funereal pace. Brendan stops and stares at them in bemusement. I can't believe he doesn't bark.

We continue. A toddler walking with its mother comes towards us, pointing and smiling. It says either "Daddy" or "Doggy" but it isn't clear and really could be either. We've decided to assume it was "Doggy".

Dad phones while we're at the field. One of the nurses has arranged it for him, as part of their new policy of bending over backwards to try and make amends for their appalling treatment. He sounds very tired, but is relatively well and in good spirits. He again says he's happy being in hospital and is enjoying the rest!

The rain is getting heavier, but I don't care. Hearing from Dad has made my day.

Breaking News: New strain of coronavirus discovered. Covid-19 is mutating.

We walk to Nicky's for tea in the evening. It's twilight. The air suddenly starts vibrating; it's alive with sound. It's not just a sound you can *hear*, you can actually *feel* it, it's tangible, it's all around. It's like a hundred discordant, chattering voices. Brendan looks upwards and stops dead. Directly above us is a V-shaped squadron of geese, hundreds of them, flying over the suburban rooftops towards the light where the sun has sunk. It's magical and otherworldly, but it also feels ominous and unsettling, because it's like an exodus, it's like a portent of doom. They disappear over the chimneypots and the noise very gradually fades away.

21st December 2020.

We meet Storm at the field. This time Brendan is less keen to play. Storm is getting older; he's no longer really a pup. He isn't, as yet, neutered, so Brendan is starting to see him as competition and a nuisance. He growls and snaps at him, but not in a playful way. Brendan very wilfully won't engage with him and poor Storm is cast out. Sadly, Storm is no longer needed, now that Remus is in town.

Breaking News: Christmas mixing rules are tightened. London and South East England put into Tier 4, meaning "Stay at home".

Following much concern from scientists, the government do something of a U-turn about the Christmas "amnesty" and put the onus on the general public: "We're not saying you *can't* have a gathering of three families, but we're saying you *shouldn't*." They receive a great deal of criticism for their indecisive and unclear leadership.

Breaking News: The first Coronavirus cases in Antarctica are reported. 36 people have contracted the virus on a research station.

My brother's just phoned. He's had another row with the hospital. Dad's procedure has been cancelled, yet again, and rescheduled, yet again. This time for Thursday.

Thursday 24th December. Christmas Eve. This means Dad will still be in hospital over Christmas and we won't get to see him at all. I feel very unhappy about it now.

Breaking News: America exceeds 18 million Covid cases.

Tuesday 22nd December 2020.

Breaking News: UK reports 691 new deaths, the highest figure since May.

Today it was Rosie's funeral. It was cold, but thankfully dry.

The service was very modern and full of fun... and sadness... but a lot of fun. Everyone had been encouraged to wear something pink or pale blue. Nicky bought me a pink tie and handkerchief to accessorize my black suit. The day is about celebrating a life, rather than about the pain of loss.

Nicky did an emotional speech, which was funny but also heartfelt and very touching. As did her Uncle Robin.

We stood at the graveside, in the bitter cold. Thirty people were permitted. It was a very nice service and everyone was so kind and considerate. No wakes or indoor gatherings are allowed, so immediately after the burial everyone has to go their separate ways, which seems odd and leaves a sense of incompleteness.

In the evening we got a Chinese. Nicky was physically and emotionally exhausted, but was pleased that the day had gone so well. It was a remarkable send-off for a remarkable mother.

Breaking News: UK reports over 36,800 daily Covid cases, the highest figure since the pandemic began.

Wednesday 23rd December 2020.

It's a dull, grey and cold morning. I sit up in bed, drinking my tea, checking the headlines. The more you read the more sinister and frightening it gets. It feels to me that things are escalating out of control and we're heading into a darker and more serious place than we've ever been since this coronavirus crisis started.

Breaking News: UK breaks yesterday's record high, with over 39,000 confirmed Covid cases.

Dad finally had his procedure today and is doing well. He's asleep now and isn't expected to be communicative until tomorrow.

Breaking News: UK reports a further 744 Covid deaths.

There are now fairy lights everywhere, festooned around porches, along hedges and in trees, and from somewhere over the rooftops comes the sound of the Salvation Army band. I remember them from my childhood. They came down our street at about this time and it really signified the true start of Christmas. And although I can hear them now, it in no way brings a festive spirit to me. It just isn't Christmas this year.

24th December 2020.

It's Christmas Eve. Or is it? It's a sunny but cold morning. Nicky comes mid-morning and we go for a walk to look at the Christmas lights, because she feels it's what her mum would like. We pass three wobbling rubber snowmen in a front garden, kept inflated by a chugging generator. Brendan barks at them relentlessly and has to be dragged away.

We get chips and peas for lunch. They are literally the nicest chips we've had this year.

* * * * * * * * * *

My top three Christmas songs

I Believe in Father Christmas
Happy Xmas (War is Over)
And possibly *Stop the Cavalry.*

I like the cynicism of these songs. There's no point banging on about good will to all men and then doing nothing about it. Like the famous 1914 Christmas Truce, largely initiated by the Germans, when hostilities stopped and the opposing sides met in No Man's Land, where they exchanged gifts and played football. Ah... but not all areas along the lines took part, not everyone was pleased. Some men were shot dead by snipers during this ceasefire. When they learned of the ceasefire – an act of insubordination – the generals were furious and some senior officers were court martialled. Plans were made to ensure that a truce didn't happen again on subsequent years. That's the kind of world we live in.

Happy Xmas. War *isn't* over.

25th December 2020

It's Christmas Day. And my mum's birthday. Happy birthday mum!

It's a sunny but frosty morning. It might not exactly be a white Christmas, but it's whit*ish*.

I take Brendan for his walk and we pass the little pub where we all used to meet on Christmas day at twelve noon, Nicky's mum, my parents, my brother and his family. Now the two mums have died and Dad's in hospital. And the pub is dark and locked up and won't be opening. Everything has changed.

We walk along the Mersey. We pass a couple. People have always been very festively friendly and cheerful on Christmas morning, so I pre-empt them and say a cheery hello, even though I don't feel cheery. Clearly neither do they; they don't respond.

Next we pass a single man. He studiously avoids my gaze. It's really odd. I decide to do a survey. Over the course of our walk, we pass 20 people, some alone, some in couples. I look at each of them, trying to engage with them. Not one person says Merry Christmas, or even a plain, simple hello. They have a look of hostility.

Is there good will to all men? No, there really isn't.

As we're approaching Nicky's, I've all but given up, when an older Asian couple come towards us, both smiling. The man raises a hand and shouts a gleeful "Merry Christmas!" It's the highlight of the day so far.

* * * * * * * * * *

Nicky had originally wanted to abort Christmas, but decided at the last minute to go ahead, as she thought it would be what her mum would want. We open our presents. We both have gifts from Rosie. It's upsetting opening presents from someone who's no longer here.

Nicky makes us a beautiful dinner. Instead of having it at the table as we have in the past, we have it on trays whilst watching TV, trying to ensure it's nothing like our normal Christmas.

In the afternoon it starts to snow while I'm out with Brendan. For ten minutes it comes down thick and fast; for a few moments it's a complete white-out, but then it stops. It stays for a while and then disappears.

Saturday 26th December 2020.

It's cold and overcast, damp but not raining. We walk to the field. The three inflated snowmen that we've passed nearly every day are now deflated and lying on the ground, rain-wet and pathetic. Does this mean the fun has gone out of Christmas? Christmas is a let-down? Does it mean Christmas is over? It does really, because today is supposedly the official end of the Christmas "amnesty" and the start of the regional lockdowns. In reality, there's no difference at all.

Breaking News: Global Covid death toll stands at more than 1.75 million.

The hospital phones and I actually get to speak to Dad. He's chirpy and eating chocolate and olives that we sent in amongst his presents. He's feeling a bit tired, but is very happy. As there are few patients left in at the moment, he's getting a lot of nurse attention and seems to be enjoying it.

Breaking News: More areas of England enter Tier 4 restrictions: total lockdown.

The weather is very bad, and perfect for a horror movie, so we watch one of Nicky's favourites, an Amicus anthology film. Unfortunately, it was also one of her mum's favourites, so it's quite poignant. Outside it's very windy and the trees are thrashing. We're apparently getting the tail end of a hurricane. There is torrential rain later on, and when I drive home many of the roads are completely flooded.

Sunday 27th December 2020.

After the hurricane, today is very still, but quite cold. Brendan is very cheerful this morning and he pulls all the way to the field; he has a definite post-hurricane spring in his step. We pass the still-deflated snowmen in the garden. They are gathering rainwater now and look abandoned and pitiful, lying sprawled across the concrete of the drive, resembling the white lines drawn around corpses. Brendan still barks at them.

* * * * * * * * * *

The hospital phoned. It was a doctor. He was calling to inform me that Dad has now tested positive for Covid and has been moved to the specific Covid wing. He's been in hospital for weeks; the hospital are responsible for him being infected. Despite the infection, they say he is apparently doing well and feeling fine. When I hang up, I am deeply disturbed and unhappy.

Monday 28th December 2020.

It's snowed in the night. The lawn is dusted with fine white powder, looking like the icing sugar on my stollen... that covers the worktop every time I cut a piece.

The hospital phones. It's a lady from Patient Liaisons. She says Dad is doing well and is eating well, which seems unlikely, because that had been an issue. She says she thinks the media are exaggerating the seriousness of the Covid symptoms and most people in the hospital with the virus are coping very well. This also seems unlikely, as it can actually kill people.

Tuesday 29th December 2020.

Breaking News: UK reports over 53,000 new

cases: the country's highest ever daily count.

I woke up at 6am, after having a weird nightmare about robots taking over the Earth. It was actually quite disturbing and I couldn't settle afterwards. I opened the curtains and it had snowed again; everywhere was white, just a pure white landscape. It was beautiful.

I have always quite liked the idea of living somewhere very cold, because I like the idea of getting home and getting warm. I'm drawn to the Scandinavian countries in particular, but I'd also quite like to be on a scientific mission in the Arctic. I tell Brendan he could be my husky and pull my sled. He doesn't respond. We go for a long snowy walk. By 11.30 though, water is dripping from the branches of trees and swathes of snow are sliding from the roofs of houses.

Breaking News: UK caught in third wave of coronavirus. NHS on brink of collapse.

I got through to the hospital. Dad is coping well with the coronavirus. It affects people very differently, sometimes it's just a mild cold, sometimes it's like very bad flu, sometimes it's very serious and affects breathing and sometimes, of course, it results in death. Dad – if he actually has Covid-19 – appears to have it very mildly.

Wednesday 30th December 2020.

We walk along the river. It looks dark, foreboding and fast flowing... and obviously very cold. There is still evidence of snow, but it's old snow now, dirty and messed up, no longer pristine and shining white. It's quite foggy close to the water and the fog appears to be getting thicker. Ahead, figures appear, lumbering briefly, then they're swallowed up again.

We call in at my Dad's flat to collect the post. I'm really cold after our walk and we stay for a while and get warm. I end up having a Pot Noodle and I give Brendan one of Dad's Big Soups, that fill his cupboards. He thinks it's Christmas all over again. Then he sits and stares at me. He seems agitated and can't settle, probably because he's out of the habit of coming here now, or perhaps he misses his granddad. Maybe he misses their arguments.

I have the TV on, which isn't like me, but it takes the empty edge off the flat and makes it sound more like Dad's home. Strangely, there isn't a programme about Alaska on today, so we end up watching a house hunting programme, full of beautiful locations. Yet again I feel an overwhelming urge to travel, to explore, to see and experience other places.

After lunch I take Brendan to the Bowl. It's basically a field, but it has steep banks in each direction, so it resembles a huge bowl. Dad used to bring us sledging here in winter. There's no snow left now, but people are still sledging down the damp grass and churning it into mud.

I'm feeling very reflective today. Perhaps because I went to Dad's flat, or perhaps it's because Dad's now got an additional illness to deal with and I'm concerned about him. Also, it really is terrible not being able to see people in hospital. On top of that, the year is drawing to an end, which always makes me question things. It's been a terrible year. For everyone.

It's a different world to the one this time last year. It's made me feel quite nihilistic, very negative, hopeless. I've been feeling this increasingly this year. No one can say what's going to happen and how our society is going to work after all this. It might be the same as before; it might be completely different. There's no point dwelling on it, because the choices are out of our hands. Once you accept this, it's actually quite liberating.

Breaking News: Many areas, including Greater Manchester, go into Tier 4: total lockdown. Work from home, stay at home, all but essential food shops will close from midnight tonight.

Here we go again. This is the fallout from the ludicrous Christmas "amnesty". The coronavirus must have thought it was Christmas. Which it was.

I manage to get through to the hospital. A bored nurse tells me: "Yeah, he's fine. He's not causing us any problems." I hadn't asked how compliant and cooperative he was being. But it sounds like he's doing well.

Thursday 31st December 2020.

Breaking News: UK hits almost 56,000 new

Covid cases. The highest daily total yet.

It's New Year's Eve. I woke up to Tier 4. The first day of local lockdown. Not that you'd know.
It's made little difference. Apart from the snow. It's snowed again and everywhere is clean and white.

I phoned the hospital. It was repeatedly engaged. Patient Liaisons phoned back mid-morning. Dad can't urinate and is having to have a catheter fitted.

As we're back in full lockdown, the golf course is closed, so we return there for our walk. I thought it would be quiet, but it isn't. It's like Aspen, or somewhere else that's renowned for skiing. It's full of families with sledges. A young couple are rolling a snowball to make a snowman. The bloke is watching as Brendan approaches. I can see what's coming and start calling Brendan to come to me. Brendan ignores me, walks slowly up to the snowball and cocks his leg. The young man throws his arms into the air and stamps off.

I throw a snowball for Brendan. As usual, he shows interest in the first one and tries to catch it, but it explodes against his muzzle, so he paws at the ground trying to find it. The subsequent snowballs he just watches warily, wondering why he's under bombardment.

We meet a lovely couple with a black dog and we start chatting. I say it's great that we can come back on the golf course again. The man nods. "You've got to look for the positives at the moment, haven't you? And when you find one, you just grab it!" That thought stays with me all day.

We're still walking at 3 o'clock. It's starting to get steadily darker. I realise this is our last full walk of the year.

We're staying in tonight at Nicky's, as we always do on New Year's Eve, but Rosie would normally join us. We're trying to behave like it's a normal evening and nothing momentous. And we will be avoiding midnight at all costs.

Breaking News: New Year's Eve: Greater Manchester police issue over 100 fixed penalty notices for breaches of Covid regulation, mainly to house parties and pubs opening illegally during Tier 4 restrictions.

The plan was to be home and in bed with my dog long before midnight, curtains shut, cocooned in lamplight and the flickering of TV images or music to avoid the inevitable New Year fireworks. But they started early; as soon as we got out of the car at home there was a barrage close by. Brendan ran inside and refused his usual late night wee walk. As midnight approached there were constant fireworks, a solid wall of sound, explosions and flashing lights. Brendan was completely traumatised. He lay on the bed, motionless, not moving, his breathing was shallow and seemed irregular and laboured. It was horrible. I gave him a marrowbone treat, but he didn't react and ignored it.

I got into bed beside him and talked to him in a calm and steady voice. For some reason, my Dictaphone had been activated and recorded everything, hours of me calmly talking gibberish to my dog and occasionally singing to him. Eventually, he calmed down and his breathing became more normal and we drifted off to sleep.

In the small hours, I was awoken by the sound of Brendan crunching the previously-ignored marrowbone treat. It wasn't a great start to the New Year. But how could it be?

Friday 1st January 2021.

It's a new day. It's a new year. But nothing's really different since yesterday, of course. The world and the future still look bleak.

I don't usually make any New Year's resolutions, but here's one: to actually survive the year.

Last year, as we now call 2020, was a terrible year. It started with me losing my van, which I really wasn't happy about, but of course, I didn't know how the year was going to pan out and how much worse it was going to get. Dad was ill, had a few falls and went into hospital for several months. Then Nicky's mum, Rosie was diagnosed with leukaemia from which she died two months later. It was a nightmare year.

Writing this diary has been very beneficial through all the difficulties and upsets of the past twelve months. It has given me a project, something to keep my mind focused, though it was intended to be a way of promoting positivity and of finding joy in a rather joyless world. The fun's somewhat gone out of it.

With the new year has come new rain, which has washed the snow away, revealing a rather drab and waterlogged world underneath.

Breaking News: SNOW AND FREEZING FOG WILL GRIP BRITAIN ON NEW YEAR'S DAY, WITH WORSE ON THE WAY.

We went to the cemetery to visit Rosie's grave. Everywhere was waterlogged and bleak. Nicky was understandably very upset. We came back and watched *The Mirror Crack'd*, which was very comforting. There's nothing quite like a series of brutal murders to help you unwind.

I phoned the hospital repeatedly. It was sometimes engaged, but most of the time it just rang out unanswered, so I haven't been able to speak to Dad "this year".

Breaking News: CORONAVIRUS SURGE SPREADING ACROSS COUNTRY FROM LONDON

Saturday 2nd January 2021.

Another day, another snow storm. Within minutes the world was transformed into monochrome.

Breaking News: UK reports a new record high of 57,725 coronavirus cases.

Another day, another 24 hours of being unable to speak

to my father.

Sunday 3rd January 2021

Brendan got me up in the night. At 3am he went and sat near the door. I took him out for quite a long walk. It was bitterly cold and eerily still. It was completely dark, but the birds were starting to sing. The pavements were shining with ice, and the hedges and trees glistened with frost.

A fox crossed in front of us and stopped in the middle of the road, turning to stare at us. Brendan tried to bound towards it. I said "It's only a cat!" and he immediately stopped pulling. He trotted sedately along and the fox slinked away at a leisurely pace. Then I think Brendan must have got its full scent, because he gave chase, pulling me after him. With all the ice on the pavements I was sliding along, virtually skiing. I had no control and couldn't stop myself. Somehow, I managed to stay upright until Brendan stopped dead at a garden wall, the fox had disappeared and the pursuit was over.

Back inside I was frozen to the bone and completely wired after my white-knuckle ride. I couldn't sleep for hours.

* * * * * * * * * *

I managed to get through to the Patient Liaisons office at the hospital. I complained about not being able to get any word about my father's condition. They said they would speak to the matron on the ward and ask her to phone me. I waited several hours for the call, getting increasingly stressed as time went by. It was so frustrating. Eventually someone did actually phone and grudgingly told me there was no change. I asked if I could speak to Dad in person and was told absolutely not, as they were too busy. That's a very valid excuse, of course, but I could hear nurses chatting and laughing in the background.

Breaking News: Britain has been one of the countries worst hit by the coronavirus, with the second highest death toll in Europe.

I put my new calendar up. It was a Christmas present from Nicky. It contains photos of London deserted during lockdown. The scenes are both beautiful and haunting. The date boxes beneath the stunning photographs remain empty. I have no dates for the coming year, no appointments, no meetings, no engagements, nothing. I've got nowhere to go and nothing to do. This is a sign of the times.

Monday 4th January 2021

I have spoken again to Patient Liaisons and they have assured me that it won't be a problem to have a phone conversation with Dad; they kindly tell me they will speak to the matron and arrange it, and I will get a call later.

I went to the doctors about my breathlessness and chest pressure. I gave blood for a cholesterol test and was wired up for an ECG, which showed nothing untoward, except a very slow heartrate and low blood pressure.

There is no word from the hospital yet. I'm really looking forward to speaking to Dad.

Breaking News: National Lockdown, effective from 6th January. Tentative exit date "middle of February".

In the afternoon, we went to Nicky's. We ordered a Chinese and were watching the government broadcast about the new national lockdown when my phone rang. It was 8.03pm. I answered. I knew it was the hospital. I was expecting – and hoping – to hear Dad's voice, but it was the matron, who I've spoken to several times. This time, instead of being brusque and awkward, she was gushing and apologetic. "I'm sorry... I'm so sorry... It was completely unexpected... There were no indications... I'm so, so sorry..." It took a moment to take in what she was saying. Dad had died. My dad. Had died. I felt an overwhelming rising of emotion, but I could hear the matron still talking breathily, apologising repeatedly: "I'm sorry. We had no idea... I'm so sorry..." In that moment I couldn't afford to be emotional; I needed to be focused, I needed to be practical and clinical; I needed to listen to what she was saying and fully comprehend what had happened. I stopped the emotion; I just blocked it and continued the conversation in a cold and business-like manner.

Dad had apparently been sitting up in his bed, in a private room off the main ward. The next time they looked in on him, he had died. He was sitting up, but he had died. She apologised after every sentence and rather than make me feel reassured in any way, it made me think she was trying to smooth over their failings or neglect. She said it had come as a complete shock, there were no signs that his death was impending, in fact they were getting ready to discharge him, which seems unlikely as he was on a Covid ward. She didn't know what he'd died of, whether it was Covid or one of his many other health complications. But she said he'd died peacefully. But he died on his own, he died without any contact with his family. None of his family or friends had been able to speak to him *for weeks*. I find that unforgivable.

My Dad.
(2nd August 1933 – 4th Jan 2021.)

Breaking News: The UK reports 407 new Covid deaths, bringing the total death toll to 75,431.

One of these figures was possibly my father.

Tuesday 5th January 2021.

Breaking News: Government call for one last major effort to defeat the coronavirus!

I woke up feeling numb. I hadn't forgotten that Dad had died, I knew straight away when I first opened my eyes, so it wasn't like it all came flooding back. I expected to wake up this morning and it all to hit me, a tidal wave of grief, but it hasn't.

Breaking News: It is estimated one in fifty people has been infected with Covid-19.

It's as though I have no feelings and no emotions. It's as though my emotions are manifesting through physical means. I've got a burning in my chest, I'm having difficulty breathing, I feel sick and dizzy and faint. I feel physically terrible, very ill, but I feel dead inside. There is nothing. I've gone into emotional shutdown.

Breaking News: More than one million people in England had coronavirus last week.

I'm thinking about Dad all the time. Constantly. I'm *thinking*, but I'm not *feeling*. I'm not feeling anything. But on paper I know I'm sad and I'm very angry.

Breaking News: Boris Johnson: "People understand overwhelmingly that we have no choice" but to impose the third national lockdown.

I've Googled grief and numbness. It's apparently quite common to feel nothing after news of a death; it's a defence mechanism.

Breaking News: UK reports new record high of 830 Covid-related deaths.

My concern is that the grief will come back when I'm not prepared for it and I won't be able to handle it. This is so me. I deal with things at the time and keep the emotions shut away, then go into a huge depression for years.

Breaking News: England's third lockdown

officially and legally commences tomorrow.

At the stroke of midnight, we're back in full national lockdown.

Dad meets Brendan for the first time. Dad was staying in a respite care home. He was very ill and weak, and I think Brendan could sense his vulnerability, because he was very gentle and patient. He would never be this gentle and patient. with Dad again, after he started to get better.

PART III

THE THIRD NATIONAL LOCKDOWN
No Light At The End Of The Tunnel?

<u>Wednesday 6th January 2021.</u>

I wake up to darkness, which slowly evolves into… nothingness. It's a dull, grey day. I still don't feel a sense of grief or loss and I'm becoming increasingly disturbed by it. The grey of the day and the greyness inside feels like the world has been anaesthetised.

Breaking News: Government warn that lockdown will extend beyond March if public ignore the rules.

The third lockdown officially begins today. There is a general "stay at home" order and this time schools have been closed again. No social gatherings – even outside – are permitted and all non-essential travel is banned.

Breaking News: USA exceeds 21 million Covid cases.

We go to meet Nicky at the cemetery. Lone people are standing in the bitter cold, heads bowed, staring at the graves. It's a very sad place; of course, no one comes here because they're feeling happy. Rosie's grave has no headstone yet, that won't be ready for several months; there is just a simple cross marker with her name on it. Already though, Nicky has started to transform the bare plot of earth into a fitting memorial garden, with plants and flowers in a riot of colour. Brendan sits respectfully for a while, but then can't resist the urge to try and wee on every single headstone.

In the afternoon, I go to Dad's flat to meet my brother. When I first see the flat, I expect it to be the trigger that will release my grief, but it doesn't. I start looking around for something that I'd like to keep as a memento, something that *means* something, something that *matters*, but strangely nothing really touches me at all. This is my first visit to Dad's flat since he died, but I still feel nothing.

Thursday 7th January 2021.

It was really cold when we went for our walk. Everywhere was frosty or covered with a light dusting of snow. We encountered a male jogger, he was tall, dressed in black and running towards us at quite a pace. I ushered Brendan in to the side. He watched the man run past, but didn't bark, growl or lunge at him, which has always been his normal response. I think this was the first time I realised Brendan had started to evolve. While all the bad things had been going on in our lives, and even though my intended dog training had fallen by the wayside, Brendan was becoming more secure and more obedient. But not less rude. On the way back, we met lovely Bruno from next door, the handsome tricolour collie. Bruno came over wagging his tail, but Brendan did all but yawn and tap his watch. Well, you can't have everything.

Friday 8th January 2021.

It's raining lightly. Everywhere is wet and grey, which feels appropriate, because it's a month to the day since Rosie died. It has been the longest month in so many ways, I can't believe it's only four weeks. So much has happened in that time, including that Dad has also died. We still haven't got a cause of death for him. They won't answer the phone on the ward, they won't answer the phone at the so-called Bereavement Suite. Someone is supposed to be going through the paperwork and coming to a decision on the cause of death. Until then nothing can move on.

Some time later, the Coroner's office phoned. The Coroner had refused to sign a death certificate for Dad, as he couldn't be certain of a cause of death, so he had ordered a post-mortem. Although I didn't like the sound of this, it didn't move me as such. I still had no feelings. A friend emailed and said this was a good thing, rather than feeling the rawness of grief, like Nicky is experiencing, but grieving is a normal process and it's all part of coming to terms with the loss. I can't even grieve for my father. It's like he's just gone, like he never existed and like he doesn't matter.

In the evening, at Nicky's, we order a Chinese again, even though we only had one a few days ago. It was my idea. We feel like we deserve treats at the moment.

Nicky said today: "I hate people!" She had been annoyed by cyclists, runners and pedestrians on the riverside path on her way to the cemetery. "I can understand why people want to move into the middle of nowhere and never see anyone!"

I gasped. "But I've *always* felt like that! And moving into the middle of nowhere is my ultimate goal!"

"I know." she said. "But you've always been a weirdo."

At ten o'clock I walk home with Brendan. He sniffs the air, searching for foxes, but there are seemingly none about. It's a Friday night, but it doesn't feel like a typical Friday night, because of course it *isn't* a typical Friday night. It's very quiet. It feels much later than it is. There's no smell of hot fat drifting over from the chippy, as is usual at this time. The chippy is closed. The pubs are closed, so there is no one staggering home. There is an eerie calm and no sound from anywhere.

Saturday 9th January 2021.

10am. Brendan's late up, so we're late out. He's limping slightly. Perhaps we walked too far yesterday, on too much concrete. It's damp, cold and foggy. There's no one about.

2pm. Walking to Nicky's, the fog has gone and been replaced by sunshine. In the park I let Brendan off his lead. It's very busy, people are standing around chatting, and blocking all the pathways. Brendan weaves his way between the bodies, visiting the various dogs that stand idly with their chatting masters. I follow as best I can, whilst trying to remain socially distanced, which isn't easy.

By the time I'm through the first heaving throng of people, I'm feeling stressed and anxious, because I can't see Brendan. Then I hear a gasp of consternation. I look into the fenced playground and see, amongst all the children, Brendan sitting happily in the centre beneath the NO DOGS sign. I can hear a parent saying "Oh dear! There's a dog in the playground!" But – as clever as Brendan is – he can't operate the heavily sprung gate without human assistance, so clearly he had an accomplice.

I retrieve him and he remains on his lead for the rest of the journey. He doesn't like children, or adults, or playgrounds, yet he's always had a hankering to go into this playground. Probably for the simple reason that he's not allowed.

Sunday 10th January 2021.

I slept in late. I say late, I got up at 8am, but we didn't go out until 10 when Brendan was good and ready. It was drizzling. At the golf course we met Bruno from next door, with his mum, Alison. She thinks the coronavirus will be with us forever, like 'flu. I'm tempted to agree.

Breaking News: Stop ignoring the rules! Health Secretary, Matt Hancock, warns public: "every flex of the rules could be fatal!"

(UPDATE: With the benefit of hindsight this headline is mouth-open astounding!)

We pass two women sitting far apart on deckchairs on a driveway, both wrapped in blankets. Clearly one lives here and one is a visitor. It's so nice to see social distancing sensibly employed. Brendan, on his long flexi-lead, wanders up to them to join the party. The women make a fuss of him.

"It's a bit cold for a picnic." I say from the gateway.

"No!" One of the women raises her glass. "Mulled wine! It's keeping us warm!" She gives a maniacal cackle. "Nothing will stop us!"

They both raise their glasses and cheer raucously.

British people are indomitable. Except when they're beaten, or their football team loses. Or they're drunk on mulled wine.

Breaking News: Police face backlash after countless Covid arrests and are now adopting a "softly softly" approach to Covid law-breaking.

The government have suggested, apparently, that people leave their Christmas decorations up to keep the place cheery, but most appear to have been taken down, so it looks like most people have chosen to ignore this official advice. But then, most people are ignoring the advice and in fact *laws* about social distancing, so why should we expect any different?

Breaking News: New mutant strain of coronavirus discovered in Japan.

Tuesday 12th January 2021.

9.30. It's like a beautiful summer's morning. It's very

cold, but it looks golden and warm. The air smells sweet. It smells *very* sweet, almost chocolatey. Actually, I realise it *is* chocolate. It's chocolate Hobnobs blowing on the breeze from the McVitie's factory.

At the field, two huge seagulls make a slow circular descent and touch down on the grass. Brendan watches them with interest, but doesn't lunge at them. Probably because he can't be bothered.

A woman with a big Labrador comes up to us beaming cheerfully. "Hello, Brendan! How are you doing?" I've absolutely no idea who she is. "Brendan's looking well!"

"Yes..." I smile down at her dog. "So's... err... she."

"*He.*"

"Yes... that's what I mean. *He's* looking well, aren't you... *You.*"

It would be so much easier to say "I'm sorry, I don't know who you are." But I can't do that. And that's why the British have a long tradition of farce. Because it's our lives.

Meanwhile, it's apparently "Kiss a Ginger Day". I've never heard of it before, but I imagine it was invented by a ginger person. Due to Covid restrictions this will probably not happen.

Wednesday 13th January 2021.

It's pouring down. We have a horrible, wet walk to the field. Remus arrives, but Brendan studiously ignores him. The most exercise he gets is from sitting down.

Breaking News: Donald Trump becomes the first EVER President to be impeached TWICE.

Thursday 14th January 2021.

We walk to the field. Brendan has a wrestle with his very best friend, Remus. I have a chat with Sandra; we don't wrestle. On the way home, we pass a Ford Focus, a blue one, the same as ours. Brendan tries to get inside. This always amazes me, because dogs are supposedly colour blind, in fact they have a much more limited range of colours than us. Brendan can, without doubt, determine vehicle colours, but also models and makes. Which is more than I can. I tend to go off the colour first, then whether the key works. Though the tell-tale clue is the dog basket on the back seat.

Breaking News: NHS staff protest outside 10 Downing St, chanting "Boris must go!"

I go into town with Nicky. She has some jobs to do. We walk through the precinct. There are a few people about, but it isn't at all busy. Only the shops selling food are open, of course; the other shops are in darkness. There are a lot of empty premises, much more than I remember from my last visit. I think this has little to do with coronavirus though, as the town was struggling anyway with the recession.

We go to the post office, the bank and then food shopping. There's nowhere else to go and nothing else to do and we're glad to leave, because the town centre is now an alien place full of alien people. It's all concrete and glass, soulless and dead. There is an air of hostility, it feels very far from home and – especially for Nicky – it is full of memories. Neither of us will ever come here again willingly.

Breaking News: Having the Covid virus is shown to provide as much immunity as the vaccines.

Friday 15th January 2021.

I slept badly. Again. This is now the norm. I had nightmares. Again. This is also now routine. I can't remember the details, but I woke up thinking about my dad. Again. I was sweating, my heart was racing and couldn't get back to sleep. It was so bad I even woke Brendan up. I got up and made a cup of tea, but I couldn't calm down. Today is Dad's post-mortem, also I'm going to see the funeral director with my brother to make some arrangements, so these two factors may explain why I'm reacting like this.

Breaking News: UK records a further 1280 Covid deaths, bringing the death toll to over 87,000.

The funeral directors was a wasted visit and could have been done on the phone. I came home feeling agitated and unsettled. Nicky came round and we chatted. In the evening we got a Chinese, using the last of the money Dad had given us for Christmas. Unfortunately, it wasn't very nice.

I was on edge all day, waiting for a call from the Coroner. I had been told I would probably hear in the afternoon, but no call came.

Saturday 16th January 2021.

It's a wet morning, raining on and off. Brendan barks at a wall because it's being rebuilt. New bricks have been stacked on the pavement, so he barks at those as well.

At the field, Remus arrives. The boys greet each other with excitement, but then nothing. Brendan seems to have infected Remus with his laziness; Remus no longer tries to get him to play, but they're very happy in each other's company and sit close by, watching any comings and goings.

Breaking News: Infamous music producer, Phil Spector 81, dies of Covid, whilst serving jail term for murder.

Sunday 17th January 2021.

Breaking News: UK Covid death rate averaging 1,000 a day.

I wake up in the night after strange, quite surreal and frustrating nightmares about trying desperately to get uphill... on a tricycle! Dad liked cycling... but not tricycling... and I'm anxious about the result of the post-mortem, so perhaps that's where it came from. Or perhaps it's just completely random nonsense.

At 5am, I'm sitting up in bed with a cup of tea, reading the headlines about the coronavirus. I read a lot, and they all say the same thing: this isn't going to end soon and it isn't going to end well. The world is in a grave mess. I stop reading.

Breaking News: UK study reveals 1 in 8 "recovered" Covid patients "die within 140 days" and that Covid can lead to heart problems.

<u>Monday 18th January 2021.</u>

Today is Blue Monday. Someone has decided it is the most depressing day of the year, based on the temperature, length of daylight, time between public holidays and a number of other rather random factors. It falls on the third Monday in January. At present, it's difficult to see it as any more depressing than any other day.

So, I'm feeling a bit blue, but no more blue than yesterday or any other day. We set off to the field, where Remus and Sandra are already waiting. While the boys sit, ignore each other and look duly miserable, it seems Sandra has also fully embraced Blue Monday. She tells me her daughter was supposed to have been attending a "living wake" at which the "deceased" has yet to decease and would herself be attending, in body as well as spirit. Presumably, this is because she wants to be the star attraction and hear what people have to say about her. It will now be postponed until after lockdown. Covid-19 is affecting all funerals, even fake ones.

As we walk home, I'm feeling a little more depressed, so perhaps Blue Monday is weaving its magic.

As soon as we get home the Coroner's office phones. They are still unsure about Dad's cause of death and are going to continue their investigations and possibly have an inquest. "But all that implies that something suspicious has happened." I say.

"No, no, not at all." the clerk replies. "It just means…" And she goes into some long-winded explanation that, at the end, seems to imply – to me – that yes, there is indeed potentially something suspicious. I don't feel very reassured.

In the meantime, we'll be issued a temporary death certificate so we can set about tying up Dad's estate and arrange the funeral, which makes it feel like we're moving forward in some way.

* * * * * * * * * *

It's Nicky's first day back at work today, though she'll be working from home, rather than going in to the office. She's got a week of half days to break her in more easily, but even so, she's struggling and is very unhappy. The work emails she's having to deal with are from the date of her mum's death and she's finding it very upsetting. She's coming here for tea.

Storm Christoph hits…

Breaking News: FLOOD WARNING! "Danger to life" as Storm Christoph expected to drop 2

months' rain in 36 hours.

It's raining from late afternoon onwards. In the evening it's tapping on the windows, but not severe yet. We're in an amber alert area, so it turns out to be Amber Monday. It rains all night solidly.

Tuesday 19th January 2021.

Early morning. As always, I didn't sleep well. Outside it's still raining; it's grey and dismal. There are pictures of flooding in the news. Storm Christoph has delivered what was promised. When we step outside it's stopped, but everywhere is flooded, roadside puddles extend across the pavements in many places. Brendan constantly barks at passing traffic.

There is a solitary seagull on the waterlogged field. Brendan stands, paws in water, looking around desperately for some canine company to ignore. No one comes, so he ignores the seagull instead.

Breaking News: UK suffers a further 1,610 coronavirus deaths in the biggest single-day jump of the pandemic.

As soon as we get home, the Coroner's office phones. They ask a lot of questions about Dad, about his medical history, his job and his lifestyle. They are going to issue a temporary death certificate and I'm told his body is ready for release.

Breaking News: More than 4 million Brits have now received first dose of Covid vaccine.

<u>Wednesday 20th January 2021.</u>

Yet again I'm aware of time spiralling by. I need to try and mark the days, because they are all starting to blend into a bland puree of sameness. Mind you, that's what Brendan likes. He hates change and thrives on routine, but today we're going to do something different. Sorry Brendan. Obviously, there's so little we can actually do in lockdown, so we're going for a walk at an alternative venue, near the cemetery.

It's raining constantly, but not torrentially. However, as we drive to Nicky's many of the roads and pavements are flooded. We pick Nicky up and continue towards the cemetery. The road is blocked off where it crosses the river. The Mersey has reached the highest in recorded history and three hundred homes close-by have been evacuated. The river is higher than I've ever seen it, but still some way below the road level. We have to drive quite a long way round to get to the cemetery. Thankfully, it is unaffected by the rain.

* * * * * * * * * *

I check out the headlines. Today is Donald Trump's last day in office. He technically finishes at 5pm UK time. Until then he still has the nuclear codes apparently. Makes you wonder if there will be a tomorrow...

Elsewhere, there is a report regarding the fears surrounding the corona vaccine, namely that people are concerned it will change human DNA, that the vaccine is untested, that the long-term effects are unknown, that everyone will be implanted with a microchip, that we are to become a cashless society and cash will be replaced by credit, which will be withdrawn if you disobey. These are all classic sci-fi tropes, but the best sci-fi is an allegory for current issues.

* * * * * * * * * *

At 3 o'clock we go out for a walk before it gets dark. It's still raining. Many of the side roads are flooded and the parked cars are standing in several inches of water. Brendan trots along surprisingly happily in the rain, sniffing occasionally.

There is a blanket of low grey cloud above and the rain is getting heavier. It hasn't stopped raining all day. It's like something biblical. It really is like the end of days; we've had the plague and now someone up there has sent the flood.

And then snow. It starts to snow.

Coincidentally, in the UK it's Penguin Awareness Day. I am aware they exist, though – despite the snow – I'm not expecting to encounter any locally.

Thursday 21st January 2021.

Sitting up in bed, I read the headlines out to Brendan. One of the lead stories reveals that Joe Biden now has the nuclear codes and Donald Trump's have been deleted. The article concludes with the heartfelt sentiment: "And the world breathes a sigh of relief."

There is a lot of flooding in the news. Two *thousand* homes have now been evacuated because of the threat from the Mersey. Despite this, there is Sunshine early on, but this has gone by the time we're heading to the park at 9.30. and it's grey and dull, but not raining. There is a solid blanket of cloud above, with a strange, unnatural hue to it. It was supposed to rain all day, but it's probably too cold for it and the water is trapped in the clouds.

On the field, a woman approaches me and asks what my dog's called.

I reply with the usual. "Brendan: he came with his name."

She nods knowingly. "Right, Brendan. He knows his own mind, doesn't he?"

"He does, yes."

Brendan is standing a few yards away. He glances at me, then looks away.

"He's quite headstrong…"

"Yes."

"And wilful."

"Yes."

"And he won't do anything unless he wants to."

I smile. "That's very true."

She pauses. "And… that's very much like you as well, isn't it?"

I'm not sure what to say, or how to react. For a moment I don't react at all, then I laugh and agree. I'm not sure where she's getting her information from. But it's a very accurate source.

I recall an occasion, many years ago, when Dad was saying to me: "No one could ever force you to do anything against your will, could they? You know your own mind and you won't be swayed. We never had to worry about you in that respect…." I was a bit confused about where he was going with it, but I decided to take it as a compliment. Quite a big compliment, because I have never forgotten it.

Breaking News: Fears that new UK Covid variant "may be more deadly".

In the evening, I watch a documentary on the sanctuary where I met Brendan. He features in it a lot, hogging the camera. He sits on the sofa next to me and I've got my arm protectively around him. I've seen the programme before, ages ago, but it's odd to see it now, nearly three years later. Brendan is undoubtedly my dog now, we are bonded, we are a pair, we are the odd couple, we are the underdogs. I stroke his ruff, which is full and healthy and he feels soft and silky. He looks identical in the video actually, he doesn't look a day older now, but it makes me sad, though I couldn't say why.

So, I can feel emotions… about my dog, but not about my dad.

Friday 22nd January 2021.

While I'm walking around the field – alone – and my dog watches from his seated position in the middle, a woman with a small yappy dog arrives; they're both wearing the same coloured (sparkly pink) coats. Brendan wanders up to them and stares at them both with disgust. I think he's appalled. The woman starts to laugh uneasily.

"He doesn't seem very happy about something." she says nervously.

"I think it's your matching coats." I explain.

She laughs, a little less nervously. "Oh… Everyone keeps pointing that out. It wasn't intentional. I just grabbed something and threw it on."

I nod politely, but I'm not convinced. The last time I saw them, they were both wearing the same-coloured coats as well. But they weren't *these* coats, so perhaps they've got a full wardrobe of matching outfits. I consider this for me and Brendan, but dismiss it. We've got quite different tastes.

Breaking News: Police break up wedding party in London where 150 people had gathered.

I heard that someone was mugged the other day, close to Nicky's flat. It happened on the main road, which under normal circumstances, would have been busy in the early evening, between the pub and the chippy. It's a residential area, only yards from people's houses and overlooked by flats.

Nicky told me of an acquaintance who had been burgled this week. His dog was in the house and had been attacked, they presumably hit him on the head and as a result the dog has gone blind. It really upset me. (UPDATE. Sadly, a couple of weeks later the dog actually died as a result of this attack.)

Later that evening, I'm taking Brendan for his late-night walk. The air is crisp and cold and everywhere is damp. A car drives past us at high speed, probably doing double the 30mph speed limit. In these wet conditions their braking would be seriously compromised and if a child or animal stepped out, it would be dead. It speeds out of sight. A moment later a police car appears, creeping along. It crawls past us. It slows right down. For a moment, it looks like they're going to stop us, but then it carries on. I don't know whether there's a Covid-induced crimewave at the moment, but it wouldn't surprise me.

Saturday 23rd January 2021.

I woke up at 6.40 after a dream. I was standing outside in the darkness, looking up at a brick building. A light came on in a first-floor curtained window. The curtains were pulled back and a figure stepped forward. It was Dad.

* * * * * * * * * *

I have selected two things from Dad's flat. The first is a painting that Dad did, of a vase of flowers. Dad got into art after my mum died. He liked landscapes and animals mainly, but he copied the flowers from a book and it was – in my opinion – one of his best. His sense of depth and scale were never very good, so a country cottage would exist in two dimensions, as though it had been ironed flat. But the flowers really capture something.

The second thing I took was an unopened gift set of "black pepper and thistle beard and face soap". Dad didn't have a beard, so it seemed an odd choice for a gift. It had been in his wardrobe for years and he wasn't interested in it. I took it along with a bag of other toiletries and household products, just because I hate waste. When I used the soap, I immediately felt a connection to Dad, which is odd, because Dad had never used it so it has no associations with him, so it's a manufactured emotion, but it was also very real and I love it.

Breaking News: Newly discovered Covid variant said to be 70% more transmissible than original virus, with a "higher degree of mortality".

10am. More heavy snow. On the way back from the field, Brendan barks ferociously at a wheelie bin. He's got really good with wheelie bins these days, after an initial bad start, but this wheelie bin has a layer of snow on top, as though it's wearing a very bad toupee. It doesn't normally have a layer of white on it, so it's out of order and needs a telling off. I can't quieten him and have to drag him away. After that he just barks at everything.

* * * * * * * * *

Apparently, it's National Pie Day. I'll do my best to take part! (Co-op apple pie served with soya custard. It's a plate pie and does four generous servings, but perhaps I get mixed up with Eat An Extra Dessert Day, because it's gone in a matter of hours.)

Sunday 24th January 2021.

Breaking News: Scientists warn: "Vaccinated people can still spread Covid."

Today it's Nicky's birthday. We're planning a very low-key day. The biggest event is going to the cemetery to visit her mum's grave.

Breaking News: Hundreds break lockdown rules and go sledging.

It's National Compliment Day, the aim being to promote admiration and politeness. I'm naturally polite, which can actually be quite a curse. If I see anyone deserving a compliment today, I will gladly pass it on. (However, I don't encounter anyone worthy of one.)

Monday 25th January 2021.

I slept well until the early morning, when I woke up following a long-forgotten nightmare. I got up, leaving Brendan sleeping peacefully, and got on with my work. Having to focus on work is such a positive thing. I'm very grateful for it.

Breaking News: As part of a Tweet war

involving Donald Trump Junior, the following damning Tweet was sent: "More Americans have died during Trump's presidency than died in World War I or World War II."

We walk across the common. It's re-snowed in the night. It's dazzlingly sunny, everywhere is bright, white and beautiful. Brendan gallops ahead, like an over-excited puppy. We encounter an old man hiking along with gusto, swinging his arms. He beams at us. "Morning! Isn't it a beautiful day? Beautiful!" He's one of those people that brings a little bit of joy wherever he goes.

We're taking our time on our walk today, because it's what Brendan enjoys most in life. Apart from *not walking,* which he also really enjoys. And it *is* a beautiful day. You don't often get days like this in January, so we're making the most of it. We're savouring it.

Brendan meets various dogs and has a bit of a play, even though I've got deadlines with work and various calls to make about Dad's funeral, we're prioritising this, the here and now.

On our afternoon walk, we pass several gangs of youths wandering the streets. They are in their mid to late teens and there are at least a dozen in each group. They are clearly not all in the same family and not in the same "bubble", but they are close together and hugging each other, so not following any social distancing. Nobody at all seems to be taking it seriously.

<u>Wednesday 27th January 2021.</u>

I woke up suddenly at 3.20am. I was wide awake and streams of words were running through my head. I was just hearing the words and hadn't realised it was actually a song. "I see fields of green..." I felt weird and unsettled, so I got up and made a cup of tea. "Red roses too..." I drank my tea and the song kept running through my head like a mantra. "I see skies of blue... and clouds of white..." Then it became apparent it was "What A Wonderful World" made famous by Louis Armstrong.

I put the lamp out and tried to go back to sleep, but the song continued. It was really strange. I've never had this before. I don't particularly like "What A Wonderful World" and don't own a copy or anything. I can't remember the last time I heard it. Not for a long time. But Dad liked it. He sang it whenever it came on the radio. Having placed the song, I thought it might stop. "...and I think to myself... what a wonderful world." It suddenly hit me. I can't believe it had taken me so long to realise. This was the perfect song for Dad's funeral. The *perfect* song. He loved the song, he loved nature, he loved the countryside and he had a very positive approach to life. I felt really excited. And then – job done – the song stopped playing in my head and I was able to go back to sleep.

* * * * * * * * *

At noon, I went with my brother to meet the vicar who will be conducting Dad's service. We're having a religious service, because that's what Dad would want. He found religion in later life. The vicar is very likeable and very helpful. Dad would love her, though he would almost certainly make inappropriate comments about *The Vicar Of Dibley* and female vicars in general. The service will open with "What A Wonderful World". I think it will set the scene perfectly.

Thursday 28th January 2021.

It's another dark and wet day. It's grey. And it's raining.

A child at the field asks if he can give Brendan a treat. I tentatively say yes. The boy approaches Brendan. Brendan gives him a dirty look, then turns and walks away. I apologise for his rudeness. The boy seems a bit put out, but it'll serve as a lesson in later life. We don't always get all our own way. And often not *any* of our own way.

As I walk along, I'm thinking about songs for Dad's funeral. We need a closing song. Singing is not permitted, as it spreads coronavirus. Even the hymns have to be piped in and listened to in silence. Nicky and Dad's partner, Val, have both independently suggested *Bring Me Sunshine,* performed by Morecambe and Wise. At first it doesn't appeal to me, but the more I think about it, the more appropriate it seems. Dad loved Morecambe and Wise and was always impersonating Eric Morecambe. And I want people to walk out of the chapel with happy memories of Dad and about happy times they'd shared. It seems a bit unorthodox, but it's also ideal.

Friday 29th January 2021.

I take Brendan out for his evening walk. It's a cold, clear night. While the Boy sniffs at a gatepost I glance upwards. There are no clouds and the sky is littered with pinpoint lights. It's quite a sight. I have always been interested in space and the mysteries of the universe, life on Mars and beyond, but right now the night sky isn't holding its usual magic, because what's happening here on Earth is weirder and more alien than anything I can imagine amongst the stars.

Saturday 30th January 2021.

It was very cold and very windy in the night. Several of our bins had blown over. It was windy all day. In the evening there was a stunningly bright full moon: Brendan – as usual – barked at it.

Breaking News: The deadliest month of the pandemic. Over 1000 people in the UK have died on average every day in January.

Sunday 31st January 2021.

It's the last day of January and the day before Dad's funeral. I still largely feel numb. I wonder whether it's because I made a conscious decision when the matron phoned, to suppress my emotions, or whether I just can't handle it so my mind and my emotions have shut down. Every time I think about anything to do with Dad, I get panic attack symptoms: tightness in the chest, difficulty breathing, palpitations, sickness and dizziness. I have learned to control the onset of a panic attack, but not the associated physical symptoms.

Today is a strange day with a silently, simmering, powder keg atmosphere.

Monday 1st February 2021.

Today is the day of Dad's funeral. I woke up at 5am. I was wide awake and knew I wouldn't sleep again. I had mild backache, but it was nothing too serious. However, when I left the house at eight o'clock to take Brendan for his walk, I was in severe pain and could barely move. I hobbled down the street, bent almost double. I kept going because Brendan needed a walk and I thought the exercise would be good for me and would loosen my back up. It didn't. It's ten minutes to the golf course; by the time I set foot on the green I was in quite serious agony and had very limited mobility. I was feeling sick with the pain and as though I was going to pass out. I was bent double and couldn't straighten up.

I don't know whether Brendan was sensing the enormity of the day, or whether he could tell that I was in pain, but he was weirdly obedient on the golf course and came immediately whenever I called, which he doesn't usually do.

The sun was shining, but the ground was frozen and covered with frost. I lay down and managed to do my back exercises, which loosened me up enough, so we were able to get home with me almost upright. Not a great start to what is going to be a very difficult day.

* * * * * * * * * *

We followed the hearse at a sedate pace, with my brother and his family in their own car. I was surprised to notice a few people we passed bowed their heads or nodded. We arrived at the crematorium where there was already a small crowd of select mourners. Because of Covid, funerals are still restricted to 30. Everyone was wearing masks and nobody shook hands or hugged.

We followed the coffin into the chapel to the song, *What A Wonderful World* by Louis Armstrong, which really seemed to sum up Dad and his view of life. My niece did a eulogy, memories of her granddad. It was humorous and touching. The service ended with *Bring Me Sunshine* by Morecambe and Wise. The one thing that was constant in people's reminiscences about Dad was his cheeky sense of humour. The service was perfect for him; I think he would have approved.

I still had no feelings at all. I was convinced I would struggle with the funeral, but it was as though I was watching it from a distance, an observer. It didn't seem very real and I felt numb to everything. I don't know whether I was traumatised or in denial or what, but I seemed completely unable to *feel*.

It wasn't as though the funeral offered any form of closure, because it isn't over: we still don't know how or why Dad died – or even exactly *when* – and there may be an inquest. And I can't feel anything, I can't grieve. It doesn't feel like Dad's gone; it just feels like he isn't here anymore.

Breaking News: Fundraising legend, Captain Tom has been admitted to hospital with coronavirus.

Today, on the day of Dad's funeral, a photographer friend, Mark Russell, sadly died. He was an acquaintance really, but I really liked him. You couldn't not like him. He was easy and interesting and knowledgeable, really funny and unpretentious. His area of expertise was in performance photography; I met him when a play I had written was being performed. His photographs were amazing.

He was 69, but seemed decades younger. I've just learned that he travelled in his twenties, inspired by Jack Kerouac's novel, *On The Road*, which I've been reading since I was 18. I've still never finished it.

Mark was a special person, one of those people I wish I'd known longer and wish I'd known better.

Mark Russell
(1st February 2021)

Tuesday 2nd February 2021.

Today, the day after Dad's funeral, my back pain has got worse. When I woke up at 7am I could barely move. I crawled across the carpet and lay on my back, unable to stand. I tried my best to do my back exercises, but the pain was too much and I had virtually no mobility. An hour later I had to take Brendan out. As usual in the morning, he wanted to go to the field, but there was no way I could make it that far. I managed a ten-minute walk, still bent virtually double and very embarrassed. He had a wander and a sniff and thankfully seemed satisfied.

It has obviously rained a lot in the night. All the paths and pavements are flooded. It's such a contrast to yesterday. The sun shone for Dad, which is so appropriate; somebody brought him sunshine. Possibly with their smile. Hopefully they'll bring him laughter all the while.

* * * * * * * * * *

Captain Tom has died in hospital of coronavirus, following a bout of pneumonia. He has so far raised over £38 million for the NHS and become a national celebrity and a national hero.

Captain Sir Thomas Moore "Captain Tom"
(30 April 1920 – 2 February 2021)

4th February 2021.

Breaking News: Concern over new Covid variants as the virus mutates.

It's been in the news for some time that new Covid variants seem to be springing up all over the place and have made it to the UK. The big fear is that Covid will just keep mutating until it's wiped everyone out.

Friday 5th February 2021.

Breaking News: The hated 10pm curfew to be scrapped when pubs re-open in May.

We return from our walk, glad to be back in the warmth. I can hear Old John next door, presumably on the phone, shouting so loud it's as though he's standing in the room next to me. "Did you hear what I said? I said the walls have ears!" Pause. "I said the walls have ears!" Pause. "*The walls have ears!* The walls... They have ears! The walls... For god's sake, I'm not saying it again. No, no... I said no. I'll tell you later. No. Goodbye!" And he hung up. So, we'll never know what scandalous gossip John didn't want the walls to hear; I'm not too sure exactly why he thinks the walls would be even remotely interested.

Saturday 6th February 2021.

My back is aching. I take Brendan out. That's about as exciting as things get.

Monday 8th February 2021.

There has been a light sprinkling of snow, like icing sugar on a freshly baked cake. (I make no apologies for my baking-related analogies.) Light flakes are blowing in the breeze, like a grated white chocolate garnish. (Nor will I apologise for my confectionary-related similes.) It's really cold; there's a biting wind that cuts to the bone. Within minutes of being outside my feet and – for some reason – my thighs are numb and painful. The temperature doesn't bother Brendan though; he's just as lethargic as usual.

We don't see Remus today. We don't see anyone. Brendan drags his paws as we head home, because it was a sad and lonely walk. I have to remind him that we're never alone when we're together, me and The Boy.

After lunch, we're just heading out when a black car pulls up. It's my brother on his way back from the funeral director, having collected Dad's ashes. He's going to scatter them in his garden. They are in a white paper bag, like a collection of pick'n'mix sweets. It just looks inappropriate and trivial and so disrespectful, to hand out someone's ashes in a paper bag. To have everything that the person ever was reduced to this small, white bag of cinders. It isn't very much to show for a life.

<u>Tuesday 9th February 2021.</u>

There appears to have been another dusting of snow in the night, so everywhere is clean and fresh again. It has once more cheered up this potentially grey and depressing world no end. Also, it's sunny and bright, which really helps. The ground is crisp and the biting wind seems to have subsided. Brendan gambols along the street, tail held high. Remus is already at the field, moping about. When he spots Brendan he comes charging over. He is like a missile, stream-lined and efficient. Brendan isn't at all afraid, he stands there as Remus does a very close fly-by. Remus circles him and nuzzles him. Brendan sighs and walks away. They do end up having a very active play though and Brendan gives as good as he gets.

In the evening, Nicky comes over for tea and we watch some telly while we eat. She sighs heavily, because there's a killing, a post mortem, a funeral. "For god's sake," she says. "Everything's about death! We can't get away from it! It's always there! Everything's *always* about death!" I point out we're watching Midsomer Murders, so it's all part of the territory. The clue's in the title really. She doesn't seem to think this is a valid reason. But she's right, you can't get away from death. If we could, we'd be very rich people.

Breaking News: Doctors reveal that the trauma caused by Covid will likely have a lasting negative effect on the population, possibly reducing average life expectancy by 25 years.

Wednesday 10th February 2021.

Breaking News: 1001 new Covid deaths reported in UK.UK death toll nears 115,000.

Wednesday. Midweek again. Already. Quite a few people have commented recently on how it's like groundhog day; every day is the same as the last one and will be the same as the next one. Nothing changes. Nothing moves forward. We're all treading water and going nowhere. Literally. That's how many people seem to be feeling. That's certainly how I feel.

As always, we walked to the field. It was very cold but very bright and sunny. I stood for a few minutes with my eyes closed, enjoying the warmth on my eyelids. It was quite blissful.

There was still a fine layer of snow on the grass and the ground was frozen. Remus arrived and the boys had a run around and a bit of a play. Then Riley, a lovely sandy-coloured whippet arrived. He was wearing a mock sheepskin jacket, looking all retro and vintage. If he'd had a beer gut and a flat cap, he'd have looked like my dad circa 1976.

The boys went charging towards him and chased him round the field. For Riley, it was barely a jog and he was playing with them, completing lap after lap without breaking a sweat, despite his ludicrous jacket. Brendan gave up almost immediately and stopped – I think to call for a taxi. Remus continued bravely, giving it his best shot, but he was out-gunned; Riley didn't even move out of second gear. When Remus finally conceded defeat, Riley did a victory lap and then he was gone. (Perhaps this is what Riley does, goes from field to field upstaging the locals, because we'd never seen him before and we never saw him again. He is now just a legend – a legend in a sheepskin jacket.)

Thursday 11th February 2021.

Breaking News: The new so-called "Kent variant" of Covid is particularly virulent and transmissible and is spreading around the world.

I awake with back ache and feeling tired. As I swing my legs out of bed, I have a heavy feeling of "here we go again". It looks sunny through the window and there is a blue sky, but I'm just not in the mood.

Breaking News: Due to mutations, scientists believe we may still be tackling Covid in ten

years time.

We met Annie at the field. Brendan went strolling over then ignored her at close range. She turned and cut him dead after that. It's a power game and there are going to be no winners. It seems that canine inter-personal politics are every bit as confusing and intricate as the human equivalent.

Breaking News: There are currently three variants of Covid at large in UK. Despite this, a spokesman announces UK should be free of Covid by Christmas.

Not having a good day.

Friday 12th February 2021.

I barely slept at all. I had repeated nightmares about Dad.

It's a cold, grey day with no sunshine as we set off towards the field. We meet a lady from along the road, returning home after a walk with her two Labradors.

"Morning." she calls.

"Hi. How are you doing?"

"OK…" she says, but sounds uncertain. She nods at her two dogs, Betsy and Tommy. "Thanks to these two! Thank goodness for dogs, eh?"

So, I'm not the only person whose dog keeps them sort of sane.

Brendan pulls all the way to the field. All the snow has gone and there's no trace of any frost, though the ground is still completely frozen. There is a sharp, biting wind and I'm really cold.

No one appears at the field. Brendan sits in the middle while I do several brisk circuits to try and warm up. It doesn't work. I'm really cold, so we head over to the Little Park, for the exercise, to generate heat, not because it's got a different microclimate. Quite a large group has assembled, deep in conversation. Their various dogs are milling around. Brendan goes up and introduces himself, firstly to the people in case they're packing treats, and then to the dogs themselves. Within minutes we have cleared the place. It seems Brendan has a reputation as "The Love Dog" and not everyone wants to be romanced.

Breaking News: Prime Minister Boris Johnson reveals his three-stage plan for unlocking the country, with the first easing of restrictions on 22nd February.

In the early afternoon, I take a break from working to sit next to Brendan on the sofa, where he's sunbathing. The sun has come out and filled the flat with its light and heat. I'm not sure my visit is welcome; I think it's seen as an interruption while he's trying to soak up the rays. (He takes his sunbathing very seriously.) I start to think about holiday locations and feel a pang of regret that we are unable to travel. However, as usual, I bring myself back to the present, the here and now. I'm lucky I have my two big windows overlooking the beautifully tended neighbouring gardens, with their exotic trees and shrubs. I'm lucky I get the sunshine and I'm very lucky that I have central heating. And I'm lucky I get to sit here with my dog. In short: I'm just lucky.

Breaking News: Covid infection rate falls: lowest since July.

Saturday 13th February 2021.

It's cold and windy. There is a pink tinge to the sky. It's 7am and already light. I'm inside, looking out of the window. Brendan is asleep on the sofa. He hasn't stirred at all yet.

When we head to the park, I have my iPod on for the first time in months; I couldn't use it before, as I was constantly on the alert and waiting for calls from the hospital. Now there won't be any calls. There is an icy breeze, cutting through me like a knife through low fat non-dairy spread.

Nicky comes for afternoon tea, by which I mean tea and malt loaf. We take Brendan to the field. It's still bitterly cold and Nicky stands there looking pinched white and shivering. She tries to get warm by throwing a stick for Brendan. Surprisingly, with a bit of encouragement, he actually trots off in the direction of the stick, but finds a nearer one and opts for that instead. He does this three times, each time locating a nearer stick. This is now "a thing". We decide to view it as a partial success.

We come back and sit in the window, watching the birds in Neil's garden next door. There are black birds, sparrows, wood pigeons, a dove and a great tit. And a lot of squirrels. We chat about the Covid headlines and drink tea. Yesterday the country showed signs of breaking the grip of the coronavirus. Could it be that things are starting to get back to normal? (UPDATE: No, it couldn't.)

Sunday 14th February 2021.

Today is Valentine's Day, when all the lovers of the world spend staggering amounts of money buying over-priced roses, chocolates, perfume or products from the Ann Summers shop. Whilst everyone not in a relationship is either extra sad, or extra relieved about it.

Actually, we quite actively don't do Valentine's Day. It has nothing to do with the inflated prices either, but simply because I believe *every* day should be as important and significant as Valentine's Day and you shouldn't need a specific day to buy a gift for your partner. By chance, we both got each other spontaneous presents this week. (Both were edible gifts and were both eaten.) This is just the way we are. Ahh...

Breaking News: New UK Covid cases number 10,972. UK death toll rises by 258.

The wind is raging and the branches of the trees are thrashing. We set off to Nicky's, with Brendan's ears flapping in the gale. Two women cycle past us and one of them shouts "Hello, Brendan!" Then she adds. "Brendan the dog" as though to clarify, in case he doesn't know. I have no idea who she is.

At Nicky's, we watch a TV documentary about Jimmy Savile. It's quite unsettling and not how you traditionally spend Valentine's Day. But at least we're together. And unsettled together.

<u>Tuesday 16th February 2021.</u>

Breaking News: Number of weekly Covid deaths falls.

In the evening, I watch an old black and white film noir, *Kiss Me Deadly*. It's quite traumatic at the end, apocalyptic and disturbing, but very effective. I can't sleep afterwards. I feel restless and energised. I take Brendan out for a night walk in the small hours. He comes out relatively willingly, which is odd. We walk around the block and past the parade of shops. Everywhere is deserted. There are no people about and no traffic at all. After the ending of the film, this isn't really what I need. It's quite unearthly. Brendan sits down on the pavement and yawns. The traffic lights near the shops turn from green to amber, to red automatically... and then back again, but no traffic comes.

<u>Wednesday 17th February 2021.</u>

Today is Random Acts of Kindness Day. It was established in 2008, but has existed as a Buddhist practise for quite a bit longer. I am not a Buddhist, but I do try to live my life according to Buddhist principles: live and let live, doing good deeds, respecting other people, animals and the environment and so forth. Being kind is part and parcel of that. I am constantly letting people out when I'm driving, especially public transport. It's great when you flash a bus, it pulls out and you get a bus flash of thanks back. But the downside is, when you don't get an acknowledgement of your kindness. This is absolutely *not* why you should do a kind act, it should be altruistic, not for gratitude, but when you don't get a quick flash or a wave of thanks you feel taken for granted. Chasing people down the street with a machete because they didn't thank you is definitely not what Random Acts of Kindness Day is all about. Apparently.

I should point out now, following a brief discussion Brendan will *not* be taking part in Random Acts of Kindness Day. He's saving himself for National Lazy Day in August.

Breaking News: Prince Philip hospitalised with unknown illness, but it has been specified it is NOT Covid.

Feeling very tired. Feeling worn out. Feeling like we've been here before. Which we have. The day holds very little that's different, yet I'm clinging desperately to the belief that we are still free. Which we really are... even if it doesn't feel like it.

Thursday 18th February 2021.

I awoke very early, but only got up at 7.30. It was just getting light and it was raining. A lot. By the time we set off on our walk, the rain had stopped and the sun was trying to break through the low cloud layer. A shaft of white sunlight appeared above the church tower, like something holy descending.

Brendan suddenly started barking furiously and jumping up and down. A jogger had appeared. Brendan does NOT like joggers coming to his field, running around the perimeter and wearing the carpet out. The jogger jogged to the next exit and jogged on. The field was quiet again. There were very few people about. There was very little movement, very little noise. Cars were parked, workmen's vans were parked, scaffolding was empty, tarpaulins flapped idly, but there was no sign or sound of the workmen. There was an atmosphere of abandonment.

Breaking News: South African Variant outbreak in Leeds. Entire postcode advised to get a Covid test.

Friday 19th February 2021.

It's mild, but very windy. There is a feeling of stagnation. Again. And pointlessness. Again. I'm starting to think the Covid situation is never going to end.

There is still no word from the Coroner about Dad. I'm waiting for some sort of result, but I'm not hopeful it will be anything revealing and I still won't know what happened to him. Even writing this I can feel my heart rate increasing and there is a tightness in my chest. I need an overhaul.

Nicky is taking part in an online forum for bereaved

people run by the Good Grief Trust. It's her first session today.

Breaking News: Government spokesman says they can't guarantee this will be the last lockdown .

Nicky came in the evening. She talked about the Good Grief Trust forum. She found it a very supportive environment and very helpful. I wondered if I should try it, but I don't want to gate-crash a forum that she discovered and besides, I just don't think it's for me. Apart from that, I'm not actually feeling any grief. I'm still not feeling *anything*.

Sunday 21st February 2021.

Sunday, bloody Sunday. A dull, grey, still, silent day.

Today's juice: apples, pears and kiwis. It was nice, with a refreshing zing.

Monday 22nd February 2021.

Breaking News: Prime Minister, Boris Johnson: England is going to start "reclaiming our freedom". All limits on social contact set to end by 21st June.

The government have released details about the current lockdown coming to a gradual end, starting with the return of children to schools and people allowed to mix with one person from another household. This seems so ludicrous, as everyone's doing that anyway.

We haven't been in a pub since before the original lockdown, so probably coming up to a year ago. It's surprising how easy it was to accept we couldn't go in one. When this lockdown ends, we probably still won't go in a pub, because we've lost whatever it was that made us want to go in. Brendan, however, is really missing pubs. We can't walk past one without him pulling to go in. Anyone would think he had a drink problem. In actual fact, he does, in that he rarely ever drinks, unless it's from a filthy, dirty, tar-coloured puddle, which he loves.

Breaking News: Prime Minister hopes we're on a "one way road to freedom" after a "wretched year".

In the afternoon it's sunny and very warm. We walk to the big field, which has a holiday vibe; people are mingling, jogging, kicking balls, sunbathing. In the distance, the towers of Manchester are sunlit and look a little bit surreal, like they're a rather false backdrop in a film.

Brendan sits on the grassy slope. I sit beside him with my arm around him. We do this a lot, because – after all – there isn't a great deal else to do.

Juice today: celery, beetroot, apple, carrot, Chinese leaf (lettuce). Surprisingly sweet, but with earthy undertones from the beetroot and a kick from the celery. Exceptionally nice and very healthful.

Breaking News: Boris Johnson: "The end really is in sight".

Yes, Boris; that seems very likely.

<u>Wednesday 24th February 2021.</u>

It's a grey, wet, miserable day. We go to the field. Brendan ignores some dogs. He sits on his hill overseeing all interactions and literally cuts everyone dead. It's his favourite part of the day.

Back at home, he has a lie down while I read him the main headlines. "Covid... Covid... More Covid... Ah, Prince Philip's still in hospital with "a" virus, but absolutely – it must be stressed – not "the" virus." Brendan is absolutely riveted.

Breaking News: Scientists warn: the UK will face another wave of coronavirus if lockdown restrictions are lifted too quickly. Some measures will be needed beyond 2021.

Many virologists believe that a vaccine is not the right way to tackle the coronavirus, insisting that it is completely and utterly the wrong way and that the vaccine has led to the virus mutating. The vaccine is believed to be less effective against newly emerging mutated strains. Virologists say a strain will eventually arrive which is completely resistant to the vaccine.

Currently, it is believed that the vaccine does not inhibit transmission, so the fact that you've been vaccinated, does not mean you cannot pass the virus on to others. Furthermore, you can still contract Covid after being vaccinated, and you can still die from it.

Many scientists insist that a certain way to stop the virus in its tracks is to observe social distancing, wash hands and quarantine infected people. This is what we were doing at first, before the vaccine had been invented. If it is done properly, it is *incredibly* effective. This is how the various other pandemics in history have been overcome. The problem with Covid is that people are lazy and don't fully observe these protocols.

People seem to think that getting the vaccine is all they have to do, and then they can forget all these simple, but effective safety measures. This is not the case. Without these simple frontline methods, it has been posited that the virus will never be beaten.

Breaking News: Government plead with the public to keep going with Covid regulations. This is a crucial point in the fight against the pandemic.

Thursday 25th February 2021.

Breaking News: Huge increase in the number of people heading to beaches, beauty spots and public places.

I actually slept well for once. I think. Until I was awoken at 6.08 by one of the neighbours slamming doors. It's a sunny morning. Next door the camelias are in bloom. It looks like a beautiful spring day. I ask Brendan if he's ready to go out. He looks up at me wearily and indicates he would like another half hour.

Breaking News: Most scientists agree that in the future Covid will remain a seasonal illness, like 'flu.

We have learned nothing. The wet markets in China are still open, where – for a time at least – the virus was supposed to have originated and crossed species.

Breaking News: Scientists predict new jabs will have to be formulated annually to deal with the increasing Covid variants.

Friday 26th February 2021.

Today, at 8am, it looks like another fine sunny spring morning. We go to the field, as usual. I'm not sure what has made the field Brendan's favourite place, outside of his home. It was the first place I brought him on his first day with me, perhaps that has something to do with it. Now he only wants to come here, and since he met Remus that has become more ingrained and if I take him anywhere else I feel I'm depriving him of his friend. They generally have a short wrestle together and then sit side by side for an hour. Remus's mum, Sandra, is the person I see more than anyone. I clock up more hours with Sandra than I do with Nicky.

Breaking News: For six consecutive weeks the number of new global Covid cases have fallen. The big question is: Why?

There are major concerns that people are less likely to adhere to social distancing and sanitising as more and more are vaccinated. I've just walked past the local park and it was like Woodstock. It was busier than I've ever seen it before and there was no social distancing whatsoever. Pavements in the area were blocked by families meeting and chatting whilst getting in and out of their cars and the pavements were restricted anyway due to poor and illegal parking. No one is doing social distancing.

* * * * * * * * * *

I spend much of the day at Dad's doing jobs. For a break, I take Brendan to the nearby park, which is next to my old junior school. The delicate spring flowers are out in force now, crocuses, snowdrops, primulas and daffodils. It's a pleasant park and Brendan's happy to have somewhere new to sit down.

I haven't been here for a long time. Many years ago, I used to meet Nicky here, when we both lived with our parents. We'd sit on a bench with a view out towards the Cheshire countryside. The view is now obscured by trees, which have grown and concealed the horizon. Before that, I used to come here in my mid-teens with my – then huge – personal stereo on and sit looking out at the countryside, wondering what I was going to do with my life and where I was going. Pretty much as I'm doing now.

Breaking News: Covid cases are rising in one in five UK council areas. Covid is a "battle we have not yet won". Despite a sharp fall in infections in much of the country, figures reflect a "stark picture".

So, things are getting better and things are getting worse. It really is the best of times and the worst of times. Should we believe *anything* these people say?

Saturday 27th February 2021.

Saturday 27th February 2021.

We spent the afternoon and evening at Nicky's, then walked home in the light of a full moon. Everywhere was eerily silvered and silent. We saw a fox, chased a fox, lost a fox.

Sunday 28th February 2021.

So, it's the final day of the shortest month. Another fine sunny morning. I always think of February as being the worst month, cold and wet, but it's actually quite beautiful.

The online bereavement group Nicky has joined, the Good Grief Trust, were discussing the end of lockdown. None of them want it to end. Many of them have lost people *during* lockdown and haven't yet gone out into the world as a bereaved person. For many people there is certainly some comfort in lockdown. You don't have to try too hard, because you can't go anywhere or do anything. The world is on hiatus and lockdown has created a protective bubble. Lockdown doesn't feel like real life; real life has been suspended. Lockdown feels like fiction. I want it to end, so we can all get back to normal, but I also want it to remain, because it's so much easier to control your world when it's just your own four walls.

Breaking News: Covid update: Vaccine-resistant Brazilian variant detected in UK. Six cases identified so far.

At the park, a bouncy young dog came sniffing around Brendan, who wasn't interested at all. The other dog was really enamoured by him and kept pestering. Because he was a young dog, Brendan was very tolerant and patient and just kept walking away. The dog eventually had to be dragged away on his lead. The next dog to pass us was an older, bow-legged female. Brendan instantly fell for her; he made her all sorts of promises and offered her his Post Office Savings book. He wanted to marry her and stay married to her for the rest of the afternoon, but their love was never meant to be, because firstly she wasn't remotely interested and secondly, she was called by her humans and scampered out of Brendan's life without even looking back. It struck me that this is one of life's ironies. We always want what we can't have.

Today's juice: pear, apple and grape. It's sweet, like sherbet. A nice colour as well, pale purple. (Sometimes – it seems – we *do* get what we want.)

Monday 1st March 2021.

Breaking News: Government scientist warns that due to the Brazilian variant, UK needs to "go backwards" in terms of lockdown, rather than easing restrictions.

It's another beautiful spring day. I'd like to *carpe the diem*, but I'm so tired. I'd actually also like to stay in bed all day. But instead, we go for a walk. Brendan spots a squirrel on the far side of the field. He charges – from a sitting position – diagonally across the grass in pursuit. For the other field users, it's such an unusual sight – to see Brendan running at full pelt – that many assume there's been a bomb warning. Brendan can run when he wants to. He doesn't run with fluid efficiency, like Remus; his legs kick out awkwardly and he looks unwieldy, as though he only learnt to run a week last Tuesday and is still unsure about it, but he can go at a moderate speed, when he has a good enough reason. The squirrel doesn't need to worry though; it disappears up the bough of a tree and before it's caught its breath, Brendan is already sitting down again and people are tentatively starting to emerge from the places they've taken cover from the perceived imminent blast.

Breaking News: A poll has revealed that two thirds of Russians believe the coronavirus was created by humans as a bio-weapon. 62% said they would refuse a vaccine due to fear of lack of clinical trials.

Tuesday 2nd March 2021.

The news is all over the place. There are positive things, promises that social distancing will be over by June, but at the same time warnings about various new strains of the virus and concerns that the infection rate has gone up again. So much of it is contradictory and very unhelpful.

Breaking News: The end of Covid is NOT in sight, Boris. Coronavirus cases ON THE RISE globally.

It's a pleasant, sunny morning again. It's blue bin day, in case you're interested.

At the field a little boy is throwing sticks for Brendan and Remus. Brendan gets quite frightened and comes and stands by my legs for support. If it had been an adult doing that, he would have seen them off, but he knows the child is vulnerable, even though he seems to be attacking him. I politely ask the boy to stop. He stares at me for a moment with his lower lip quivering, then runs away.

In the night, I wake up suddenly when I think I feel Brendan jump onto the bed behind me. The mattress dips and I roll slightly towards the depression. I wonder what he's doing, then realise he's actually asleep in front of me. I don't know what the hell that is behind me. I turn, but – perhaps thankfully – there's nothing there. I wonder if I'm asleep, but at the same time I know I'm fully and totally awake. My heart's racing and I'm sweating.

The bed dipping happens several times. It doesn't disturb Brendan, so I assume it's either something to do with him, or it's in my mind.

Friday 5th March 2021.

Look, it's Friday again; the end of another week. Yet another week. Already. It's a dull, grey day. There's no movement in the bare trees. No movement at all. Anywhere.

Breaking News: Almost 125,000 people in Britain have been killed by the coronavirus.

An article I read inspired me to ask: IF LOCKDOWN FINISHED RIGHT NOW, WHAT WOULD BE THE FIRST THING I'D DO? There's no easy answer, but let's assume the virus is unequivocally dead and is never coming back – what would I do? My first thoughts would be a holiday... or many holidays. But we can't go anywhere, because we've got animals that hate travelling and a sick cat who would find the journey to a holiday destination too stressful. So, we wouldn't be able to go away.

What is emerging from this question, is that our personal world is very insular, very local. We can't go anywhere and we can't really do anything. Covid restrictions haven't really cramped our lifestyle. Our lifestyle was already restricted. So, if restrictions were lifted, I'd probably take Brendan to the field and then come home again. Depressing, isn't it? Except for Brendan, who is throwing a party to celebrate not having to go on holiday.

In the evening, I ask Nicky what she would do if lockdown ended. She shrugs dejectedly and answers the same as I did. "Nothing... because of our animals." She doesn't particularly like going away anyway. Holidays are much more my thing. She shares Brendan's love of staying at home. They have that in common. As do the cats. So, I'm the odd one out. As usual.

Saturday 6th March 2021.

We're at the field. It's a grey, still, cold day. There's nobody here. We walk around the perimeter, listening to the wood pigeons making their odd calls. I watch Brendan ambling along with his tail up, looking like a meandering dodgem car. He loves being here. There is the sound of somebody hoovering from one of the houses nearby, it's that quiet.

Monday 8th March 2021.

It looks like another grey, featureless day. Two words spring to mind: drudgery and nothingness.

I take Brendan out at 8am; his idea not mine. Everywhere is quiet. There is hardly any traffic, pedestrian or vehicular. We barely see anyone. We pass two uniformed schoolboys on our way back, then I realise it's the 8th March and pupils are supposedly returning to school today. The pavements should be flooded with young people by now, but they aren't.

Breaking News: Schools are reopening today. A person can meet up with one person from another household, but outside, not inside, which remains illegal. Care homes can allow one regular visitor per resident.

This is all a bit of a joke, as only eight people and a confused dachshund have been observing the rules anyway.

Tuesday 9th March 2021.

In the evening, at Nicky's we're watching an old comedy which ends up revolving around a funeral. Nicky sighs and starts bemoaning that we just can't get away from it. I have to agree; death is *everywhere*. Presumably it always is, but after you've had a bereavement – or several – you become much more acutely aware of it. I suppose death is one of the primary human concerns; birth, sex, death are the big events and a lot of drama and comedy revolves around these issues. It's just we're getting a bit sick of death being forced upon us all the time.

Wednesday 10th March 2021.

They had warned about the bad weather and they were right. All night rain hammered on the window. Then it was a windy and wet morning that looked set to continue throughout the day.

We walked back from Nicky's over the common. We passed the pond. Even the ducks had sought shelter in the long grass on the bank, because seemingly the pond was too wet for them. Brendan trudged along sniffing, but looked fed up and miserable.

Breaking News: A plant-based diet could help reduce the risk of contracting Covid-19, as it is known to boost the immune system; it is believed it can also reduce the symptoms of the virus once contracted.

With that in mind, today's juice is grape, grapefruit, apple and blueberry. Nice and tangy but not bitter. It explodes on the tongue in an unexpected riot of zesty freshness. Gorgeous.

Thursday 11th March 2021.

It's windy and wet all night. The rain stops in the morning, but the wind carries on.

Breaking News: Four more cases of the Brazilian variant have been identified in England.

I'm going shopping in Didsbury today, which feels like a big, decadent holiday. I'm far more excited about it than I probably should be.

I buy a coffee and a bag of Co-op custard doughnuts; *that's* why I'm excited and it feels like a decadent holiday, no other reason. I sit in a seating area outside the library, often full of drinkers and rough sleepers. Today they've obviously sought refuge elsewhere, as it's deserted. It's very windy. Slim, white-barked saplings are thrashing wildly, bending to 90 degrees. My doughnut bag starts to slide away across the bench and tips over, but I catch it before any roll out. I sit there, sugar crystals in my beard, wondering why American cops are famous for sitting in their patrol cars eating doughnuts. Probably because they can. People walk past eyeing me suspiciously or perhaps with pity. I must look like a vagrant, hat on, hoody up, bearded, wrapped up, rucksack beside me, greedily eating takeaway food, covered in sugar and not caring.

I call in Aldi. Because of Covid, they currently have a traffic light system to limit the number of people inside the store. One in one out. It seems like another world, alien. I wait in a short queue for the green light, then I enter. As usual, everyone is all over the place until the till, when they obediently stand two metres apart.

And that's it, that's my day out. There's nowhere else to go, so I return to Nicky's, eager to collect my boy, who I've missed. We're never apart, so it feels really odd without him. Brendan comes to the door to meet me, tail wagging. He seems as happy as I am.

Breaking News: The rate of new Covid cases in England continues to fall.

Friday 12th March 2021.

Breaking News: A new Covid variant from Antigua has been identified.

It's a dull, dreary, grey day. We walk to the field and come across an elderly lollipop man, complete with hi-viz jacket and STOP CHILDREN lollipop, having a wee up against the wall. Brendan's so shocked he doesn't react at all, despite it being like a greatest hits compilation of all his top triggers: a man, an *old* man, an old man with grey hair, wearing a hi-viz jacket, carrying a stick of some sort (in this case the lollipop), in a confined space and out of place (he isn't normally there, so to Brendan this implies a crisis of some sort) and – the final insult – weeing on one of Brendan's wee spots. This should be like red rag to a bull, but Brendan just stares open-mouthed. His world no longer makes any sense.

I expect the old man to say something like: "Oh sorry, son... I was desperate." He's in view of a nursery and a special needs school and the path is usually very busy. If it had been a mother with a young child passing instead of me and my apparently easily-shocked dog, this story might have ended with the old man having to hand in his over-sized lollipop.

Remus isn't at the field. The field is waterlogged. We wait for quite a while, but he never comes. The rain stops eventually and the sun comes out. But Remus doesn't.

We walk home a little dejectedly, but don't encounter any more pissing septuagenarians.

Saturday 13th March 2021.

There is a swirling grey sky, which looks like ink in water. The grids are all blocked and the rainwater has flooded the edges of the streets. At the field there is a sudden hailstorm, which Brendan hates. He trots towards the gate; he's heading home whether I come or not.

When we get home, the post has been and there is a letter from the hospital in response to my various complaints about Dad. I was quite anxious as I tore open the envelope. It was mainly a load of waffle and excuses, though they did admit some errors and short-fallings. I was impressed by the thoroughness of the report, but not satisfied overall with the reasons given. I can take it a step further, but I'm not sure whether I want to. It's something else to put to one side and think about.

Sunday 14th March 2021.

It's Dog Theft Awareness Day. Dog theft is a growing crime. Many people currently have small, designer dogs that cost a fortune, breeds like French bulldogs which thieves can sell on easily. There is often talk at the field about Transit vans crawling along, watching dog walkers. They say dog theft has escalated during lockdown. It might seem common sense, but people are advised not to tie their dog up outside shops, never let their dog out of sight, ensure their garden is secure, think about getting CCTV installed and change their routine regularly. Dog kidnapping for a ransom is on the increase and there are disturbing reports of pets used as bait in dog fights. It really is a sick world.

Brendan isn't a French bulldog or a designer dog of any kind, but he's adamant he doesn't want to be stolen and sold to a new owner, unless he's thoroughly vetted them first, which will necessitate full financial disclosure.

Apart from the hoopla and pageantry that is Dog Theft Awareness Day, it's apparently also Mother's Day. Nicky has gone to the cemetery to take flowers.

At the field Brendan and Remus excitedly play wee on this/wee on that. It never gets boring. Apparently. Sandra and I elect not to take part.

Monday 15th March 2021.

When I wake up at 7am, I am hit with that familiar feeling of hopelessness, a feeling that every day is a repetition of the last and that we have no freedom at all and have nothing to do and nowhere to go, so everything is pointless. Then I look at my boy and everything seems so much better. I reassess and realise I'm free and I'm very grateful for the liberties I have.

Tuesday 16th March 2021.

Breaking News: UK Covid vaccination programme way ahead of schedule!

I woke up at 4am. I don't know if I'd had a nightmare, but I lay in the dark thinking about the letter from the hospital about Dad. I found myself going through the various points I need to respond to. There are many inadequacies in the reply and many things are just plain wrong. While I have no wish to just bash the hospital for the sake of it – because that won't bring Dad back – I think it's important to highlight areas that were unacceptable, areas in which they failed badly – and at times they did – in the hope that these problems can be corrected in the future. The hospital has a terrible reputation, but it's all we've got.

Brendan started having a dream, yelping and whining, I spoke gently to him and he calmed down.

Wednesday 17th March 2021.

I'm not sure where my time is going. There are usually around 24 hours in most days, but they seem to run out so easily and I have very little to show for them. And my time isn't taken up sleeping... as I hardly do any of that. I know immediately that up to three hours is taken up at the field or in the garden or walking around the block in the dark. (For Brendan's benefit, not my own.) As for the other 21 hours of the day though, it's a mystery.

Thursday 18th March 2021.

There is thick fog this morning, obliterating the view from my window; the world has been smothered with grey. I love fog.

Breaking News: Daily Covid deaths falling at a greater rate than expected.

When we got back home after our walk, Brendan went straight to bed and fell into an exhausted sleep. Perhaps he was preparing for tomorrow, as it's...

Friday 19th March 2021.

...World Sleep Day. Ironically, but not unexpectedly, I had a terrible night. I barely slept at all and when I did I had bad dreams. When I sat up in bed in the morning, I couldn't remember the details of the nightmares, but I was left with an uneasy feeling that time was running out. Which it is. Always.

World Sleep Day exists to raise awareness of the importance of sleep and to encourage better management of sleep disorders. I am quite aware of this already; I just don't know what to do about it. Brendan is embracing this special day and celebrating... with a nap. This day could have been custom made for him.

He loves sleeping. On a list of his top five hobbies and pastimes he would place sleep at all five positions.

Breaking News: New study reveals that vaccination alone is unlikely to achieve herd immunity and fully contain the virus.

It's another grey morning, but the branches are stirring slightly and I can hear the birds. I have my tea and I read the headlines. None of the news stories are positive or uplifting, lightweight or trivial. There is much talk about a third wave of the coronavirus reaching Britain. Is this our lives now? Lurching from one lockdown to another?

Breaking News: Boris Johnson to receive Oxford/AstraZeneca jab in an attempt to prove it is safe.

This is fine, assuming anyone actually believes a word he says. We've no proof that was the AZ vaccine, or a vaccine at all, it could well have been a Tequila slammer he was injected with.

Breaking News: World Health Organisation warns more people are dying of Covid in Europe NOW than this time last year.

Saturday 20th March 2021.

So much death surrounds us at the moment. Perhaps when you're young you feel invincible, I think I did in a way, whilst simultaneously also thinking we faced inevitable nuclear holocaust. I think when you're young, you feel like death is for others and it will never happen to you. I might have felt that once, but I no longer do. I don't feel invincible. I feel distinctly... *vincible.*

Breaking News: Vaccinated people are dropping Covid protocols. Because of the vaccine, people are thinking the pandemic is over and are "not following Covid-appropriate behaviour".

While the boys had a brief wrestle at the field, I was talking to Remus's mum, Sandra. She was telling me about her husband's illness, death and funeral. We got on to funerals in general and the current restrictions, which at present remain at thirty mourners, but still no wake is allowed. There's no way I could get up to 30 mourners without hiring people in. It started me thinking about my own funeral and what I'd have. Perhaps it's a useful exercise, or perhaps it's just morbid. I would want a non-religious service, certainly. But then I wouldn't actually want a service at all. I don't want any fuss. I thought about songs, but I came to the conclusion that I'd be dead so I didn't really have any preferences. But scatter my ashes at Portmeirion. And make sure I'm dead first.

Breaking News: STAY AT HOME! Protestors clash with police in London as anti-lockdown demo turns violent.

Sunday 21st March 2021.

It's World Poetry Day. So, here's one for you:

<u>An Ode to Brendan</u>

Brendan – he came with his name.
He's different and just not the same.
He'd rather sit down
Than wander around
And he's terribly awkward to tame.

* * * * * * * * * *

It's grey and still outside. The air is hazy; it might possibly be raining. It's another of those motionless days, there's no movement and no sign of life. The stillness is eerie and deadening. There are no birds; there's nothing.

I'm up at 6. (Brendan isn't.) I'm out at 9. (Brendan deigns to accompany me, reluctantly.) There are lots of dogs at the field today, but they all seem to be affected with Sunday lethargy, as none of them are particularly keen to play. This is fine with Brendan.

At 12 noon, I'm sitting reading the headlines. The situation in Europe is getting worse with the coronavirus running rampant. There are fears this will transfer to the UK. In accordance with the grimness of the world situation, the sky has gone darker and it looks like it's going to rain.

In the afternoon we walk to Nicky's. It's very busy in the region of the park – our usual route – so we walk a different way to avoid the Sunday crowds. Brendan doesn't like changing our routine, so he's in a mood and dragging his paws, sometimes stopping completely and gazing back wistfully in the direction we've just come from. We turn down the road where I used to live in our family home. I see it often and rarely think or feel anything, as it was another life. We had a lot of friends here and in many ways, it was a classic and wonderous childhood. We had long summers of sunshine; we all played out all day and only came home for meals. You can't really ask for more as a child. It was a nice area – and still is – and the houses are good-sized, semi-detached. Most of the old families have gone now. The children grew up and moved away and the parents downsized to retirement flats, as my own parents did. Most of them will have died now.

I've always lived in this area, which has its downside. I continually bump into people who say "Hello! How's your dad doing? I haven't seen him around for a while." There are ghosts and reminders everywhere.

Breaking News: Violence and rioting in Bristol as hundreds gather for demonstration against the increase of police powers due to the Covid pandemic. 20 officers injured.

The news is full of scenes of violence which broke out at a demonstration, where police were attacked, a police personnel carrier was set alight, whilst full of officers. Several police officers were injured. It is being described as the worst violence displayed on this scale for decades.

Monday 22nd March 2021.

It's Monday again. It always seems to be Monday. Unlike

Bob Geldof, I like Mondays. Usually. I feel it's the start of a new week, there are new possibilities and anything could happen. But then again, I seem to recall very recent Mondays when I felt like it was the start of yet another identical week, there were no possibilities and nothing at all would happen. That turned out to be correct. It's all a matter of perspective, I suppose.

Today I'm tired, but far less tired than I ought to be, as I haven't slept well for days... or probably weeks. Months even. Perhaps I should try some revolutionary action and maybe stay awake until 4.07am, to shock my system and break this cycle of sleeplessness.

At 8am it looks like another of those static grey days of nothingness, but that's not a problem. Today is another adventure. I've got to go into Stockport to do some errands relating to Dad. It will be my second trip this year. It will be disappointing and strange, I already know that, but it will be different. It will be *something*.

I drop Brendan off with Nicky and then head into Stockport. I seldom come here these days, whereas I worked here for well over a decade, for many years in a bookshop from my teens. I pass a community centre, where I also worked, that served as a drop-in resource for people with mental health problems. This seems to be currently in use as a Covid Testing Centre, though there is no queue and I don't see anyone going in.

Many areas in the town centre have now been pedestrianised, though there are no pedestrians about. There is no passing traffic, no walking feet. It's a ghost town. In the precinct, it's just as deserted and post-apocalyptic. Thorntons is shut, though obviously it sells an edible product, though the Vape Shop is open. Bakeries are operating as normal, and the big chain cafés, like Costa and Nero, are open for take away drinks, but the privately owned cafes are closed. It's all very eerie.

I'm happy to get back to Nicky's, where Brendan gives me a lovely welcome at the door, then rushes back inside to eat the treats that he's been ignoring for the past two hours. Nicky says he hasn't eaten, or drunk anything or even been to sleep, he just lay on the settee looking forlorn and abandoned. Well, that's exactly how I've felt, wandering through the concrete centre of town on my own. We have a symbiotic relationship. Sort of. We complement each other. In a way. We're definitely more than the sum of our parts. When together, we make up one truly great person. Or possibly a really bad one.

* * * * * * * * *

Today, I filled out my census form online, which was due yesterday. I was quite annoyed that they ask for your sexuality and religion. These are not mandatory, so on principle I didn't answer. If you subscribe to the conspiracy theory that Covid is just a hoax to cover the Powers That Be gaining control over the populace, then the Census – with its probing questions – seems to be trying to ascertain which members of the public are worth keeping and which are surplus to requirements and have no place under the new regime. In that case, my answers will ensure that I'm one of those to face the culling.

Tuesday 23rd March 2021.

Breaking News: 23rd March. A year since Britain went into lockdown.

Today is the anniversary of the first lockdown. A year has gone by. A year like no other.

The Prime Minister has referred to the past year as one of the most difficult in the country's history, during which there have been 150,000 Covid-related deaths. He also warned that a third wave of the pandemic was likely.

Looking through the news items about the weekend demonstrations and the eruptions of violence, I'm shocked that so many people believe the pandemic is a hoax. There are photographs of protestors carrying banners saying "WE'RE SAFE. THERE IS NO COVID". If there really is no Covid, then it's a highly efficient global conspiracy.

Once we're up to speed with the news, we head out. It's a cold and breezy day. We meet a neighbouring couple with their dog. The dogs stand aloof and avoid eye contact. I say how I think people are ignoring social distancing, at which point they both, in perfect unison, take a step backwards. Not *every single person* is ignoring the warnings, obviously, but many people are.

We carry on to the Big Field, at Brendan's request. What a difference! There are two people running and exercising, and us sitting down. Gone are the hordes of people partying. I can hear the cacophony of the nearby school, it's obviously breaktime.

It's very cold. The air is grey and grainy and the towers in the city centre of Manchester stand out dark and ominous against an ash-grey backdrop. Those towers seem to get closer to the sky every time I see them.

Breaking News: A minute's silence at noon is to be held in remembrance of the 150,000 people who have died during the Covid pandemic.

I was sitting at home and waiting for noon, so I could join in with the Minute's Silence. Not that there was much noise here anyway. Brendan had just been sick on the carpet and I left it. At about 11.59 there was a noise, like a cannon firing – which I don't think it could have been – probably a fluke, possibly a car backfiring. There was also bumping and banging from one of the neighbours. I sat quietly with my dog, looking out of the window at the trees stirring in the cold breeze, trying to contemplate the enormity of the death toll.

I cleaned the sick off the carpet and then made a curry; these two events have no connection, though the curry did look like the sick and probably tasted similar. I slaved over the curry, but it wasn't coming together. Nicky came for tea. We ate the curry. It was horrible. At eight o'clock she wanted to go out into the street as there was another Minute's Silence. She had brought a candle. We duly went outside at the appointed time. Doug and Alison from next door were there. People had been asked to take any light source, even a mobile phone, to create the illusion of a national beacon. It could have been a touching spectacle, a very moving moment, but no one else from along the street came out. At all.

Wednesday 24th March 2021.

I had another bad night. I went to bed really late on purpose, thinking this might reboot my natural sleep cycle, but it didn't work. I barely slept at all and the left half of my body went numb, I thought I'd had a stroke.

Breaking News: Fears that mutant Covid strains could be entering UK, as 68% of people arriving from France – including lorry drivers – are exempt from British quarantine rules.

According to my day-of-the-week socks, it's a Wednesday. And I've no reason to doubt that. Because it's a Wednesday, we do what we do every Wednesday; we walk to the field. The fact that we do it six other days a week – on average – is irrelevant.

Brendan and Remus have their usual violent wrestle, during which Sandra always worries that Brendan's being bullied, but Brendan loves it. He rarely plays without being forced into it; he's always reluctant and standoffish at first, but Remus doesn't give up with him and keeps pestering until he starts to retaliate, probably out of annoyance. Once his engine's running, he can't get enough. Until he's had enough, that is. Then he'll usually have to snap at Remus in a way that means business, then they sit together in companionable silence.

Neil and Annie arrive. Annie wees on some trees; Neil doesn't. Instead, he announces that he's ordered some bamboo underpants. I picture bizarre Y-fronts made from strips of bamboo, but they're actually made from fibres, he tells us, so it's like normal material. They are apparently soft, breathable and anti-bacterial. I'm not too sure why Neil feels the need to share this, but this avenue of conversation is not pursued. At least Neil's bamboo underwear made this day stand out and memorable; it isn't every day you're introduced to the concept of bamboo pants.

Breaking News: More worries over Oxford-AstraZeneca jab: concerns over blood clots and efficacy amongst elderly.

Nicky now prefers working from home and her company is considering keeping this a permanent arrangement. Is this the future? Us all in our little pods, alone? On the one hand it's sad, because we're basically social animals, yet we're all working in our home offices, all segregated. On the other hand, it's safer, cuts down travel time, removes unwanted interruptions and is preferable in so many ways. When I worked in an office, I would have loved the opportunity to work at home.

Breaking News: CONFUSION AND CONCERN. AstraZeneca admit they used "somewhat outdated" information in their vaccination press release, which "might in fact be misleading a bit".

Thursday 25th March 2021.

Breaking News: North Korea launches two banned ballistic missiles.

Perhaps the world *will* end with a bang rather than a whimper, after all. The coronavirus pandemic has taken all the limelight and we've not heard much from Kim Jong-un, but early this morning North Korea fired two ballistic missiles. They travelled 279 miles and then landed harmlessly in the sea.

It is believed to be a challenge to the US and the new Joe Biden administration.

Breaking News: NHS emergency alert level downgraded, due to falling numbers of Covid patients in hospital.

Saturday 27th March 2021.

I already knew what the time was before I looked at the clock. It was 6.05am. I look at the clock at 6.05 every morning. Sure enough, it was 6.05. Some mornings I turn over and doze for an hour, some mornings I get up. This morning I got up. I opened the curtains. It was bright and breezy.

I've got the familiar Ground Hog feeling again today. It's a Saturday, which of course doesn't really mean anything any more. A Saturday has little more relevance than any other day. Except perhaps there is more pressure to do something fun and memorable.

I leave Brendan in bed dozing while I get washed and dressed. A bizarre stranger looks back at me from the bathroom mirror. The moustache part of my beard arrangement is now so long it keeps getting in my mouth. This has nothing to do with lockdown, of course, but because I want it longer and now seems the best time to do it, while everyone has been looking dishevelled and tousle-haired. It's really interesting and – I think – gives me a bit of a 'Sixties look, by which I mean something like a Beatnik. I like it.

Breaking News: 55% of Germans and 61% of French think Oxford-AstraZeneca jab unsafe.

Brendan comes swaggering towards me across the field. It strikes me that if I'm a Beatnik, he'd probably be a Teddy Boy, because he's got side-burns and his over-sized paws could resemble brothel creepers, and his long legs are like drainpipes. He sits down and casts me a sidelong look, then surveys his field, enjoying the scenery that he sees every day – sometimes several times a day – never tiring of it. I wonder what he's thinking. He sits there, seemingly so contented. Barring heavy rain or a nuclear strike, I think he'd happily sit at the field forever. It really is his home from home.

I sit beside him and chat to him. I often remind him of happy times we've had together. We disagree on these, as very few of the occasions on my list include being at the field, whereas very few on his list include being anywhere *but* the field. But our happiest times are when we're together. Mind you, we're very rarely apart.

"We've been to some places, haven't we, eh boy? The West Country... The south coast... East Anglia..."

He leans against me. You might assume this is a sign of affection, brought on by the happy memories, but it's simply because he wants a back rest.

"We've had some adventures, haven't we, Brendan? Breaking down in Portishead on our first trip! That was funny, wasn't it! Not at the time, of course. We didn't laugh much, did we? We didn't laugh at all... Anyway..."

People say its mad to talk to yourself, but I'm not talking to myself, I'm talking to my dog. People also say it's mad to talk to your dog. Yet some say it's only madness if the dog replies. Brendan thinks for a moment and then disagrees.

Sunday 28th March 2021.

Last night, at 1am, we moved to British Summertime, which means putting the clocks forward. (Spring forward, fall back.) Before I went to bed I moved all my clocks on, so it's safely done. It's a strangely disorientating action, but it really shouldn't be. I was so tired, I was in bed by 9.30pm old time, which is ridiculously early, but I was exhausted. And so was Brendan. But then he's been out for many hours today and although he's happy at Nicky's, there's nowhere like home for him; he loves getting back and getting himself settled down. He usually sleeps very soundly when we've been out for any length of time. He's curled up neatly next to me, fast asleep. He looks so happy and so secure. I'm sure this is the happiest he's ever been.

<u>Monday 29th March 2021.</u>

The big news is that today is another step forward in the easing of restrictions, including being allowed to meet outside in groups of up to six people; outdoor sports facilities, including outdoor swimming pools can reopen, and the travel restriction is lifted, though people are advised to remain working from home where possible. If anyone thinks this hasn't been happening all along then they are unstable. This "Freedom Day" is an exercise on paper, that's all.

Breaking News: Friends (and families) reunited. Groups of up to six can socialise in parks and gardens.

Headlines: perceived threat from China, "land-grabbing" territories, such as Hong Kong or Beijing, and the UK is currently cutting the armed forces, but investing more in upgrading the nuclear arsenal. With China, no longer Russia, as the main threat. Nostradamus, never one for political correctness, said "beware the yellow men". This feels like we've gone back several decades into the icy heart of the Cold War. The world has come to a standstill with the Covid pandemic and now we've all this to contend with.

Breaking News: The government have revealed a new slogan to stress the importance of ventilation in reducing the spread of Covid: "Hands, Face, Space and Fresh Air."

We walked to Nicky's for a visit, and then walked home

in the sunshine, wearing way too many clothes. We sat on the common. Brendan was in his element, loving every sight, every sound, every smell. When we got to the Big Field though, it was like Glastonbury and Woodstock rolled into one, with groups of teenagers in tight huddles. There were no restrictions being observed whatsoever. So, it's no surprise that the prime minister has announced an increase in Covid infections in young people.

We bump into Gus, a gentle Labrador, out with his mum. He and Brendan used to play quite vigorously together. They are still very friendly, but the excitement and energy has gone. They stand side by side, tongues lolling out, watching what's going on. Gus lives in the next street to us. His mum tells me they were broken into the night before. The patio doors were blow-torched, to melt the lock out. They didn't get away with much as the interior doors were all locked. Everyone was asleep upstairs, including Gus; he didn't raise the alarm.

Brendan quite often sits upright and growls or barks in the night; he has obviously heard something. I always assume it's the badgers or foxes, who pass through our garden regularly, but it may well be scouting burglars. Brendan's bad attitude might be the reason this property has never been burgled since we moved in. Old John next door told me it was broken into a lot before I came.

Breaking News: Third wave of Covid expected to hit Britain.

Tuesday 30th March 2021.

I wake up to a beautiful, sunny, spring day. Brendan keeps on sleeping during the beautiful, sunny, spring day. The birds are singing, it's the Easter school holidays. And the country and indeed the world is facing socio-economic collapse. There's a lot to be thankful for. Probably. I just don't know what it is.

There is a lot of litter at the field, food wrappers and cans, including a bottle of champagne by the look of it.

Breaking News: "Horrendous" scenes in UK public parks, where hundreds gather to drink and socialise. Social distancing is being completely ignored.

We went back to the local field in the afternoon; it was very busy. It seemed very good natured at the time we were there. A police car drove slowly past, but didn't stop. Brendan sat down and didn't seem phased by the number of people, but he was disappointed because no other dogs came at all. Dog walkers are studiously avoiding it.

When we got back home, a house a few doors down was having a loud, raucous party. Although we couldn't see, it sounded like there were several dozen people there.

Breaking News: Over 1000 gather at Nottingham Arboretum. Social media shows scenes of hugging and brawling, pushing and shoving. Nottingham has a higher Covid

infection rate than the national average.

<u>Wednesday 31st March 2021.</u>

At the field, Sandra mentioned that she had seen a photo of a Bosnian Barak hound and she thought it was the spitting image of Brendan. While Brendan was playing with Remus, I did a quick Google search. People have suggested many breeds for Brendan, from Airedale to any number of terriers, a "collie-hound" (whatever one of those is), to the regular Alsatian and Retrievers. None of them are right. Until now.

I've never before heard of a "Barak hound". There were several varieties, but they all had a look of Brendan. Some had the wrong beards, some had different fur, some were bushy, but they all looked like Brendan wearing a very poor disguise. I'm sure he's not a pure breed, but there is undoubtedly some Barak in him. I showed him the photos. He was so overwhelmed that he had to have a sit down.

Breaking News: Germany, Canada and France amongst the growing list of countries to suspend use of the AstraZeneca vaccine in younger age groups, due to side effects.

Over 30 people have so far died from blood clots after receiving the O/AZ virus. Deaths have occurred 4 to 16 days after receiving the vaccine. Originally, the government declared that the clots were natural and incidental – nothing to do with the vaccine – though it has now been admitted that the clots are indeed a direct result of the vaccine.

Vaccination centres are reporting massive no-shows for Covid jabs, but this is officially being blamed on the hot weather, rather than the people being afraid due to the increasing stories about the deadly side effects.

Breaking News: Mini heatwave sees Platt Fields Park in Manchester overrun with an estimated 3,000.

Thursday 1st April 2021.

Today it's Brendan's birthday and he is 8! It was a grey start to the day. I allowed him a lie in and then brought him breakfast in bed; a marrowbone roll.

Nicky texted to say it was bitterly cold; it looked dull, but mild. We set off to the field, Brendan wearing a BIRTHDAY BOY badge. Remus was at the field and then the vizsla, Sunday arrived. They all had an extended run and play and lots of treats. After Sunday had gone, the boys got down to their usual wrestling, and did quite a bit of running around as well, initiated by Brendan, which is unusual for him. He's never been eight before; perhaps it's gone to his head.

We came home after 90 minutes and Brendan had a special breakfast of a full luxury pouch and then went to sleep next to me.

The day was all about Brendan. But then, very few days aren't all about him. Nicky came to his party in the evening. There were games (Don't pass the parcel), nibbles, (Marrowbone rolls and chews) and a Brendan-related quiz, in which Nicky had her knowledge about

Brendan tested and had to win prizes for him. (Where is Brendan's favourite outside place? (The field.) What is one of my favourite Brendan moments? (Sitting on a cliff overlooking the translucent sea on a baking hot day, near Land's End, my arm around The Boy). What were Brendan's two worst water experiences? (The Sea Tractor at Bigbury-on-Sea and the Plymouth Ferry.)

Brendan and Remus on Brendan's 8th birthday.

After all the excitement, Brendan went to sleep surrounded by shreds of wrapping paper. Well, you're only eight once.

Friday 2nd April 2021.

It's Good Friday, though there's nothing very good about it from what I can see.

Our friends in Gloucestershire, Steve and Jess have had to have their dog, Erik, put to sleep. Steve said they're devastated as he meant the world to them. It rams home that everything is finite. I sit next to Brendan and cuddle him, making sure that I appreciate him every moment. And I do. I couldn't appreciate him any more.

Sunday 4th April 2021.

It's a dull, grey Sunday morning with no movement. No sunshine. No anything actually. But it isn't a normal day. Oh no. It's three years today since Brendan came to live with me. It seems so much longer. (No offence, Boy.) We've passed the anniversary of the day we met at an animal sanctuary. On Nicky's insistence we had gone to volunteer as dog walkers. Brendan was the first dog we met. He wandered into the room, climbed onto my lap, curled up and went to sleep. The staff were shocked and warned us about how aggressive he was, but he really wasn't. He was vulnerable and needy; he'd sought and found solace.

We came several times dog walking and each time all the dogs we'd walked had gone, been re-homed, which was great. Except for Brendan. I realised that if, one day, we came and he wasn't there I'd be very upset. I couldn't technically have a dog in my flat as it violated the lease, but I agreed to foster him for one night while they were having work done at the sanctuary. He was brought to me by a volunteer, Debbie. He'd been sick in her car and looked very sorry for himself. But he came into my flat, hopped onto my bed and that was that. In those days he was neurotic, psychotic and dangerous to know. But we never looked back.

Monday 5th April 2021.

At 7am when I got up it was grey and still. At 7.30 while I was drinking my tea, it started to snow, just a few flakes, like petals on the air. Ten minutes later there was a blizzard. By 8 o'clock it was sunny.

While the snow swirled outside, I was sitting with Brendan, thinking about the world. I think about the world a lot. I wonder whether things can ever go back to any form of normality. I don't think they can for us. I think everything that went before is over now and gone forever. Our world has changed. Our lives have changed irreparably. Only my boy remains unchanged, thankfully.

Wednesday 7th April 2021.

Today Nicky saw her dad for the first time in months. He's 89 and has been shielding. He's very worried about the Covid situation. They visited her mum's grave, kept masks on and kept a safe distance. It wasn't a very social visit, but Nicky said it was good to see him again and it feels like she's crossed another barrier back towards some sort of normality.

On our way to Nicky's, a small boy passed us. He looked at Brendan and said "Nice dog." I was expecting some sarcastic juvenile punch line, but there wasn't one. So Brendan let him live.

Breaking News: In the UK there have been 79 reports of blood clotting following the AstraZeneca vaccine, resulting in 19 deaths so far.

We're assured that it's very unlikely that you'll have side effects and die as a result of the vaccine. 19 deaths isn't many out of 20 million jabs so far, unless you're one of those 19. And zero deaths would be so much better.

I read an article by a scientist, Mark Pickles, who pointed out that the "Big Pharma" (huge pharmaceutical corporations) are making MILLIONS from this pandemic. It is in their interest to encourage everyone to have their jabs as soon as possible, before the virus starts to abate naturally, as has happened with previous pandemics. As, when and if the virus does abate, it will be attributed to the success of the vaccine. He raises the issue of – as yet unknown – long term side effects and cites the 2009-10 swine flu outbreak, which disappeared "as quickly as it came". A vaccine had been produced; hundreds of people – especially in Sweden – are still suffering side effects, including narcolepsy.

Another article stated that 1,000 doctors and scientists had signed a letter condemning the vaccination programme. None of these "vaccine negative" stories make the mainstream headlines, strangely.

Thursday 8th April 2021.

We walk a long way along the river valley. At least it's a long way for Brendan. He's so obedient and sticks close to me and obeys my commands. This has all come about during lockdown... which is ironic, because training him was one of my original objectives for lockdown. After a few sessions I gave up, because he wouldn't respond to treats and completely ignored me until I got cross, then he'd come slinking over like a recalcitrant teenager. And he's not a teenager... he's eight. But now he's very responsive and keeps quite a close eye on me at all times. I'm not too sure why or how this has come about, but I'm very pleased it has.

Breaking News: According to scientists, Britain is set to achieve "herd immunity" against Covid-19 within days.

Herd immunity was the much talked about state when most (60-80% for Covid) of the adult population (of Britain) had been vaccinated against Covid-19 or had already contracted the virus. This is the official reason for the big push to get everyone to have the jab. Once herd immunity was achieved via the vaccine, then we are told the virus would have nowhere else to go and would die out. (UPDATE: Guess what... it didn't. Strangely, we achieve this goal of over 80% vaccinated, but it doesn't crush the virus, though we won't really hear about herd immunity again. As a concept it will be quietly dropped.) Herd immunity? Never heard of it.

Breaking News: Covid cases have plummeted to lowest level since July.

Juice of the day: grape, grapefruit, apple, blueberry and pear. I love the bitterness of the grapefruit. Thick and bittersweet with a sherbet-like texture. Gorgeous.

Friday 9th April 2021.

Breaking   News: Buckingham   Palace announces   Prince   Philip,   the   Duke   of

Edinburgh, has died at the age of 99.

The scene outside the window at 7am is drab, grey and motionless. At 9am I stand at the door holding Brendan's lead and encouraging him to follow. He looks at me, yawns and flops back down on the bed, so I sit working at my desk, with my coat on, until he's ready to go out. I give up waiting and force him out at 11am.

We walk to the Big Field. In the distance, the tall towers of Manchester look dark and foreboding, as usual. Beyond them are the backbone hills, the Pennines, not always visible, but today they're catching the sun and are bare, bleak, bold and cold. A plane flies over at one point and Brendan runs to the far side of the field, barking, chasing it off. He wins and the plane retreats.

Breaking News: Another potentially dangerous side effect has been reported due to the AstraZeneca vaccine. "Capillary leak syndrome", if untreated, can lead to organ failure.

Sunday 11th April 2021.

It's National Pet Day, which encourages people to love their pets. I think I can safely say I've already ticked that box. To honour the day, I ask Brendan what he'd like to do most in the world, which is why we end up walking to the field and having a sit down.

While we're out walking at 9pm, the air is heavy with a smell of smoke. A few moments later there are flashing blue lights, but no siren. A fire engine drives slowly past us and disappears towards the park. (It turns out to be part of the playground on fire, set alight by teenage arson vandals.)

Monday 12th April 2021.

Brendan got me up at 2.30am, wanting to go out. It was very cold and still. There were no cars and all the houses and flats were in darkness, only the street lamps shone their sickly orange light. There were no sounds, no background hum of traffic, just the intrusive and solitary deep thrumming of the police helicopter quartering repeatedly above. I remembered the local crimewave and felt unsettled.

When we got back inside, I was energised and wide awake. Brendan went out like a light, but I didn't sleep again.

Breaking News: Hospital admissions and deaths have fallen sharply. Even Covid infection rates are down. Things are looking up.

Today is actually a big day in the easing of lockdown. You can now get a haircut, go to the library, go to the gym or have a bikini wax. You can have four weddings and a funeral, but you can only invite 15 people to the weddings and 30 to the funeral; we must conclude that people mourning are less contagious. You can have a meal or a drink outdoors, but you may not have a meal or a drink inside. You can shop for non-essential items, have a driving lesson and have your nails painted in Union Jack colours. If you really want to.

Tuesday 13th April 2021.

Breaking News: Russian general warns World War 3 "WILL happen" if NATO interfere in the Ukraine.

It's a sunny but cold morning. We didn't sleep well, me and the boy, so we're tired and aching. I walk to the local shops. It now looks weird to see them all open, so many of which have been shuttered and in darkness for months. A café bar is full of people sitting outside. The only clue that everything isn't completely normal is that people going into the shops are wearing masks.

Breaking News: Over 150,000 people in the UK have so far died from the coronavirus.

Thursday 15th April 2021.

Breaking News: New official figures reveal that in the cases of almost a quarter of the registered Covid deaths, the people had died *with* the virus rather than *from it*, so Covid was not the actual cause of death.

On our walk, we pass two hairdressing salons. One is using masks and visors, while in the other, the staff and customers have no masks or visors or anything.

We pass the chippy. I'm feeling really hungry and I'd love some chips. I throw caution to the wind and buy chips and peas. I feel very decadent, sitting in the park at a picnic bench in the glorious sunshine, with Brendan stretched out on the grass beside me. The chips are perfect, though Brendan turns his nose up at his share. He hates vinegar, so I lick any trace of the offending acid from a selection of chips and offer them to him, but he still isn't interested. He's becoming distinctly Middle Class. He's probably holding out for some brioche and tapenade.

Saturday 17th April 2021.

It's a really beautiful day. As usual, we're galloping along the street towards the field, to meet Remus and have an energetic... sit down.

Breaking News: The nation mourns the Duke of Edinburgh.

In the afternoon, we walked over to Nicky's. At the big field, just before 3.15 there was a loud crack, like a gunshot or an explosion. Brendan bolted off, terrified. I called him, with more than a sense of urgency, and he stopped dead. I went to him and cuddled him. I was very impressed that he stopped, that he even heard me, because at one time he would just have kept on running if he was afraid, but he now trusts me enough to overcome his fear, knowing that I'll save him. I don't know if the noise was connected with Prince Philip's funeral, or just a fluke.

I didn't dare let him off his lead again and he pulled all the way to Nicky's, where we watched the second half of the funeral, which was surreal. Very noticeably, the chapel was almost empty, with just the immediate

Royal Family and no crowds. The Queen sat completely alone, which looked very sad. It was an historic occasion and I suppose, the end of an era.

Sunday 18th April 2021.

I awake early. I stay in bed until 7.40, which constitutes a lie in. For me, not Brendan. (For Brendan a lie-in can last up to 24 hours.) It's a dull day. It feels like a day of drudgery. I'm tired and my back is aching.

It's a Sunday. In my childhood I always hated Sundays, for a number of reasons. I loved Friday night, because it felt like there was an age of freedom ahead. Saturday was beautifully sublime and I felt free, because tomorrow I still didn't have to go back to school. But on Sunday, I was so aware of the weekend running out; the following day it was school. I hated school. Plus, Sundays were static days when everything was closed and there was a soporific, suffocating, sterile atmosphere. That's sort of how it's felt in lockdown. There's nowhere to go, there's nothing to do. Everywhere's closed, many places are closed down completely.

We walk to the field and the sun comes out; everywhere seems just a little bit better. Remus arrives. After the boys have had a play, Brendan lies down. Remus always stands over him, so it's like Brendan is sitting under a grey bridge. This is a display of dominance. Brendan tolerates it for so long, then snaps at him and Remus scoots away. This is the beauty of their relationship; there is no lasting animosity, they bicker, but are ultimately very happy together.

Breaking News: The World Health Organisation warns that global Covid cases are increasing at a "worrying rate".

<u>Monday 19th April 2021.</u>

We're on holiday! (For the day.) I have decided to throw a curveball – even though I don't know what that means – and treat this week as a holiday and have some days out. It'll be weird!

We start early. I take Brendan out and drop him with Nicky. He doesn't want to go in; he knows exactly what's going on. I leave him lying gloomily on his settee with his head on his front paws. It's an Oscar-nominated performance. I manage to leave him anyway, despite his efforts.

I walk to the tram stop. As this is the first stop, the tram is very quiet. There are less than half a dozen people on and everyone is wearing a mask.

The first part of the journey is very suburban. We accelerate past people's back gardens, then it gets very interesting, all canals, rivers, locks and bridges. The buildings get taller, there are riverside apartments, but no longer any houses, then we're sliding along the windy city streets, past the portico of the library and through open squares. It is almost deserted.

I walk through the Arndale centre. Again, everyone is wearing a mask. There is a one way system, though no one is following the signs, but it's quite hard to follow.

I have a browse around Waterstones. I love bookshops, I love the atmosphere and I love books. I used to work in a bookshop, for twelve years. To this day I can't go in one without straightening piles of books and rearranging them, so a visit to Waterstones is like a busman's holiday.

I buy a Costa coffee, which seems to have increased dramatically in price since I last bought one. I also buy a bag of custard doughnuts from the Co-op. I sit outside near the cathedral. It's warm and sunny, but there are still very few people around. The cathedral is surrounded by blossom; it's beautiful. There are several new apartment blocks and office buildings, already it's a different city. I'm not sure when I last came to Manchester, but obviously it was well over a year ago.

I text Nicky to ask how Brendan's doing. She's bought him a new chew toy, but he won't play with it. He won't eat any of his treats and is just lying awake being miserable. This is probably the longest we've been apart since lockdown and I'm missing him.

I weave my way across the city via the river and canal paths mainly. I'm too hot and wish I'd worn my shorts. I notice some stickers on a bus stop: I'M SICK OF THE TYRANNY, FUCK SOCIAL DISTANCING and THERE'S NOTHING SOCIAL ABOUT DISTANCING. There's also nothing even remotely anarchic about putting a sticker on a bus stop.

I pass a huge sign on the side of a building inviting me to DISCOVER MY WORK LIFE BALANCE, which makes me question whether I've got it right. Have any of us? Usually not. I sit in some formal gardens, a little oasis in the city. Because of that sign, I'm thinking about what I want from life. Money doesn't come into it; I don't want to win the lottery or anything like that. I don't want loads of money, I want simple things, such as this: sitting somewhere beautiful, sitting on a clifftop with my dog looking at the sea. I want the freedom to travel, to go where I want to go. With my dog.

I'm feeling hungry, so I head back into the Arndale Centre to try and get something to eat. It's a total contrast to earlier. It's packed out, there is no social distancing, the one-way system is being completely ignored and a lot of people don't have masks on, but they aren't being challenged by the security staff.

I don't like it, so I head home before the rush hour starts. On the return journey on the tram, several people don't have masks on, or have their masks pulled down and are chatting with friends.

It's been a trip of two halves: an enjoyable and quiet morning followed by a busy and stressful afternoon. I used to go into Manchester a lot and I felt comfortable there, but – after the lockdowns – it no longer feels like the place I once knew. Manchester might still be basically the same, but I've changed.

<u>Tuesday 20th April 2021.</u>

I read the headlines while I have my morning tea. All the news is depressing. Carbon emissions are expected to soar this year as the world tries to race back to consumerism after the wilderness of a year of lockdowns. Over 800,000 people have lost their jobs in the UK, due to the pandemic. I convey these facts to Brendan. He's speechless.

We later go for a walk along the river. It all looks very natural and normal, you wouldn't know anything had been wrong at all, and you wouldn't know that people had died, lost their jobs and pollution was going to skyrocket. But right now, there is a wealth of birdsong filling the clean air. People jog along the river path, cycle and walk their dogs. It's idyllic.

Breaking News: NASA successfully flies remote controlled helicopter on Mars.

Not content with having destroyed one planet, the aim is now to destroy another.

Wednesday 21st April 2021.

Today, it's the Queen's birthday, just four days after Prince Philip's funeral. She's 95 and is Britain's oldest monarch ever!

It's also National Tea Day, when everyone is encouraged to drink tea! That's my kind of day and I'm going to do my bit! My favourite type of tea is Assam, which is strong and malty. Nicky likes Earl Grey, which is delicately perfumed. Apparently the most popular tea is Darjeeling, also known as "the champagne of teas". It is believed people have been drinking this intoxicating dark golden nectar since 2700 BCE.

In between cups of tea, I manage to have some juice: blueberries, grapefruit and apple. It's very sharp, which I don't mind, but it wouldn't suit everyone. I think it would benefit from some sweet grapes.

Breaking News: UK should expect a new surge of Covid cases over summer months.

After 9 o'clock we go for our evening walk. The streetlamps are on, but the sky is still bright. It's quite cool and I'm in a sombre mood, having just looked at the headlines again. Understandably, as the world is going into an irresponsible frenzy of unlocking, everyone is becoming more lax towards Covid, so there will be an increase in cases and there are dangerous new variants to contend with. All we're doing is careering towards the next inevitable lockdown with a recklessness akin to suicide.

I'd be happy to go for a long walk, ambling along as the darkness increases, but Brendan doesn't want to. He stops at a white car and stares up at me. He seems to think that any car parked along the road will do to get us home. I explain again that it doesn't work like that. I think his suggestion is that if I can jemmy the door open, he can hotwire the car and we can drive in luxury the two hundred yards back home. We continue around the block. On foot.

Breaking News: "Troubling new variant" located in UK, especially prevalent in Midlands.

Thursday 22nd April 2021.

It's sunny from the moment I open the curtains at 7.01, when the room is flooded with golden sunlight.

This week was supposed to be a week of "holiday days", which hasn't quite worked, but today we're going to Alderley Edge in Cheshire, which is a tree-covered ridge immortalised in Alan Garner's *Weirdstone of Brisingamen* fantasy book.

Brendan strolls along, under the trees, as happy as Larry's supposed to be, sniffing and weeing, weeing and sniffing. We get a view over the Cheshire Plain, to the huge white dish of the radio telescope at Jodrell Bank, which dominates the landscape for miles around, to the Welsh fringes, and all the places I'm longing to visit.

The weather is flawless, the scenery is stunning and we've had the perfect day, me and my dog.

Breaking News: India ravaged by coronavirus. 314,835 infections reported on Thursday, the world record for daily Covid cases.

Friday 23rd April 2021.

It's a sunny day and considerably milder than it has been recently.

The situation with Russia and China set to invade bordering territories is apparently worsening and there is a real threat of nuclear war. This is getting very little coverage in the main news though, as it's not about

Covid, specifically the easing of lockdown, which steals all the headlines.

It's no exaggeration to say that my childhood – at least my teenage years – were ruined by fears of nuclear holocaust. It was all I thought about. It must have affected so many people, but not everyone, some people just didn't think about it, which is a far healthier way to live. And now here it is back again. But this time I'm not prepared to be concerned about it. It either happens or it doesn't - and worrying about it isn't going to make any difference either way.

Breaking News: Prime Minister warns we cannot "delude ourselves" into thinking Covid has gone away: it hasn't.

Continuing our theme of holidays, I take Brendan on a different walk, to a park and ornamental gardens. After an energetic run, Brendan wants a sit down, so I get a coffee and cake and sit in the mottled shade on a bench, with the sound of a choir filling the air, they are close by, but concealed within a rose arbour and are telling us insistently that it's going to be a bright (bright), bright sunshiny day. They're not wrong. There's a relaxed yet vibrant feeling, like a royal park in London. The singing, the birdsong, the shifting canopy of leaves, the scent of blossom, the sparkling sunlight. It's all magical. Until a bird shits on me. Then it's suddenly less than magical. It's meant to be good luck, but I'm not feeling very lucky.

Breaking News: Experts say Britain is now no longer in a *pandemic*, but *endemic* situation as Covid cases continue to fall.

Saturday 24th April 2021.

I awoke after a dream which featured the Joni Mitchell song *Both Sides Now*. I'm not especially familiar with this song, but I felt there was a message there, but I was missing it. I sat up and put it in Spotify and listen to the Joni version several times and then renditions by a number of other artists, including Judy Collins, Neil Diamond and Glen Campbell. Brendan, lying beside me, put a paw over his ear and sighed loudly.

The hours rolled on. I was completely wired and left with a feeling that something very important was happening. But I don't know what, except the realisation that I really don't know life... at all.

Breaking News: Covid no longer the leading cause of death. It has fallen behind dementia and heart disease.

Sunday 25th April 2021.

It's a sunny day. It's not a great day really. I feel we should have gone somewhere, anywhere and done something, anything, but we didn't. We stay in all afternoon at Nicky's and watch programmes, trash programmes, while it's sunny outside and Nicky keeps falling asleep, her head suddenly lolling forwards.

"You're missing the only bit of plot." I say.

Her head jerks into an upright position and she waggles her leg. "I wasn't asleep! "she says defensively.

"You were!"

"I was just resting my eyes."

"You were asleep."

"My eyes might have been shut, but I was still listening."

"What just happened then?"

Long pause. "Well, I might have dozed for a second."

Within a minute, she's asleep again. And so is Brendan. And Hector. And Pixie. And I'm awake on my own, inside on a sunny day.

Monday 26th April 2021.

I slept relatively well, but awoke feeling very despondent. It's impossible to think about the future in a positive light, so it's better to narrow your vision and focus on the immediacy. This is how dogs live: they enjoy the moment. Though, it's not really how Brendan lives. He seems to go out of his way to avoid living in the moment and always wants what he hasn't got, or what he had until recently but didn't appreciate, or what he's no chance of having. He's not a good role model.

Breaking News: WORLD WAR III WARNING: RUSSIA POSES AN 'EXISTENTIAL THREAT' TO THE UK, AS PUTIN MAY CHOOSE TO USE NUCLEAR OPTION

I look through the leading news articles. The news

is all bad. There has been more violence at anti-lockdown demonstrations. Countries around the world are expressing their mistrust of the various Covid vaccinations, as the Pfizer jab has seemingly caused a "small number" of heart problems in Israel. India's Covid situation is still running rampant; the world's highest ever coronavirus spike has been recorded there for the third consecutive day. Indian hospitals are running out of much-needed oxygen, are over-flowing with patients and people are dying on the streets.

I have been watching the X Files over the months and tonight finished the final episode, series 11, the last one ever. I had forgotten, but it chillingly involved a global pandemic, a plague designed to wipe out the human race. It showed scenes of hospitals swamped with dying people, which echo the terrible situation in India. It was not comfortable viewing.

Wednesday 28th April 2021.

I didn't sleep well. I was anxious and preoccupied. First thing in the morning, I finally did my reply to the NHS regarding my Dad's treatment and ultimately his death. I had thought about letting it lie, but – even though it won't make any difference – I feel I should speak my mind. I spoke my mind. Can't say I feel any better or any sense of closure. But how could I? We still don't know how or why Dad died.

Whilst I'm getting dressed, a phrase comes into my mind: Make Today Matter. I resolve to do just that... by any means necessary.

On the way back from the field, a neighbour who I only occasionally see, crossed towards me. She said she just wanted to tell me that one of her dogs, Tommy, had died. She started crying. I felt helpless. I almost hugged her, which would have been odd at the best of times, but these aren't the best of times, so I stood awkwardly and tried to comfort her verbally with all the usual trite cliches that you wheel out because there is really nothing else you can say. I felt so sorry for her. Instead of offering support, Brendan sat at a distance with his back to us and shunned us all.

* * * * * * * * *

We go for a walk in the early evening. There's no denying we're well into spring now. There are daffodils – past their best – bluebells, forget-me-nots, primulas and camelias, and all the trees are now clothed with young leaves. The air is heavy with the sweet scent of blossom. The sky is blue and the sunlight is slanting as the sun sinks towards the artificial horizon of rooftops. It's beautiful.

* * * * * * * * *

There is a full moon tonight, with shreds of horror movie clouds filling the sky. It looks ominously chilling. Thankfully, Brendan doesn't notice it, or he'd have barked at it. He hates the moon.

So, did I make today matter, as planned? Well, I did try my best. I've no car at the moment, so all I've got is what's on my doorstep. Though I didn't do anything that wasn't part of our routine, I certainly made the most of it and appreciated every second of the day with my dog.

<u>Thursday 29th April 2021.</u>

The sunshine this morning is coming and going like someone's messing about with the dimmer switch. (Do we still have those?)

We go to the field. We walk a long way round to shake things up. It's busy today, full of dogs, including some that haven't been since before the original lockdown, so is this a sign that people are treating the pandemic as though it's over? Brendan sits down and ignores all of them.

<u>Friday 30th April 2021.</u>

It's a beautiful sunny morning. I'm going to Make the Day Matter. Again. I take Brendan back to the river for a walk. He has a good run around and gets really tired. He has a lie down and a chew stick: he never needs much encouragement. I have a sit down and a coffee: I never need much encouragement. I also have a cake: I need even less encouragement.

We sit surrounded by blossom; the air smells like a perfume shop. We eat our chew and our cake and watch the world go by; we're very similar in that respect; we study people (and dogs) and think. Sometimes our thoughts are so deep that we might need an extra chew and an extra cake.

Two ladies pass by; they stop and smile at us. "You two

look very relaxed and happy."

I laugh. "Coffee and cake helps."

They heartily agree and do an about-turn, heading back towards the café.

After we've relaxed, we go for a walk through the wetland area, where raised wooden walkways lead through a kind of overgrown swamp-jungle, with rushes, reeds, mosses and a tangle of trees, with no space for any sky. It's like the everglades, but there are no alligators. Probably. Even in the dull light it's vibrantly green and full of life and birdsong. Then we walk across the grassland, which is like the Pampas, or somewhere else that's grassy. It's very hot now and we're both tired, so we lie down together. I can feel the black parts of Brendan's coat throwing off the heat. We stay there for some time, watching the waist-high grasses stirring in the breeze. It's quite wonderful. It really doesn't get any better than this.So yes, today we *did* make the day matter.

Saturday 1st May 2021.

The first day of May. Mayday! Mayday! It's a sunny morning, but I already know it's cold. The sun keeps coming out, so people are dressed for summer, though it keeps clouding over.

Breaking News: India daily Covid cases exceed 400,000.

As lockdown is clearly coming to an end, do I buy a van? I haven't thought at all about the future; I've been too busy trying to focus on the present. Being in lockdown has put everything on hold. It's been very much a day-to-day existence; a very limited existence. This has suited Brendan no end. He is trying to persuade me *not* to get a van, so that we never have to leave home again.

Despite what he'd have you believe, we've had so many lovely shared experiences on holiday, discovering new places together, seeing new sights, weeing on different trees, sitting on different fields – some of them even without goalposts – watching the sun setting over the sea instead of Manchester, then the joy of returning to our van for the evening, closing the curtains over the darkness and arguing about who should sleep on which side of the bed. Such happy times, so many memories.

Getting a van is quite a big job. I hate buying vehicles; it's a mine field. And buying a campervan has so many more pitfalls than a car. It would be so much easier not to bother or to live vicariously through clips of travel on Youtube. But I'm going to start looking for a van. I've decided. Sorry, Brendan.

* * * * * * * * * *

At Nicky's we get a Chinese for tea. I seem to say that quite a lot at the moment. That's because we're currently getting Chinese a lot, I suppose. I crack open a fortune cookie and read the motto. I roll my eyes. "How absolutely *ludicrous!*"

Nicky appears from the kitchen. "What does it say?"

"It says: You will soon be surrounded by good friends and laughter!"

She squeals in delight. "Yes. *Ludicrous!* That was such a Victor Meldrew moment." She laughs, thus fulfilling a prophecy.

Monday 3rd May 2021.

It's a dull, grey morning and rain is forecast for the whole day and most of tomorrow. Well, it is a bank holiday after all. I get repeatedly soaked taking Brendan out. He gets soaked as well and doesn't like it at all.

Breaking News: Scientists now say Deadly third wave may NEVER hit UK.

Tuesday 4th May 2021.

Again, it rains most of the day. I'm back in wellies for the field. The clouds are low and heavy and dark; the colour of slate; the colour of Remus. Not that we see Remus. We don't see any other dogs at all, but there are four pigeons pecking at the wet grass. For no apparent reason, they suddenly take off in unison; three fly off in one direction, the fourth in another.

Breaking News: England lockdown to be eased on 17th May after no Covid spike.

In less than a fortnight, things will be back to almost a state of complete normality. The old normality, that is. This will mean *all* businesses can open, along with inside seating at pubs, cafes, restaurants. Cinemas, theatres and stadiums can also open. Even social distancing rules will change, with people allowed to hug. It's this last one that concerns me, as I think people will automatically stop any form of social distancing and I think it's a good habit to keep.

Breaking News: Grim milestone. India passes 20 million Covid cases.

I take Brendan to the field again in the afternoon. For a few minutes it's raining and sunshining at the same time, but there are no rainbows.

Wednesday 5th May 2021.

It's a bright, sunny morning. After two days of wet weather, we want to get out in the sunshine and make the most of it. I take Brendan to the fields alongside the river. There is so much colour, so much blossom, so many flowers. It's beautiful, but a bit damp. It used to be a landfill site, but you'd never know.

Brendan seems to get tired quite quickly these days. I'm a bit worried about his joints and am going to get some joint-specific vitamins and improved-quality food. He's really tired when we get home and sleeps for several hours, while I start actually *looking* for a camper van instead of just *thinking* about it. It always seems like an insurmountable task. I don't have any success.

Breaking News: "Vaccine failures". UK report shows more than 500 people died of Covid *after* vaccination.

Nicky comes for tea. It's curry again. It just doesn't work very well and looks like brown slop. I think I've lost my curry magic and will have to broaden my culinary repertoire.

Nicky has been planning wreaths for her mum's birthday. She got very upset at one point about the prospect of lockdown ending and real life resuming, because without her mum it won't ever be normal again.

Breaking News:Four more Covid deaths. UK death toll stands at 127,543.

Thursday 6th May 2021.

On a concrete fence near to the field, someone has sprayed in huge pink letters the word FEAR, alongside smaller words in blue: FUCK TRUMP.

The morning is fine, but it rains on and off for the rest of the day. Every time I take Brendan out, we get soaked.

Friday 7th May 2021.

We set off to the field. Our smiling postman is coming up the drive. He says a cheery hello. Brendan walks past him without a word. This is such a contrast, as he used to issue a barrage of barks at the poor postie. He's always happy and always friendly. The postman, of course, not Brendan. Despite him being out in all weathers, the wind and the rain, pounding the pavement, verbally and physically abused by dogs and probably their owners, yet he always seems contented and upbeat. He's an inspiration. Again, the postman – and in no way Brendan.

Saturday 8th May 2021.

It was the local and mayoral elections yesterday. Most of the results are now in. Perhaps surprisingly, the Conservatives – the current government – have wiped the floor with all opposition. I thought they might do badly, as the party in power is always seen as the enemy, and voters always think a new broom will sweep clean... but it doesn't. I thought criticism for the Covid handling – and there has been plenty – might affect results. But people don't necessarily vote the same locally as they do in a general election. The main opposition, Labour, appear to have been trounced.

Breaking News: THE PEOPLE HAVE SPOKEN! Tories win by a landslide!

If this was a film, it would be a somewhat repetitive film. My brief for lockdown (one of them) was to try and make each day different, but I'm so tired, I'm ground down and just getting through the day is a big enough challenge.

9.05am. The rain is drumming against the window like a thousand cliches. There's a gale blowing outside and the branches are being thrown about. Brendan has looked towards the window and is now avoiding my gaze, in an attempt to dodge a walk, but it's not going to work indefinitely.

9.45am. We're heading to the field. It's still raining. The roads are flooded. We have to negotiate an alternative – and drier – route. I walk around the field while Brendan sits in the middle looking miserable. No one else comes. We head home, both soaked through.

Breaking News: Over a third of the people who catch the coronavirus don't display any symptoms, but are still passing the virus to others.

Monday 10th May 2021.

Breaking News: Face masks no longer required in England in classrooms from 17th May.

Today is a rare day out without Brendan; he stays with Nicky and I go to Chorlton, a suburban shopping area with the feel of a village. Apart from anything, I'm going to cruise the recently re-opened charity shops for old picture frames.

Strangely, there are still a lot of shuttered shops in Chorlton, I'm not sure why. Possibly they've gone bankrupt during lockdown. I buy several suitable frames, but the highlight of the trip is sitting outside a café and juice bar, my first such experience in a long time. (Apart from my outdoor coffees in the park, which I'm not counting, as I sit on a wall rather than in a designated seating area.) I'm the only customer. It's 11 o'clock and I have an Americano and a vegan chocolate bun. You go inside to order, wearing a mask, but have to sit outside. I had to sign in with my name and phone number, in case there is a Covid situation, you will be alerted and will have to self-isolate. I couldn't remember my phone number; I haven't given it to anyone for ages, so I had to look it up!

So, I sit outside. This is a momentous occasion, as I'm actually in a café. Well, outside one. It's mild today and the weather seems to have stabilised. It's really fun sipping my coffee, reading, but also being aware of snippets of conversation from people passing by, having a brief window into their lives. An elderly man sits at the bus stop opposite. He coughs repeatedly. He's not wearing a mask. Many buses come and go, and I realise he's not waiting for a bus, he's just sitting there. This is probably his day's activity.

Two young women arrive and sit at another table. They are typical Chorlton types, it's quite a Bohemian area and they seem quite radical and arty, but once they've finished checking their phones and start talking, their conversation seems to revolve around floor tiles, which is quite disappointing.

I'm enjoying this experience so much, I feel a little bit liberated, so I order a soup of the day, which is carrot, ginger and... something else. It's very nice and very home-made.

I've had a nice morning, but I've missed my boy. I pick him up at 2 o'clock. Nicky says he's been miserable, and wouldn't have any water and wouldn't eat his Bonio. He greets me at the door, then goes back to the settee and promptly eats his Bonio. We go for a walk, until it pours down, then we head home. Once inside he goes straight to bed; he's exhausted. He loves being at home.

Today has been a memorable day. It feels like I have taken a step back towards normality. I just hope I haven't contracted Covid along the way.

Breaking News: Boris Johnson expected to completely scrap social distancing rules.

Tuesday 11th May 2021.

Whilst looking online for the main news stories, I inadvertently stumbled across a couple of websites dedicated to "end times predictions". What a happy little read that was. It featured everything from war with Russia, war with China, war with Iran, natural disaster, civil unrest and much, much more. If watching the "real" news isn't depressing enough for you, you might want to tune into websites like this. One site came complete with a question; DO YOU KNOW IF YOU ARE GOING TO HEAVEN? BE SURE: CLICK HERE. I didn't click.

Breaking News: Concern as the faster-spreading Indian Covid variant becomes more prominent in UK.

Nicky came for tea. We had sausage and mash. It was nice. (I said it was nice, I didn't say it was exciting, challenging or took very much effort.)

I didn't sleep well. I had a dream about Dad. He was seriously ill. It was very realistic. I woke up sweating. It was still dark and I was exhausted, but I couldn't sleep again.

Wednesday 12th May 2021.

Another sunny start to the day. Today's highlights include Pets At Home and vegetable shopping. Remember, not long ago someone said I was "living the dream". And I think I definitely was, but clearly, I'm not anymore. But is anyone? Anyway, the dream is what you make it. And I think living your life as well as you can, at any given time, is the best you can possibly hope for.

Breaking News: Experts warn: Third coronavirus wave could hit UK in summer or autumn if easing of lockdown continues at current rate.

I've just noticed, this is exactly the same warning from 30th May 2020. And they were right then, there was of course another wave. This was followed by the contrasting:

Breaking News: UK could be back to normal by end of year.

And then the further contradictory:

Breaking news: Indian variant calls into question planned UK reopening on 17th May.

So, who knows? For every positive you read there is a negative. I don't consider myself to be a pessimist – or an optimist – I think I'm a realist and my opinions are formed rationally, based on the information available. It doesn't take a genius though, to realise that the Covid infection rate is climbing all the time, yet there is no talk of postponing or even curbing the ending of lockdown, so it isn't looking good.

Breaking News: Bolton, Greater Manchester, is Indian variant hotspot.

We drive to the river and walk across the fields and meadows. It's lush and fresh, the air smells of mown grass and blossom. Someone has set the birds to maximum volume; they appear to be competing with each other to see who can make the most noise.

We pass three workmen presumably from the Environment Agency, cleaning out a sluice in the river. I'm worried Brendan might react to them, due to their hi-viz uniforms and the fact that they're carrying things, and the fact that they aren't normally there, but he just gives them a cursory glance, then carries on with his meandering and sniffing. Again, his nonchalance astounds me; at one time this would have been a major incident with socio-economic repercussions.

The river looks beautiful, quite full, chocolate brown. There's a cool breeze and the sky is blue. We sit in the grassy meadow. A woman with three dogs walks close-by and Brendan goes over to introduce himself. I realise there's a little dog's head sticking out of the woman's rucksack. Apparently, this is her friend's dog and the little dog is blind, but she likes to have a run in the grassy areas when it's quiet and there are no obstacles. She's a beautiful little Jack Russell; she keeps closing her eyes and sniffing the air. She seems to be very contented.

Brendan tires of the dogs and wanders off to sit by himself and ignore everyone. The woman laughs and says she admires his attitude.

"I think we get the dog we deserve." I say, "And it constantly surprises me how similar we are."

She actively agrees. It turns out only one of the dogs is actually hers; a small, slightly scruffy and quite grumpy-looking little terrier. "She's exactly like me. She doesn't really like socialising... and I *love* being on my own. I used to have a really high-pressure job with Formula One, but I turned my back on it. I just thought I don't need this stress in my life. Now, although I have children and a partner, I get up really early, do my exercises, go for a run, then sit and read with a cup of coffee, so I've had a full day before the rest of the family get up. Or in the evenings I go for a run with the dog, run to a pub and then have a pint and sit there reading on my own. I just love my own company."

I nod enthusiastically. "You've just described me perfectly!" I say, quite incredulously. "Apart from the working out bit... and the running... and working for Formula One. And I don't have children... Or a husband... But I do like coffee."

She laughs. We say goodbye. She wanders off with her dogs and I cajole Brendan back to the car.

Thursday 13th May 2021.

Today is International Hummus Day, presumably aimed at raising awareness of the plight of hummus.

It is a middle eastern dip made predominantly from chickpeas, tahini, garlic and lemon juice. I have very occasionally made my own. Nicky's mum, Rosie, said my hummus was the best she'd ever tasted, but I prefer the creaminess and texture of shop-bought. You can have it with toasted pitta bread, on sandwiches or I like it as a filling for jacket potatoes, which will be my lunch today. It is very versatile. My own hummus tip is to stir it into homemade curry, which really gives body to the otherwise potentially watery sauce and it gives the curry a certain taste of authenticity, despite it not being an Indian ingredient. So, enjoy Hummus Day. Enjoy hummus.

Breaking News: Prime Minister announces full inquiry into government handling of Covid pandemic... in a year's time.

The Prime Minister has now warned what everybody already knows, namely that there could be another Coronavirus surge in the winter. There is growing concern that the situation with the increasing spread of the highly transmissible Indian variant of the coronavirus could cause delays for the planned final easing of lockdown, currently scheduled for 21st June. UK cases of the Indian variant are believed to have tripled in a week. The Prime Minister issued an "extraordinary warning" that there might be "greater suffering" next winter due to the new variants. Perhaps for his next trick he might discover gravity.

Breaking News: Israel descending into "senseless civil war" amid street violence

between Jews and Arabs, as rockets strike towns and cities.

I take Brendan to the park. We can hear, but not see, the regular personal trainer, who's at work behind a hedge. He seems to be giving his instructions to his victim in rap: "You need to learn, twist and turn, go for the burn: *go for the burn!*"

We don't do any of those things, but we do walk away. Quite quickly.

Breaking News: Prime Minister refuses to rule out local lockdowns.

In the afternoon, Brendan wants to go to the field to show off his new attire, as he's sporting his new harness, which makes him look like a member of a crack military unit. It's gone to his head and he's so far cautioned three whippets and frisked a Labradoodle.

Sadly, there are no dogs at the field and no people. No one is sitting smoking a joint or sending a stinking blue haze up from a disposable barbeque, despite it being a nice evening... and not the constant rain that was forecast. Brendan sits for a very long time, following the letter of the law, looking cool and slightly stern and officious. Then we go home, having made no arrests.

Dog Fact: Police dogs are now called PD, followed by their name. Imagine PD Brendan, PD Remus, PD Bruno, PD Dougie, PD Daisy, PD Evie and PD Annie.

Breaking News: Prime Minister assures public:

"At the moment" the easing of restrictions "will go ahead on Monday".

Friday 14th May 2021.

It was a dull, grey morning. There was no early sun today. We went to the field in the morning and then again in the afternoon. Brendan was a bit sluggish on the walk. He did bark at a plane, but even that was very half-hearted. I made a point of smiling at the people I encountered en route. A middle-aged man scowled back; an older woman did smile, but nervously; a young gardener actually *did* return the smile in a fairly genuine manner. As an experiment it was inconclusive. (Requires extra study.) But all the smiling made me feel good.

Breaking News: Indian variant more transmissible and set to become dominant UK strain.

I saw a comment on Youtube: IN THE 1980S PEOPLE THOUGHT: "THE FUTURE'S GOING TO BE GREAT!" IN THE 2020S PEOPLE THINK: "LET'S GO BACK TO THE 80S!" I'm not saying I agree, as the threat of nuclear annihilation was ever-present in the 'Eighties, but hey, we've got it back again now! And I don't know if we should ever go back to 'Eighties fashions; they are a thing of the past and are safer left there. The past is a foreign country; they had different hair.

Breaking News: The Indian variant continues to cause concern.

Nicky's Covid app shows there are 348 active cases in this area, which is an increase of 142 from last week, which means it has virtually *doubled*. Perhaps Boris Johnson has got wind of this because:

Breaking News: PM does U-turn. End of lockdown in jeopardy due to Indian variant surge, creating "the risk of disruption and delay".

Saturday 15th May 2021.

Breaking News: Coronavirus vaccines "almost certainly less effective" at reducing Indian variant transmissions.

I have nightmares. Again. I wake up early, lie awake and finally get up and make a brew. It's 6.22am and it's raining.

I take Brendan to the common. I again spot two magpies. I'm not at all superstitious, not even slightly, but in these dark times you have to seize the joy when you find it. There are also two ducks at the pond, but unfortunately you don't get any points for ducks; they don't come with their own allocation of good will or bad fortune.

The pond is awash with alliteration today: mallards, moorhens and magpies. I also spot two coots building a nest very noisily in the bullrushes. Brendan watches with interest but doesn't bark. And then it starts to rain again.

Breaking News: Step 3 of reducing lockdown will go ahead on Monday, but Step 4 on 21st June may be in jeopardy due to Indian variant.

Driving back from Nicky's at 10.10pm, it's like a normal day from the past, before Covid was unleashed on the world. The pavements are busy and groups of people are heading home from the pubs. There are a lot of cars about and there's a lot of noise. Obviously, there's no sign whatsoever of any social distancing.

Breaking News: Four in UK have so far died of Indian variant.

UK cases of the Indian variant have leapt from 520 to 1,313 since last week. There is pressure on the government to ensure that the final stages of the easing of lockdown should go ahead. Various surveys are showing increasing numbers of people are concerned about the lowering of restrictions and are reluctant to travel abroad for holidays.

Sunday 16th May 2021.

Breaking News: Eric Clapton hits out at "propaganda" over vaccine safety after AZ jab caused "disastrous reactions" lasting weeks.

More Breaking News.... Old John next door hasn't shaved for four days and is growing a beard. I only know this because he was obviously on the phone again and shouting at the top of his voice as he imparted this information to someone. I then heard. "I'm going to

Tesco now... Are you at home? Right... And where's your wife? Is she out?" Pause. "She *is* out? She's not in? Are you sure? Good. In that case I'll call round." Then it went quiet, until I heard his door slam.

Breaking News: Global death toll stands at well over 3,300,000.

Monday 17th May 2021.

Breaking News: UK OPEN FOR BUSINESS! Finally, indoor hospitality – pubs, restaurants – can open, as can cinemas, theatres, concert venues, indoor sports halls, hotels.

It felt like just a Monday, another Monday, but it turns out it's *the* Monday. The Monday when Britain opens its doors to virtually everything... including the coronavirus.

Breaking News: Significant rise in Indian variant across UK: Over 2,300 cases reported.

Tuesday 18th May 2021.

It's a nice sunny morning, as promised, so we head out to Alderley edge again. When we arrive, it's quite cool and breezy, but it's very beautiful and green and lush. We go to the café, which has outside seating only. Brendan has a Bonio, I have coffee and cake. There are amazing views across Cheshire to the distant hills. I'm lucky to be here with my dog and I really don't need anything else.

Breaking News: When will social distancing end?

What social distancing? There literally isn't any! People stopped bothering a long time ago. And that's why the virus is still running rampant.

Thursday 20th May 2021.

We go for a walk to the river. There is no break in the clouds, which are solid watercolour grey. There's no blue sky, there's no sun. It's breezy and cool and it's promising rain. En route, we pass close to Dad's flat. Brendan always pulls to go and see his granddad, which is odd, because they rarely saw eye to eye. I miss my dad. We were very dissimilar in many ways, but we both loved the countryside and I certainly inherited his back and sinus problems. It would be nice if I could skip his cholesterol, prostate cancer, Alzheimer's and heart disease though.

The little pub, The Crown is now open. There are people standing drinking inside. As we walk past the side door, Brendan pulls to go in. I do a double-take, because there is a man in a green coat and a flat cap, wearing glasses and clutching a wooden walking stick. It's the spitting image of my dad. I stop and stare for a moment. The similarity doesn't fade as I stare, but I just assume it's a man who happens to look remarkably like Dad, but it isn't actually Dad, because Dad has died. Dad used to go in this pub, though he did complain bitterly about the price of the beer.

We finish our walk and go to Nicky's for tea. We have Indian snacks and salad whilst watching *Jeff Wayne's War of the Worlds Live*. The invading Martians are killed by the common cold, so they wouldn't stand a chance against Covid.

Breaking News: Five more deaths, bringing UK Covid death toll to 127,721.

Friday 21st May 2021.

I wake up at 3.48am and Brendan is trembling beside me. I don't know if he's heard thunder or perhaps a firework, but something has frightened him. I cuddle him and chat to him and we have the light on after that. As usual, once reassured, Brendan goes straight back to sleep, but I don't. I get up and open the curtains to a wet and blustery day. Rain is forecast for all day.

11am. Quite unexpectedly, the Coroner's office phones. They've had the results from my dad's post-mortem and subsequent laboratory analysis of tissue samples. It has revealed that Dad died primarily of heart failure, but he also had sepsis. I'm not sure what I expected the cause of death to be; heart failure was certainly on the cards, but it was very sad to actually hear it. Dad was in hospital and no one was with him when he died. We don't know how long he had been sitting there before any staff noticed. His sons and his partner hadn't seen him *for months* and he died alone. And really, coronavirus lockdown or not, that's unacceptable.

12.05 pm. It's raining lightly and it's dull and grey. Brendan was sitting with me, but has taken himself off to bed. I'm just looking out of the window and feeling disturbed and unsettled. I have been very stressed recently. By which I mean for months. I wonder whether knowing Dad's cause of death will actually – in time – be part of the healing process. I hope so, but I don't really believe that.

Saturday 22nd May 2021.

Nicky has taken her aunt to see her uncle in hospital, where he's had a heart by-pass. This means, rather than our usual Saturday together, I'll be staying at home with Brendan. Brendan is delighted: it's his idea of an ideal Saturday.

Breaking News: Covid infection rate highest since January.

In the evening we walk to the Big Park via the shops. It's really busy and there's a holiday or weekend feeling. The takeaways, bars, pubs and restaurants are all heaving and the pavements are full of hurrying pedestrians. We are normally at Nicky's at this time on a Saturday, so we don't usually see this. But also, this is the first Saturday since the "big opening".

By contrast, when we get to the park it's completely empty. This is opposite to how it was during full lockdown, when this park was the hub of the community with people sitting out, bringing deckchairs, having picnics and there was a drinks caravan. Now, despite it being a sunny evening, it's deserted.

Breaking News: UK has suffered one of the

worst death rates in the world; government blamed due to "dithering" over lockdown measures.

In the shower at night, I always think about places I've been to, that I'd like to revisit, one of which would be the Outer Hebrides, but that would involve a long ferry crossing and Brendan would be terrified. It wouldn't happen, and if my dog doesn't go, I don't go. We're a team and being together is more important. Instead, we need to visit somewhere on Brendan's approved list of travel destinations, which includes The Field and... actually, that's it... Just The Field.

Sunday 23rd May 2021.

Breaking News: WW3 warning. China feels it can "do what it wants" and is set to spark nuclear war.

They say that when tests were carried out for the hydrogen bomb, there was real concern that the reaction would ignite the Earth's atmosphere and the whole planet would be consumed in flames, ending all life here forever. But they still pressed the button anyway. I wouldn't put anything past the human animal.

Our current potential fireball, in the mooted war with Russia and China, is receiving very little mainstream media attention. All the stories are about the coronavirus, new variants and the further easing of lockdown. It seems that as long as the average Britain can be vaporised with a pint in their hand and not wearing a mask, then they'll die happy.

I feel quite depressed about the worsening situation. The lesson is: enjoy the moment... it might be your last.

Breaking News: Defence Secretary: "RUSSIA IS OUR NUMBER ONE THREAT." Russian submarines circling British coast.

Last night I had a series of nightmares, about being in tight spaces and feeling very claustrophobic. I've no idea where this came from.

On the common, Brendan is dragging his paws and sighing a lot. We meet a mother and son walking their dog. We often bump into them. The son is an adult with Downs Syndrome. I say "Hello, how are you doing?"

The woman frowns. "Getting a bit fed up of everything to be honest."

The son says defiantly: "*I'm* not fed up! I'm not getting fed up! I'm staying positive!" It really touches me.

Breaking News: There are 908 Covid patients in hospital, 123 on ventilators.

We arrive at Nicky's. Brendan leaps onto the settee and settles down for a long rest. We watch the film of *War of the Worlds*, the Tom Cruise version. Nicky likes Tom Cruise. Miraculously, she manages to stay awake throughout the film. We order a Chinese. Yes, again.

Breaking News: Despite an increase in Covid

cases, hospitalisation figures remain similar to last week. Positive spin: there hasn't been an increase in deaths. Negative spin: despite the vaccine an awful lot of people are getting infected and are seriously ill.

The government has been criticised for trying to sneak a serious news story out late on Saturday night, where it might go unnoticed. After releasing a positive story about the vaccine, they quietly revealed that troubling new data on the Indian variant had been assessed as a condition red and that the vaccines were considerably less effective against it: 20% less effective.

Breaking News: Covid vaccine effectiveness against the Indian variant: one jab 33% effective; two jabs only 51% effective.

Meanwhile, on a lighter note:

Breaking News: Italy wins Eurovision. UK gets nil points.

Monday 24th May 2021.

It's a nice sunny morning and there's not much news, but the general gist is that things are looking up whilst simultaneously looking very bleak. The death rate is down, yet the country is being ravaged by the Indian variant. The vaccine might possibly be very effective against the new strains, whilst also being not very effective at all.

I am sick of the contradictory news reports. I think that's how it's supposed to be. The government are coming under heavy fire for their handling of the Covid crisis in general and in particular the Indian border closure. And as for the situation in India, it is no longer news. In the UK we're only concerned with the easing of lockdown. Today, so far, there is no mention of World War III that was being threatened yesterday.

There is no *new* news today, just a re-hashing of all the previous news. There is no definitive and factual story, because everything you hear or read is laced with perspectives and opinions. It's impossible to say what's happening with any degree of accuracy. Perhaps that's intentional.

* * * * * * * * * *

A new couple appears at the field. They're not new to the area, but they're new to the field, and their dog is new to them. She's from a rescue centre. "They said to us 'What type of dog are you looking for?' And I said 'Really, we just want a dog who won't hate us!'" I really laughed.

I introduce The Boy. "This is Brendan: he came with his name."

The little dog, Blossom, looks like a very small Alsatian. Sort of. She's gentle and quite shy and blinks constantly. She's beautiful. Brendan graciously welcomes her to his field, assuring her that she's permitted to come at any time, even when he's not on duty, though advanced booking is preferred.

Breaking News: 39 year old British woman dies in "blood clotting incident", days after AstraZeneca jab.

<u>Tuesday 25th May 2021.</u>

It's bin day again. Is it sad that bin day marks the week to the degree that it clearly does?

Today, I need to go to hospital – as an out-patient – for a chest X-Ray, to check my heart is in good working order. It's raining and very grey. It strikes me out of the blue while I'm making the bed, I'm focused on the task in hand and right at this moment I'm actually quite happy. I also realise that this might be the happiest I am today because of the hospital, depending on what the X-Ray reveals.

10.15am. I've dropped Brendan at Nicky's and am driving to the hospital through the town I've always lived in. I never intended to stay here, but I've never left. All the cars have their headlights on and the surrounding distant hills are all lost in the low clouds and mist. I pass the crematorium and the cemetery. I pass Nicky's school, the grammar, and then my own school, the comprehensive. I pass the bus stop where I first saw Nicky; we were both in our school uniforms. This journey seems laden with history, with meaning. It suddenly feels like I'm passing all the significant places from my life, if feels like it's a final journey and this is a sort of farewell.

I pull up at traffic lights. A lorry in front has a tail flap with LIVING THE DREAM emblazoned across it. I smile, then stop smiling, thinking it must be a message.

I turn off the main road, into the hospital. The hospital where Dad died. The hospital where my mum spent the last weeks of her life before being moved to a hospice for her final 24 hours. My brother was born here. (I wasn't. I was born in the centre of Manchester. I'm a proper Mancunian by birth.)

I park and check my phone. It's dead and won't switch on. Everything seems like an omen or portent. I walk into the hospital beneath grey skies, and I don't expect to come out again.

* * * * * * * * * *

I sit in a windowless waiting room. There are Perspex screens separating all the chairs and everything is laid out on a socially distanced basis. Sitting there, looking around at the half dozen other out-patients, I'm very aware that of all the people who pass through this X-Ray department today, some will have good news, but some will have terrible, terminal results.

My name is called and I'm led along a strip-lit corridor into a darkened room, humming with electronic equipment. The procedure is very quick and efficient. The staff are all friendly and helpful. I won't get the results for a week but I'm going to forget about this and not allow it to hang over me. I leave the hospital and step back out into the damp air, beneath the grey skies.

Wednesday 26th May 2021.

It's Nicky's Mum's birthday today, so it won't be an easy day for her. She's going to Rosie's grave with her father and taking a huge wreath of pink roses.

There is a low blanket of grey cloud smothering everything as we walk to the field. Brendan is scampering perkily ahead, with no sign of the stiffness he's been suffering from for several days. Perhaps his new food, oil and medication is taking effect.

A little pug-faced dog stops on the pavement to say hello to him. She stands staring at him adoringly. Unfortunately, Brendan has his dismissive "Yeah, whatever, love" attitude and walks off.

Breaking News: Covid chaos at number 10 is like an "out of control movie".

Today, the news is dominated by former adviser to the prime minister, Dominic Cummings, giving evidence to an enquiry about the government's alleged mis-handling of the Covid crisis. The upshot is, Boris Johnson failed to grasp the seriousness of the situation in time and Health Secretary, Matt Hancock, should have been fired on 15-20 different occasions.

Breaking News: People suffer stroke after AstraZeneca jab. Doctors told to be vigilant.

Thursday 27th May 2021.

Outside it's grey and miserable. We head to the river for our walk. I'm wearing wellies, long trousers, fleece and waterproof jacket. The sun comes out and it goes warm, very warm. I'm the only person not wearing shorts and T-shirt. I feel like an incongruous idiot and am way too hot. Brendan is embarrassed and refuses to walk with me.

Today, Nicky has gone on an adventure on the bus, to the semi-rural area where she spent part of her childhood. I wasn't allowed to accompany her; she wanted it to be a solo pilgrimage. It will be a day of memories and certainly quite emotional for her. Our day is punctuated by frequent texts from her, letting me know where she is and how she's doing. It sounds like she's covering a lot of ground and is enjoying it, though it's tinged with obvious sadness.

Friday 28th May 2021.

Breaking News: More side-effects of AstraZeneca vaccine: reports of life-threatening capillary leak syndrome.

Yesterday's fine weather seems to have gone. It's dull and grey and the forecast is for rain, yet it feels like a holiday. Nicky is off today and is coming over this afternoon and we're having afternoon tea. Proper afternoon tea; she's bringing her cake stand!

We walk to the field. Despite the grey clouds, it's very hot and humid and I get soaked with sweat. Brendan barks at a plane, then lies down with his paws crossed and has a much-needed rest. After a suitable amount of relaxing, we head back home, where there is repeated machine gun fire from the Polish bloke's flat directly below. It's presumably a game. Hopefully. I can reveal that "Argh, bollocks!" is the same in Polish.

Nicky arrives – along with her cake stand – and we have our afternoon tea, sitting at my table in the window: finger sandwiches, mainly cucumber, with a variety of little cakes. It's really nice and makes the day quite memorable. We should do this more often. Preferably daily.

Breaking News: "Two more months of lockdown needed" say experts. UK not ready for easing of restrictions on 21st June.

<u>Saturday 29th May 2021.</u>

I have the usual disagreement with Brendan; he wants to go to the field, I want to go somewhere else. I win. We drive to the river and go for a walk in the meadows and to the ornamental gardens, where we meet a big, friendly man with three dogs of varying sizes and models. The man laughs constantly. He's carrying a folding deckchair over his shoulder. As we're chatting, he slumps down into it with a sigh. "I've been out for an hour and a half. Every day, I bring them here for an hour and a half. Every single day." Something tells me, in that hour and a half they probably cover an average distance of fifteen yards. Brendan considers jumping ship, because that sounds like his sort of walk.

"Ah, he's an old boy. How old is he?"

"He's only eight. He's not exactly old. He's just bone idle. And he's in a mood. And he prefers sitting down to walking."

The man laughs riotously. "So do I!" He stops laughing abruptly. "I *hate* walking."

"Oh, I love it."

"No, I hate it." I'm not actually sure whether the big man or Brendan said that, but they are unanimous.

One of the dogs, a little female Jack Russell is sniffing around Brendan. The man claps his hands. "Come away, come away, you stupid bitch! He's an old dog; he's not interested in you!" He manages to offend virtually everyone.

We make our excuses and move on to the outdoor café. I have a coffee and a cake and Brendan has a handful of complimentary gravy bones. There are silver dog bowls of water dotted about. I try to encourage him to have a drink. He looks at me aghast, a look that says "Do you know how many dogs have drunk out of that? It's *disgusting!*" He goes home thirsty.

Breaking News: Boris Johnson's public popularity nosedives after Dominic Cummings revelations.

Former advisor to the Prime Minister, Dominic Cummings – himself disgraced and ridiculed after he broke lockdown rules – has said that Boris Johnson is "unfit to lead the country", was neglectful and very unfeeling, reluctant to react against the approaching pandemic in the early days, allegedly declaring "only the over 80s are dying" and then "let the bodies pile up!" It is claimed that Johnson was prepared to let enough people catch the virus, so that herd immunity would come about naturally.

Health Secretary, Matt Hancock, is accused by Cummings of "repeated lying". Polls show the public have "little or no trust" in Hancock and that he should resign. Dominic Cummings, however, isn't the hero of the hour, as he is generally seen as an unreliable witness and 80% of the people surveyed do not trust him to tell the truth.

Breaking News: Man. City 0, Chelsea 1.

As it's National Biscuit Day, it seems only right to dunk plain chocolate digestives in my tea. So I do.

Sunday 30th May 2021.

Breaking News: PRIME MINISTER'S SECRET WEDDING. Boris Johnson got married yesterday in a secret ceremony. It is said it was to blot out the negativity surrounding his popularity slump.

As you'll know, it's World Otter Day, so... happy ottering!

It's a warm and sunny morning. It's actually a beautiful day and we set off to the field. This is, I think, the first day of the year I am wearing short sleeves, without the emergency back-up of a jacket.

Brendan goes straight to the hill and sits down whilst I do a circuit of the field, which is a mass of yellow and white; the buttercups and daisies are really shooting up in the sunshine.

Neil and Annie from next door arrive and we all sit on the hill. Annie gazes at Brendan, but it was just a garden flirtation for him and he's moved on. Neil chats about his medication and his lupus. I'm not sure exactly what that is, but I think it means he's a lycanthrope.

Breaking News: British spies "believe Wuhan lab leak theory is feasible".

This is a surprise U-turn. We were told the Covid leak couldn't possibly have come from the Wuhan Institute of Virology, but now it is being vaunted as a likely contender. UK and US intelligence is investigating the theory, after President Biden ordered an inquiry into the origin of the pandemic.

Monday 31st May 2021.

Breaking News: Other countries restricting UK travel, as we are considered a Covid risk.

Another sunny morning, blue skies, gentle breeze. We're now heading into the English summer. There's nothing like being in lockdown and sitting watching the seasons come and go. And of course, as I keep saying, this is nothing like lockdown. Every day the news is full of contradictory stories about the will-they/won't-they remove the last vestiges of social distancing on 21st June? It's all the press are talking about. Yet no one I speak to ever mentions it. Is wearing a mask in a supermarket such a big problem? Is keeping your distance from a stranger an intolerable issue? Is washing your hands regularly an unbearable hinderance?

Rattling endlessly on about the 21st June is clearly considered to be a good news story. It isn't even news, because it's the same old rehashed nonsense and supposition. I know I'm like a dog with a denti-stick, but the vaccines are seemingly not very effective against the Indian and other new variants, so logic dictates that only the social distancing measures will save us. It's that simple. Yet bizarrely there is so much resistance to all forms of social distancing.

Breaking News: Covid infection rate increasing, despite three-quarters of the population now vaccinated – more than enough for herd immunity.

In the light of the Dominic Cummings revelations, and they weren't really revelations, they amounted to assertions that the government reacted too slowly, public opinion has fallen away from Boris Johnson and his government. It looks like history will record that they acted sloppily and slowly as the coronavirus raged in other countries. There was a warning, as we saw how it was ravaging other parts of the world, but the government failed to act in time. And they're still failing to act or react.

Breaking News: Sunshine and Bank Holiday: Britons flocked to beaches and beer gardens. As far as Covid goes... expect the worst.

Today we drove into the countryside at the edge of

town, where Nicky spent part of her childhood. We went for a walk over green, rolling hills and had a picnic. It was warm and sunny, but there was a cooling breeze. Brendan loved it, because it involved a lot of sitting down. It was actually a fairly perfect day. In the evening we got a Chinese takeaway. Naturally.

Breaking News: Ex-US health official says lab leaks occur "all the time", even in the US. He alleges that the last six SARS-1 outbreaks originated in laboratories in China.

Tuesday 1st June 2021

Breaking News: Covid variants renamed to remove stigma. The Kent variant is now Alpha, South African variant is Beta, Brazilian variant is Gamma, the Indian variant is now Delta.

Catchy new names for the same old variants. These new Greek alphabet monikers are so much more "sci-fi" than the dull old geographical ones that made sense. "The Delta Variant" is a readymade sci-fi film title. "The Kent Variant" is so much less Hollywood.

Breaking News: Tensions rise between Russia and America. "Like new Cold War".

It turns into a sunny and warm morning, but it isn't unbearable, however, we're keeping our walks to a minimum and sitting down in the shade more. This is, of course, what Brendan prefers anyway. We sit at the field under the canopy of an ash tree. Neil and Annie from next door join us. Annie's quite aloof now that Brendan's broken her heart. Neil tells me about various local burglaries and the increasing number of car thefts recently. There have apparently been a couple of carjackings, in the immediate area: thieves have stopped vehicles with people in, forced the drivers out and driven off. And they aren't only going for expensive cars, they are stealing old wrecks as well - to use in robberies - so no one's safe. He says the thieves are putting false number plates on the stolen cars, so police cameras are not reacting to them, then they drive round in them technically invisible. I'm not sure where he gets all his information from, but Neil's very well-informed.

Breaking News: No Covid deaths reported in UK, which shows that the pandemic is coming to an end!

Does it? I really don't think so. This seems very unlikely when the infection rate has been climbing over the past few weeks. This is being celebrated as the first time this has happened since the pandemic began 15 months ago. It's big, exciting news! It's headline material! No one seems to remember that it also happened on 30th July 2020. And then it got worse again.

<u>Wednesday 2nd June 2021.</u>

Today it's very hot, *incredibly* hot. We've come to the river; we're avoiding any concrete paths, only walking on grass and sitting in the shade. We pass a field full of horses grazing methodically. One strains his neck far over the barbed wire fence to get some interesting grass which is just out of his reach, like we all do in life. Brendan gives him a warning bark. The horse blinks at him and chews apathetically.

We stroll along, Brendan sniffs and wees and sniffs again. Willows weep at the water's edge. There is a hum of insects and the sub-tropical heat. There are clear blue skies and sunlight glinting on the river. We're enjoying being here, dawdling along. We're in no hurry, after all, there are no deadlines and there's nowhere to go.

Breaking News: Expert claims UK has hit a "dangerous moment" in Covid pandemic and warns that "vaccine beating variants" will emerge.

I get a call from my GP. The results from my chest X-ray are back. I really haven't thought about it much over the past week and I've just got on with life – as far as is possible. The results were favourable, though the doctor tells me my cholesterol – after being perfect for many years – is heading towards the high end of the scale and I should be aware of this. The result about the scan is great news; the cholesterol less so.

Breaking News: Covid cases expected to dramatically increase, as infection rate rises due to Delta/Indian variant.

At lunchtime, Nicky cycles to nearby Didsbury Park to meet us and we sit on the grass and chat. She isn't having a good day, but it's very nice to see her. Brendan celebrates by having a nap.

Breaking News: 12 Covid deaths were reported today by UK, after a day of zero fatalities yesterday.

Thursday 3rd June 2021.

Breaking News: FINAL UNLOCKING. The Prime Minister can "see nothing in the data at the moment that means we can't go ahead with Step Four".

Twenty cases of a newly discovered, so-called "Nepal variant" have been detected in the UK. But the Prime Minister can "see nothing in the data at the moment that means we can't go ahead with Step Four".

More countries have been added to the red "forbidden" travel list, including Portugal, due to Covid outbreaks. But the Prime Minister can "see nothing in the data at the moment that means we can't go ahead with Step Four".

A survey has revealed that more than half of the British people would prefer a delay to the planned Step Four unlocking, scheduled for 21st June. But the Prime Minister can "see nothing in the data at the moment that means we can't go ahead with Step Four".

Tracking shows that Covid-19 is advancing in all but three parts of the country, but still the Prime Minister can "see nothing in the data at the moment that means we can't go ahead with Step Four".

The government have announced over 5,000 new Covid cases in the last 24 hours. But the Prime Minister can "see nothing in the data at the moment that means we can't go ahead with Step Four".

In the week ending 26th May, Covid cases had risen by 22%, and yet *still* the Prime Minister can "see nothing in the data at the moment that means we can't go ahead with Step Four".

In other news, the heatwave is forecast to continue for the next fortnight. And yet the Prime Minister can "see nothing in the data at the moment that means we can't go ahead with Step Four". (Sorry. Force of habit.)

Friday 4th June 2021.

Breaking News: Step Four unlocking may be delayed by two weeks after 21st June as government draw up new plans.

Apparently, the Prime Minister *can* now see something "in the data at the moment that means we can't go ahead with Step Four" of easing lockdown.

Breaking News: New study reveals that people receiving Pfizer jab have lower antibodies targeting Indian variant.

I had nightmares throughout the night. Repeated nightmares. About zombies. I was being chased by the undead. I don't know why... but if I know zombies like I think I do, then it would be because they wanted to eat my brain. The dream also had something to do with dog food. Brendan wasn't there visually, but he was important to the dream somehow and he was present, but off-screen, as it were. It was disturbing and each time I went back to sleep, the nightmare carried on where it had left off, so it was like a film in instalments. And not a very good film, to be honest. I woke up trying to work out what it meant and I woke up tired, but I woke up to a beautiful sunny day, still and golden, even at 7am.

* * * * * * * * * *

We walked to the Big Field. It went very hot, so hot that it sapped Brendan's energy. Not that he's very energetic most of the time. There was very little shade. I expected the field to be packed on such a nice day, but it was very quiet. There were three dog walkers and one family with children. Presumably everyone else was in the shopping centres, as they're open as normal at the moment.

Nicky came in the evening. She is finding things very difficult at the moment and really missing her mum. She got a call; Pam, one of her mum's closest friends, had just been rushed into hospital with suspected coronavirus. This has further upset Nicky.

* * * * * * * * * *

The news features photos of people on beaches in the sunshine, packed together like sardines.

Today's headlines:

Breaking News: Infection rate increasing, but it's still safe to continue unlocking.

Breaking News: Infection rate increasing, but it's not safe to unlock.

Breaking News: Yes, it is.

Breaking News: No, it isn't.

You get my drift.

Saturday 5th June 2021.

We met Neil and Annie at the field. Brendan walked slowly up to Annie and kissed her on the nose for old time's sake, then wafted off and sat down some distance away. Their relationship is very complex; it is damaged, but poetic.

We talked about the new variants and tried to remember all the letters of the Greek alphabet, more of which will presumably be employed as additional variants come to light. We didn't get very far. Alpha, Beta, Gamma, Delta, Epsilon and Omega. And I feel there's a Theta and Omicron. Lambda? Sigma! (I should have got that straight away, it's the name of one of my publishers!) Well, that was today's excitement.

Sunday 6th June 2021.

Breaking News: UK Covid infections continue to increase. Total fatalities now stand at

127,840.

It's cooler today. I'm quite cold in my short sleeves. The field is busy with dogs. Brendan jogs right up to them, because he likes to ignore them close-up. Remus has returned from his holidays in Wales. He says he's glad to be back. The boys have a reunion wrestle and then a reunion sit down together.

There is organ music and singing coming from the nearby church. It's nice, it sounds like it's from a bygone age, not just pre-corona, but rustic and pastoral. Presumably, singing is allowed again; it had been banned as a spreader of the virus.

They say romance is dead, but somebody has spray painted a new black heart near the field.

Breaking News: Poll reveals that the government is losing public confidence after the Dominic Cummings revelations.

I do a lot of my most profound thinking in the shower. Tonight, whilst soaked and soapy, I decided I really should try and build up my interactions with the outside world. I'm well aware that if I didn't have Brendan with his demanding routine, I would see virtually no one.

Monday 7th June 2021.

Breaking News: Scientists call for lockdown exit delay as Third Covid wave appears.

It's a sunny morning and the start of another week.

The car is having its MOT today. We've had it a year. Its longest journey has been a few miles. It's not really been out of our postcode.

Because I shopped locally and it was the day after a bank holiday, there was virtually no food.

I stayed in, worked, did the washing, walked the dog.

Breaking News: Two U.S. experts reveal that genome sequencing of Covid "seemingly proves it was made in a lab".

China this week refused to participate in any further investigations into the origins of the pandemic. Apparently, the Chinese government have already admitted that the wet market theory was wrong and possibly a cover-up. Less people are sniggering about the lab escape theory; more scientists and experts are coming out and saying they had postulated it was a lab escape all along.

Breaking News: New evidence reveals that three workers at the Wuhan Institute of Virology fell ill with "Covid-like symptoms" in November 2019. The odds on a lab leak are mounting.

Tuesday 8th June 2021.

Breaking News: Covid rates up in more UK areas than at any point since January.

Well, it's Best Friend Day again. Unbelievably, a year has gone by since the last one. Equally unbelievable, is that my two best friends haven't changed since then, which is pretty good going during lockdown. I asked Brendan who his best dog friend was. He's very diplomatic and declined an answer. It doesn't matter, I know it's Remus. They share a calm friendship that very few people get to experience.

Breaking News: 90% jump in Covid cases since last week.

Today was virtually a carbon copy of yesterday, until the evening, when Nicky came for tea. She was quite upset, because it is exactly six months since her mum, Rosie, died. As usual with time, it seems incredible that it's that long, and equally incredible that it's not longer. It's been a traumatic six months.

Wednesday 9th June 2021.

Breaking News: 8 out of 10 UK adults have Covid antibodies, but it isn't halting the virus.

There are sirens at 9am. I hear a lot of sirens now. These sirens seem to stop somewhere very close by, but I see no sign of them.

The sun's shining, but it's not overly hot. The birds are singing, there is a gentle breeze stirring the trees, and the air smells dry, like summer. On the common, the trees create a mottled canopy high above. It's like a green cathedral; the ground is speckled with sunlight, like the light coming through a stained-glass window.

It's beautiful, quite breath-taking and has the same cool, calm reverence as, say, York Minster, but without the obligatory giftshop selling over-priced bookmarks and pens.

There is no traffic sound, no aircraft tearing open the sky, no chatter of people, just birdsong and the stirring of the branches above. The tranquillity is suddenly broken by a familiar sound:

"Oreo! Oreo! *Oreo!*" It's the voice of the professional dog walker, heard but not seen through the foliage.

We carry on walking. It's a lazy summer's day. Everything seems to be moving in slow motion. It's idyllic. Yet I'm completely aware that this could all be swept away by the press of a button, as tensions between the superpowers increase. All you can do is appreciate the moment and live the day.

Breaking News: Expert warns: Vaccines will not be enough to beat Covid and humans must adapt and alter their lifestyles.

So says Doctor David Nabarro from the World Health Organisation. He recommends that people continue to wear face masks and behave responsibly. "The future of humanity is going to require that we adapt our lifestyles so that we make it hard for this virus to spread."

Thursday 10th June 2021.

We're on the Big Field. There is no sun at all, just an

unbroken blanket of low grey cloud. A group of boys are playing football. Brendan is getting exhausted just watching them and I know as a result he'll sleep well tonight. I also know, by the law of averages, that I won't.

We continue to Nicky's, where I leave Brendan. I go into Didsbury for a coffee. I get an Americano in Costa and sit upstairs. It's quiet and the tables are suitably spaced. If I had my dog at my feet this would be another of my ideal moments. Brendan loves coming in cafes. He doesn't beg for treats or anything, he just lies down quietly and relaxes and watches the coming and going – and I suspect he eavesdrops a bit. We are both very much observers of life; I think we're both always looking for something, but we're never sure quite what. In all likelihood, we've probably already found it.

Breaking News: Face masks and social distancing should continue "forever" according to Professor Susan Michie, a senior government scientific adviser. When asked if this was realistic she replied: "There's lots of behaviours we've changed in our lives. We now routinely wear seatbelts, we didn't used to."

Friday 11th June 2021.

Breaking News: "We're going in the wrong direction!" Covid cases rising in all parts of England, with the sharpest rise in the Northwest.

We were at Millgate Fields on the river, walking through the vast area of grasslands. Brendan suddenly started barking and bounding a few paces through the tall grass, then stopping and barking again urgently. In the distance there was a blue bench. The bench didn't used to be there, so Brendan wasn't happy. He urged me forward to investigate, following tentatively a few steps behind, effectively using me as a human shield.

It was a bench made rather crudely out of rough wood and painted sky blue, decorated with flowers and bearing the words "the forget-me-not bench" along with a series of names: Jenny, Sam, James, Laura and Alex. It seemed very poignant. Were these the names of people who had died this year of coronavirus? Or – more likely, given the youthful or juvenile appearance of the artwork – is this a group of friends who are all going their separate ways after this final Covid summer together. Are they all going to different universities, spread across the country? Is this their commemorative bench, a reminder of their friendship and the happy times they'd spent here, times that – no matter what they think now or what they promise themselves or each other – they will never see again. It just seems so sad.

Brendan – however – wasn't sad. After all the excitement he was now having a sit down.

Breaking News: Over 42,000 cases of the Indian variant have been confirmed in the UK.

<u>Saturday 12th June 2021.</u>

Breaking News: Delta variant makes up 91% of all new cases.

I sat up in bed and read Brendan the headlines. He didn't say anything, but I know he's sick of the Covid news. We both are.

Breaking News: Dr Jenny Harries: "While vaccination reduces the risk of severe disease, it does not eliminate it."

Today's juice: carrot, celery, apple and beetroot. Beetroot is a superfood, but for me it rather spoils what would otherwise be a really nice juice. It is often earthy and sometimes has an overpowering peppery taste which catches me at the back of the throat and can make me cough for hours. It's so good for you that I keep persevering with it, but as a juice ingredient I'm not a big fan.

Breaking News: The British Medical Association add their weight to the call for a delay to the 21st June end to lockdown.

Sunday 13th June 2021.

Breaking News: June 21 will no longer herald a full return to normality after Boris Johnson resigned himself to a delay of up to four weeks in lifting the remaining Covid restrictions.

Brendan wants to go out early, which is very unlike him,

so we're out on the streets at 8am. There are very few people about at this time. A lone jogger, then two Lycra-clad cyclists going for a big day out. It reminds me of Dad. Not that he ever wore Lycra, but he did love cycling when he was younger.

I watch Brendan pottering around the field. There is very little trace of his limp today.

We meet a lady with a collie, having a quiet walk. We have a brief conversation... about the weather, of course.

"Not as hot as I was expecting."

"No, but I think it'll get warmer."

"So do I!"

"*He* doesn't like it too hot, do you, boy?"

"Neither does he."

"Neither do I."

"No, I don't."

"Well, better get on."

"Nice to talk to you."

"Cheerio."

You can't buy moments like these.

Breaking News: Prime Minister "all but confirms" that the 21st June easing of

restrictions will not go ahead as planned.

According to Nicky's Covid app, there are currently 1,218 covid cases in this immediate area, up from 359 a week ago.

Breaking News: Scientists warn that more than 40,000 people could die this summer as the Delta variant sweeps through the country.

Monday 14th June 2021.

If you're suffering from pain, exhaustion, a smothering sense of hopelessness, chronic lethargy, sleeplessness, a deep-seated dissatisfaction it could be indicative of a psycho-social malaise... or it could just be that it's a Monday.

This particular Monday is much cooler. (Unforecast.) There are some light showers. (Unforecast.) I suggest we go to Alderley Edge. Brendan suggests we go to the field. We go to the field; I can't be putting up with the sulking.

The Prime Minister has announced that lockdown will continue for another four weeks. The new

"Freedom Day" will be 19th July. The only restrictions though are social distancing and masks, and nightclubs can't open. It's not exactly causing a hardship to most people.

Tuesday 15th June 2021.

I had a terrible night's sleep. I have decided to look into hypnotherapy, but I haven't got a lot of faith in it.

I decided I'd do an internet search when we got back from the field. By a huge coincidence, while Brendan and Remus were wrestling and Annie was cheerleading, I was speaking to one of the regular dog men at the field, Dougie's dad. He mentioned that he used to have terrible trouble getting to sleep, so he went to a hypnotist and it was very successful. He said he had trouble switching his mind off at night. I agreed. He said he was quite a stressed person. He really doesn't give that out; he comes across as one of the most relaxed and jovial people I've ever met. But then people seem to think I'm calm and relaxed (I'm not!) and that Brendan's really laid back (He's *really* not!) Clearly you can't judge a book by its cover. Speaking for myself, I suppose I'm like a swan. A swan that likes a cup of tea and a cake. I'm gliding along, looking sedate and calm, but under the surface I'm paddling like mad. Brendan *isn't* like a swan. He refuses to swim.

(UPDATE: I eventually DID go for a hypnotherapy session. I paid a substantial sum of money and then spent an hour listening to the "hypnotherapist" complaining about how bad his life was. After the session, perhaps not surprisingly, I still couldn't sleep.)

Breaking News: 19th July is "Terminus Date" for Covid rules. Only an "unprecedented and remarkable" change could derail it.

Wednesday 16th June 2021.

It's gone really hot. Dangerously hot. It's so hot that for most of the time I have no socks on. My socks have the days of the week on, so without them I'm in a wilderness without days.

With socks securely in place, we go for a walk in the fields by the river. The grasslands are up to my chest and I'm well over six foot tall. They are waving majestically in the warm breeze. Brendan is tunnelling through the stalks, trying to make himself a cool nest.

We can't sit still for long. The sun is high overhead, blazing down. We lurch from one patch of shade to another. A small group of students pass us. Two girls remark:

"Ah, he's gorgeous."

"Angelic!"

There's a chance they're talking about Brendan. But he isn't being very angelic. He starts growling at them. The girls squeal and giggle, while the boys pretend they aren't intimidated, though they start walking considerably faster.

We pass a bench with a memorial plaque on it, which I haven't noticed before. It's for a young man who was found hanged. He was just 18. Under his name are the words: "Love, laughter, music". It's very sad.

Breaking News: UK report over 9,000 new Covid cases, the highest daily total since February.

As usual, I watch *Hancock's Half Hour* in bed. Tonight, Tony's got a bad cold. He's coughing and sneezing all over Sid James. It's like a public information film on how *not* to behave during a pandemic. At the end, Tony survives his cold, but – sadly – only for another eight years, after which "Things just seemed to go too wrong too many times."

Breaking News: UK has the highest Covid rate in Europe.

The government keep banging on incessantly about the amazing number of people who have been vaccinated. But something clearly isn't working, is it?

Thursday 17th June 2021.

I read the headlines every morning. Brendan has the right idea; he sleeps beside me and pays them no attention. I'm bored of them. I'm really bored. I'm bored of the same re-hashed stories that say absolutely nothing about the current situation, and I'm bored of the general disinformation, I'm bored of personal opinions presented as facts. Everything you read in one report is contradicted in the next one. What I'm seeing is that Covid cases in England are rising exponentially and the situation is out of control.

Breaking News: New "Delta-plus" variant may affect vaccine efficacy.

Breaking News: Covid cases "rising exponentially" in England.

Breaking News: The number of Covid cases is

doubling every 11 days.

Breaking News: 20% of hospitalised Covid patients have been "double-jabbed".

Breaking News: We have achieved herd immunity level figures, but haven't achieved herd immunity; it just isn't working.

We go to Nicky's for a pizza lunch, which is lovely, then I take Brendan for another walk along the river, where we pass a depressed heron standing on the opposite bank staring into space.

Brendan is limping occasionally, so we sit down surrounded by wild flowers. (Germander speedwell, buttercups, kidney vetch, dog rose, oxeye daisies, red campion, red clover and meadow cranesbill. Yes, I've got a guidebook.) There's a kind of soporific laziness to everything. (Not just Brendan.) Bees glide around collecting pollen. We hear lots of birds, but don't actually see any, though I do spot a butterfly, I think it's a red admiral.

After some time, I realise I've been sitting on an ants nest and my arms and legs are crawling with them. (I'll be itchy for the rest of the day.)

Despite the good forecast, it starts to rain. Again.

Breaking News: 9,055 Covid cases reported.

Today's juice: kiwi, pear, apple. A tarty and slightly dangerous juice. Mysterious, with an edge. A femme fatale of a juice.

Friday 18th June 2021.

Breaking News: Covid death rate falling. Only 11 new deaths. Covid drops to 24th leading cause of fatalities.

I took Brendan out; he weed on a few trees; he weed on a few lampposts. It's all in a day's work.

Breaking News: Tories face humiliating by-election defeat. According to senior Tory, voters think Boris is a "charlatan".

Saturday 19th June 2021.

We walked over to Nicky's flat in the late afternoon. She was just on the phone. Her mum's friend, Pam – who is in hospital with Covid – is having great difficulty breathing, so she's going to be put on a respirator. I didn't know how they worked, but she will be anaesthetised and fed via a drip. She will remain unconscious for several weeks, so it's like being put into suspended animation. It seems quite sinister and weird. Apparently, some people are kept like that for months. It's all very sci-fi.

Breaking News: New study finds Covid may lead to loss of brain tissue.

Sunday 20th June 2021.

I'm awoken by heavy rain in the night, hammering

on the window. It doesn't seem to bother Brendan at all. When I fall asleep again I have a long, convoluted nightmare about the river bursting its banks in the town centre. I awoke at 5am and lay awake. Something about the dream had unsettled me an made me think of Dad.

Apparently, it's Father's Day. Not having a father any more, it had escaped me.

Monday 21st June 2021.

It's a busy day on the British calendar today. Firstly, it's National Yoga Day. Obviously, I began the day with my daily yoga. But I did a bit extra to honour the day. Yoga – when done properly – is not only good for the body, but it balances and calms the mind. Even yoga done badly is good and is some energetic stretching. Brendan loves a spot of yoga, his favourite position being the dog stretch, obviously. He is quite partial to any lying down positions.

It's a week until my birthday, so I'm trying to do some sort of treat every day. Today I'm taking the Boy for a trip into the countryside. I know he'd much rather just go to the Field, and when it's *his* birthday he can do just that. Nicky has made me a picnic lunch with lots of treats. It's gorgeous.

Within minutes of us heading off on our day out, three cars go through blatantly red lights. Not amber, completely and utterly red. Nobody gives a shit.

At Alderley Edge, it's cool and shady, green and

beautiful. Brendan snorts and drags his feet. "It's not exactly the field, is it?" Then he spots a squirrel scampering past and gives gleeful chase and the field is quickly forgotten.

Today, apart from being National Yoga Day, it's also National Selfie Day, so we take a few selfies. Of ourselves. (None of them are very good.)

In the afternoon, the weather nosedives. It's really windy and really cold. The sun has completely gone behind a low blanket of grey cloud. We were intending to stay and observe the sunset, as it's the longest day. Is it though? Is it really? Because it doesn't feel like it. It feels like a day in November. It' so cold and wet that we head home long before dusk, but after tea we go to the Big Field to watch the sunset.

We come here because it's probably got the best views, towards the Cheshire plain in one direction and towards Manchester in the other. It's very quiet. Two runners are going around the athletic track and two boys are playing football. The sun is like liquid gold, sinking towards the horizon. Purple and red leak out into the clouds. The sun sets and it's quite spectacular.

Tuesday 22nd June 2021.

Breaking News: Prime Minister warns of "rough winter" ahead with "new horrors", but insists things are looking good for 19th July, the so-called "terminus point".

Continuing my birthday week, I'm heading into

Manchester on the tram. Our local stop is the very first, or the last – depending on which way you're heading... you could almost call it the "terminus point", but that would make far too much sense and be so much more appropriate than the government's ludicrous use of the term... but I digress. So, as the tram starts from here there are very few people on board. I'm pleased to notice everyone is wearing a mask. At the next stop though, two older women get on, one has a mask and the other doesn't. They sit right in front of me, even though the tram is still virtually empty. This is very annoying and not etiquette, just as you don't stand next to another man at a urinal unless there's no other space. I assume the woman without a mask is exempt. They start talking. Though I'm trying to read, I can't concentrate on my book.

The next time I glance up, half way through the journey, No-Mask is wearing a mask and she says: "Well, I'm really proud of everyone for wearing their masks." What a hypocrite! She wasn't wearing a mask a moment ago! "Mind you, you said you'd been on the bus and no one at all was wearing one?"

"It was the train, actually. But no one was wearing one on the bus either."

"Well, it just shows you."

I don't know exactly what it shows you, but she's probably right.

In Manchester I go in Costa and order an Americano.

"Would you like a cinnamon bun with your coffee today

for you please thank you?" asks the automaton at the till.

If I did I'd order one. I'm not the sort of person to forget to order a cake if I want one.

Signs on all the tables tell you not to sit there unless it's been cleared and sanitised, but every single table has dirty cups and plates on it and is littered with screwed-up serviettes and crumbs. I clear a space and then sanitise my hands. It isn't a great experience.

Next, I go into the Arndale Centre, where 40 per cent of the people are NOT wearing masks. (Yes, I counted.) On the way home, on the tram, there are 12 people and 4 are not wearing masks, which equates to 33%. (I was never this good at maths at school.)

I walk back from the tram. Nicky has brought Brendan to meet me. I see them approaching and can hear Nicky saying: "Who's that? Look Brendan... who's that?"

Brendan comes towards me, but it's almost like he's in slow-motion. He's overcome with excitement; he does a strange two steps forward, three steps back manoeuvre and his head is wobbling. When we finally meet, we have a lovely greeting. He's overjoyed. And I'm overjoyed. I wish I could frame these moments.

Breaking News: UK records highest number of daily Covid cases in over 4 months: over 11,600 cases and 27 deaths.

Is this a surprise to anyone at all?

<u>Wednesday 23rd June 2021.</u>

It's cold, it's breezy, it's grey, it's miserable - and it's the third week in June! Everything feels a bit bleak and miserable. I'm aware we're trapped in a dystopian novel set in the near future, the part at the beginning that will be glossed over when it's made into a film because it's not actually all that interesting.

Breaking News: New variant of concern, "Delta plus", identified in India.

It's National Pink Day. Apparently. But no one seems to have told the nation. Nicky's having trouble buying pink flowers for her mum's grave. Rosie loved pink.

Breaking News: Health Secretary: "Delta variant is 40% more transmissible.

Sometimes, at the field, when he's been interacting with another dog, Brendan will suddenly come running over to me and lean against my legs, looking up at me, as though to reassure me that I'm still his favourite (for the time being). He knows which side his bread's buttered. (It's both sides, because that's how he likes it.)

Breaking News: Number of Covid patients in hospital highest for two months.

My moustache is getting longer again, which I like, because it makes me look not like me. I think I look and feel like a different person, but then after all that's happened recently, I am a different person. I look like an insane walrus and I approve of it.

Breaking News: Chinese scientists have deleted vital data from an international database about the earliest Covid patients, that could have revealed the true origins of the virus.

Thursday 24th June 2021.

Breaking News: World Health Organisation expert: "The virus is still mutating".

It's Midsummer's Day. It's grey and gloomy, it rained earlier and it doesn't look remotely like summer – mid or otherwise. The Summer Solstice on Monday is the official start of summer, and now, three days later, we're allegedly mid-way through summer; I'm no expert at maths, but I can see that something doesn't add up there. But technically, we are almost half way through the year. Another year flying by. Another year of doing nothing and going nowhere. This can't happen again.

As I've said before, I'm absolutely NOT superstitious, but walking to the field, I can only see *one* magpie. One for sorrow. You never see one alone, they always drive around in packs. This is unheard of. Only one magpie, but a dozen or more wood pigeons, pecking at the grass. Brendan charges at them and they take off in a flurry of wings and feathers. A few of them seem to be struggling to break free from the gravitational pull of the field. Like most of us, it looks like wood pigeons are also carrying an extra lockdown pound.

Breaking News: Dr David Nabarro of World

Health Organisation: We will have to continue social distancing as well as using vaccines "as part of our defence" against Covid.

<u>Friday 25th June 2021.</u>

Today is Take Your Dog To Work Day. Technically, I take my dog to work every day, because I work from home. Not that he helps much.

It's raining. Rain is forecast for the whole day. I leave my wet and sad-looking dog with Nicky and I go to Costa in Didsbury. There are a group of young women chatting together in an amiable manner. I had friends once: strangely they all moved out of the area. Now I don't need friends; I've got a dog.

I realise I've not really honoured Take Your Dog To Work Day, as I'm sitting in a coffee shop without him, and I'm actually working on my iPad, so I'm technically at work. If Costa accepted dogs he would be here, but they don't. It's like being in the Victorian times.

I have a quick look round the various charity shops. Charity shopping has been ruined in recent years, because of the current trend for "retro" and "vintage" goods. You used to be able to buy old crap at a relatively good price, but now old crap costs a fortune and it's cheaper to buy it new. I spot a book on dinosaurs in the pet section. Despite my bookshop tidying issues, I leave it there because it makes me smile. (Kids, dinosaurs do not generally make good pets.)

I queue to get into the Marks & Spencer Food store to

buy a sandwich. The nice female staff policing the line gives me a wide smile; even through her mask I know it's a lovely smile. "D'you mind waiting until someone comes out." she says, "Shouldn't be a minute."

She disappears inside momentarily, then reappears with a tabloid newspaper and holds it up to me. "Have you seen this?" There is a blurred photograph of the health secretary, Matt Hancock, "embracing" (their words not mine) his female aide and thus breaching Covid guidelines. The "embrace" looks like more than an embrace to me. "He's married. Three children. She's married. Three children. And *that* is *not* social distancing, is it?"

"It's not." I agree. "No."

Unfortunately, someone comes out of the shop, so I have to go in rather than stand there chatting with her. This brief exchange with this lovely woman made my day.

Saturday 26th June 2021.

Brendan's leg problem is very intermittent. When he finally got up at 9.32 this morning, I was worried he wouldn't be able to walk, but he hopped up and had no problems getting downstairs to the front door. He trotted perkily along the pavement, then suddenly seemed to react, go into a spasm, as though he'd had a seizure. He held his paw up and looked at me. I examined it and found a dried holly leaf sticking into the pad. I freed it and he scampered on happily. I then noticed all the leaves on the pavement. We're already gliding towards autumn. Of course, the seasons don't stand still. It isn't summer for three months and then it changes to autumn overnight. The process is continual; it goes on all the time, but we don't always notice it. We aren't always aware.

After a dull, grey start, it suddenly went sunny and weirdly hot. A crowd of regulars arrived. Brendan, Remus, Annie, Blossom and Dougie, along with attendant humans. Neil announced wistfully that he'd like to be a teenager again. I said I'd never want to be that young again. Sandra said she hated school. I also hated it and couldn't wait to leave. There was a point when I was in my thirties, when I suddenly felt I'd come into my ideal age. I knew who I was. It was quite empowering. I suddenly understood life; all the pieces fell into place and everything made sense. I think I'm much less certain now. Suddenly, none of the pieces fit together – they're probably from different jigsaws – and absolutely nothing makes any sense.

Breaking News: Calls for Hancock to resign or the Prime Minister to sack him.

Sunday 27th June 2021.

Looks like rain. Feels like rain. I imagine it'll rain.

Breaking News: Hancock resigns as Health Secretary after breaching social distancing rules and kissing his aide.

Matt Hancock has resigned. There was so much pressure against him, there was no way he couldn't.

He openly admitted he had let the people down. Boris Johnson said he was sorry to receive the resignation. Despite the awkwardness and the shame, Hancock has bowed out with some degree of dignity and recorded a video apology to the public which *seemed* humble and genuine, but he's gone now. That was Hancock's Half Hour. Next up, starring as Health Secretary, former chancellor Sajid Javid.

<u>Monday 28th June 2021.</u>

It's a Monday. But not just any old Monday. It's my birthday. I'd rather save them up until I can have my *ideal* birthday, which would involve going on holiday, but apparently I can't. So, I've started the day with a box of goodies from Nicky. And we're going for a day out. I've not yet decided where. The weather is grey and suspect.

We end up at the little church we went to a few weeks ago, because it isn't very far at all, but it feels like the bucolic depths of the countryside. It was strangely still, there was no movement in the trees at all, despite being at the top of a hill and very exposed. It was almost like a film set. We sat on a bench having our lovely picnic that Nicky had (again) made, when a local came along. After Brendan had finished barking at him, the man stopped and chatted. It turns out he knew Nicky's family, who had lived in the area. He was a red-faced country type, thickly accented like a BBC yokel, and full of ancient wisdom, like: "Best say nothing, know what I mean? A still tongue in a wise head, that's the way." and "As me dad used to say, 'When you wake up in the morning, if you can get out of bed, you're a millionaire.'" Classic country common sense.

Brendan enjoyed his day, sitting down for several hours. His limp was completely absent. Even when he stood up.

In the evening we got a Chinese. Obviously. I got lots of presents. Brendan thoughtfully gave me a dog seatbelt and a collapsible, lightweight travelling dog water bowl and a dog treat tin. He buys great gifts. Nicky gave me a huge pile of brilliant presents, including a weather station (expect more weather reports!) and enough chocolate and sweet things to cause serious injury to someone less dedicated than me. It was a great day.

Tuesday 29th June 2021.

Breaking News: Tens of thousands defy Covid rules after Matt Hancock's affair.

Erm... Breaking News... tens of thousands were defying Covid rules anyway and continue to do so.

Wednesday 30th June 2021.

Brendan's leg isn't so good today. He's limping very badly a lot of the time and it seems that his front legs are painful when he first stands up. He's generally very lazy, but he seems worn out all the time. It's like he's aged several years in a matter of weeks. But it's not constant, sometimes he doesn't limp and seems absolutely fine. All the dogs at the field have pulled muscles at one time or another, Remus, Annie, Daisy, little Evie. It took them quite a few weeks to heal, but I'm thinking it's getting beyond that now.

I phone the vets to ask what their policy is at the moment. You can't accompany your animal inside, which greatly concerns me, as Brendan panics and if he feels threatened, he can be aggressive. It's irrelevant anyway, as they have no appointments in the near future and there is quite a waiting list. Instead, I order a canine food supplement, a powder that you sprinkle on the dog's regular food. You are guaranteed to see startling results, or you get your money back. It's horrendously expensive.

Breaking News: Daily UK Covid cases highest since January.

Brendan was quiet all afternoon and quite inactive, but in the evening, we went back to the little church. It was Nicky's idea. She made another picnic. It was mild and sunny, but there were dark clouds and a steady breeze. It was quite stunning. We should do more of this. Brendan was inexplicably back to full power and his leg was perfect. He was very affectionate. And he seemed to travel well. It was a lovely evening.

Thursday 1st July 2021.

Breaking News: 80% of hospitalised Covid patients develop a neurological condition.

July the first. A new month. It's a hot and sunny day, but also breezy at times and with cloudy spells. By the way, I'm loving my new weather station. Daytime temperatures are ranging from 21 to 22 degrees C. In case you're interested, humidity is around the 45 mark. (But I'm not sure how humidity works and need to research it.)

Breaking News: Covid cases are surging in nearly every area of England. The Northeast has the highest rate, followed by the Northwest.

I'm trying to limit Brendan's walks to rest his leg, so we don't go to the field at the usual times; as a result, we don't encounter any of the usual crew. Because of this I don't see anyone at all. I don't speak to a single person. Brendan is the only one I talk to all day.

Breaking News: The Queen voices concern over climate change and says we must "change our ways".

Friday 2nd July 2021.

I did my yoga this morning. I missed yesterday. It was surprising how much I'd started to seize up in just 24 hours.

I dropped Brendan at Nicky's and left him looking very miserable, lying on the sofa surrounded by treats and toys, but ignoring all of them, while he worked at making me feel guilty. And I *did* feel guilty, but not guilty enough to abort my plans, because the lure of a bag of Co-op custard doughnuts will keep the guilt at bay for a while. I went into Costa in Didsbury, along with my secreted doughnuts. As it's still officially part of my birthday period, I had a medium – not small –

Americano. Well, you only live once. My new healthy eating, raw food and wholefood regime begins next week. Not perpetually next week, like the average diet, but actually on Monday.

Breaking News: 7,125 more Coronavirus cases in UK.

Nicky came for tea, we had curry. Again. It was gorgeous. She's been doing Covid "Lateral Flow Tests" for some time and has been encouraging me to do the same. With her help I finally did my first one today. It's a home kit for Covid, along the lines of a pregnancy test, but you don't wee on it. You take a swab from the back of your mouth, right at the back, it's not comfortable and it makes you gag. Then you take a swab from up one nostril; right up, it's not pleasant at all and it made me sneeze, and then my nose ran for an hour. You shake the swab in some liquid and then put two drops onto a tester, like a sort of thermometer. It will show you if you are carrying Covid. Thankfully, I wasn't. I notice the kits are made in China. But then again – apparently – so was the coronavirus.

Breaking News: So far there have been 153,000 Covid-related UK deaths.

Brendan's new food supplement powder has arrived. It's a green-grey colour and smells awful. It was no surprise when he refused to eat his food with it on. I had to disguise it in a lot of margarine, and then he ate it, but begrudgingly, as though he was doing me a big favour.

Saturday 3rd July 2021.

There is much controversy about the potential axing of face masks, and much contradiction.

Breaking News: The British Medical Association insist that keeping protective measures is "crucial" to stop spiralling Covid numbers having a "devastating impact".

Breaking News: Face masks may remain after 19th July Freedom Day due to Covid surge fears.

Breaking News: Poll reveals more than half of Brits want all face coverings to go.

Breaking News: Poll reveals more than half of Brits want face coverings to stay.

Breaking News: A *Times* poll reveals over half UK citizens will continue to wear masks even if not required to by law.

Sunday 4th July 2021.

Breaking News: Expert warns new "mutant strain" will hit UK soon.

So, it's American Independence Day. It's a still, grey day at the moment and I'm not feeling particularly independent. But then, I'm not American.

Breaking News: Cases of Delta variant up 46% on last week. Delta accounts for 95% of all UK coronavirus cases.

It's cool at the field and very quiet. Until Neil from next door arrives with Annie. Annie wafts across the grass and pointedly ignores Brendan, but he's too busy staring into space to notice he's being snubbed.

Neil gets his phone out and starts jiggling with his weather app, trying to upstage my weather station. He predicts we'll be having rain shortly, at which point I can feel occasional drops on my head. We set off for home, with the rain getting steadily heavier. We're lucky; when we get home it comes down seriously. I sit down with a cup of tea and watch it for a few minutes from my double windows, while Brendan has a nap; ignoring people can be exhausting.

At one point the rain gets so heavy, I can barely see the apple tree and it sounds like someone is shaking maracas. Brendan sits up and looks at the window, then looks at me, to ensure I'm in control and capable of protecting him from the downpour. Reassured, he flops down again and continues his sleep.

Breaking News: Despite expert advice to the contrary, mask wearing and social distancing to end on 19th July.

The newly appointed Health Secretary, Sajid Javid – replacing disgraced Matt Hancock – has made it clear that he wants a return to normality as soon as possible, despite the elevated infection rate.

Breaking News: Health Secretary, Sajid Javid says "we have to be honest about the fact" that without masks and social distancing measures Covid cases will rise significantly.

People are saying that the government have surrendered to Covid, that they have abandoned the people. There is currently global criticism for this government and general disagreement about abandoning masks and social distancing.

Breaking News: Professor Adam Finn, from the government's own Joint Committee on Vaccination and Immunisation says mask wearing is extremely valuable and he will continue to wear his.

Perhaps it's just a fluke, but Brendan hasn't limped at all today and he definitely has more energy. Can this really be the miracle food supplement acting already? It's *really* expensive, but I'm sure it's having a positive effect. I was starting to get very worried about him. I thought perhaps it was his age and that he'd just continue going downhill, but he's gone from acting like an eight-year-old to a six-and-a-half-year-old. It's amazing.

Monday 5th July 2021.

Breaking News: Health Secretary, Sajid Javid: "We must learn to live with Covid, as we

already do with flu".

I am sick of this diary now. I am sick of having to read the endless contradictory news stories. I'm sick of the situation. As of yesterday, the government have announced they are abandoning face masks and all forms of social distancing. They are saying people need to be responsible and make their own choices, but people *aren't* responsible, if they were, we wouldn't need a government, we'd all be self-governing.

The coronavirus hit when there was a Conservative government in power. At first, I actually thought they were handling it moderately well. It has since transpired that mistakes were made all along the way, some stupid gaffs and delays in closing borders, slow reactions and so on. This was a freak scenario and there was a lot of guessing. But as time has gone on, there have been revelations about the government being incompetent, unprofessional and self-serving. (UPDATE: Over time, there will be many more damning revelations about the government!)

Breaking News: British Medical Association: "It makes no sense to remove restrictions in their entirety".

Breaking News: Government determined to axe all restrictions on 19th July, despite advice to the contrary from experts, and in spite of the huge number of Covid cases.

Breaking News: Public Health expert,

Professor Robert West likens removing all Covid safety measures to removing all road safety rules. "Absolutely bonkers".

Breaking News: Trade Union says plan to scrap masks on public transport as Covid cases still rising is "negligent".

Breaking News: Labour's Jamie Driscoll: "We can't leave it to personal choice as to whether people wear face masks. We wouldn't make obeying the speed limit a personal choice. The point of a face mask is that you're protecting other people not just yourself."

Breaking News: Unlocking to go ahead despite rise in infections.

Breaking News: Scientists warn that an end to social distancing could result in a more transmissible and totally vaccine-resistant variant emerging.

Breaking News: Boris Johnson tells public to "learn to live" with Covid.

Breaking News: Labour leader, Sir Keir Starmer brands the Prime Minister "reckless".

Breaking News: Boris Johnson: "We must reconcile ourselves, sadly, to more deaths from Covid."

Breaking News: Rushing Roulette. Boris Johnson's eagerness to unlock is a callous gamble with the lives of the public.

Breaking News: "Boris Johnson surrenders to Covid. He should never be forgiven."

Wednesday 7th July 2021.

Breaking News: Nobel medical laureate warns: In ditching Covid restrictions, the UK risk making a vaccine-resistant Covid variant.

It was an all-male dog walking day today. This doesn't happen very often. I'm talking about the humans, in dog terms there were two males and two females. Everyone had a grey or greying beard. And I was the youngest, by quite a few years. That seldom happens now.

I learnt today that Chris has a motorbike with a sidecar and he sometimes takes his dog, Dougie, out for a ride – and he loves it. I can't see Brendan liking that at all. The other Chris makes mandolins in his shed as a hobby. Of course, everyone has a life, a history and aspirations, but we generally only get to see the dog-side to the people at the field. Today was filled with revelations.

Breaking News: UK quietly sneaks out vaccine warnings: "Pfizer and Moderna vaccines may cause heart damage", without any formal announcement.

Whilst Nicky was here for tea, England played Denmark as part of Euro 2020, which was delayed from last year by lockdown. We didn't watch it, but later on I heard raucous, drunken shouting. It was happy shouting, so I assumed England had won.

Breaking News: England beat Denmark 2:1 in an extra time thriller and secure a place in the Euro "2020" final. Our first major tournament for 55 years.

Thursday 8th July 2021.

I've come to dread looking at the headlines and every day my resistance to checking the news increases, because it very rarely says anything I want to hear and I end up quite stressed. At the moment, it seems a monkey in a wig could run the country better than the prime minister.

There is a buzz about last night's football result. England beat Denmark and will now go on to play Italy in the Euro 2020 final. I'm reliably informed that football's coming home.

Breaking News: Global death toll surpasses 4 million.

In the afternoon, I sit in the garden reading, so Brendan can have a sit down on the lawn. There is a loud thud beside me. An apple has fallen off the tree and thunked into the grass. Brendan reacts, surprised. He gets up and comes to investigate. He snorts around in the grass and undergrowth, and actually locates the offending apple. He picks it up and carries it to where he was sitting. For a few minutes he examines it thoroughly. It looks like he's going to eat it. I promise him a fiver if he'll take just one bite, but he gives up. Instead, he starts barking at the neighbour's cats sitting on the windowsill, so we have to go in.

Today's juice: Kiwi, pear and apple. Thick and tantalisingly tarty. A promiscuous juice.

Breaking News: Over 100 international scientists sign a letter accusing the government of conducting a "dangerous and unethical experiment" over "dangerous and premature" 19th July easing, which will lead to "both acute and long-term illness" and create a "fertile ground" for vaccine-resistant Covid variants.

Friday 9th July 2021.

It's warm today and intermittently sunny. Brendan scampers along to the park with no trace of a limp and he seems to have boundless energy. He even has a bit of a play with another dog, The Other Bruno. The Other Bruno's mum is in the fenced playground, she shouts over: "Hello, Brendan-I-didn't-choose-his-name!" She means Brendan: he came with his name, but this is close enough and I don't correct her.

We also meet Neil and Annie, setting off very late for their walk, Jack Russell Bob and Next Door Bruno.

Brendan interacts with all of them, so I'm very impressed with him. He spends some time sniffing the hedge, sniffing relentlessly. Can it really be that interesting?

Breaking News: Delta variant is re-infecting people who have already had Covid-19.

It hasn't been a good week. I feel like I've got cabin fever. I feel trapped and restless and agitated. It's mainly down to the weather, because it's too hot for Brendan outside, so we're having to stay in and try and keep cool. Because of the heat, the usual dog walkers haven't been sticking to their routines, so we haven't seen Remus or any of the others for some time. Also, Brendan became virtually lame and for a few days the car was in the garage, so we had no transport. We have really felt like prisoners.

Today's juice: apple, carrot, celery and Chinese leaf. Nice. A sensible juice. It won't offend anyone, but it won't thrill anyone either.

Sunday 11th July 2021.

Breaking News: Manchester's Mayor, Andy Burnham, has warned that 19th July could turn into "Anxiety Day" and argues that face covering should remain enforced by law.

Last night was a loud and raucous night. There seemed to be several parties at neighbouring houses and throughout the small hours there was chanting and shouting. It sounded like people were having their football celebration parties a day early, perhaps because of having to go to work on Monday morning. Though I'm sure there will be a lot of people phoning in sick, whether England win or not.

Despite all the noise, Brendan slept soundly. At one time he would have been terrified, but generally – as long as he's in his beloved flat – he feels secure.

Nicky reports that her Covid app states there are 1629 cases locally and it is climbing all the time.

I've just done my lateral flow test. It makes me cough and makes my eyes water, but it isn't too bad. I'm doing it several times a week.

Breaking News: The Government – in a partial U-turn – now claims people will still be "expected" to wear masks in public places, even though it will no longer be a legal requirement.

We watched the football at Nicky's. England v Italy. Italy played very well in the second half. It was 1:1, then England lost on a penalty shoot-out. Still, it was a really good match. England came second, they got silver, that's quite an achievement.

When I headed home with Brendan, there was a lot of chanting and fireworks. We also passed a number of lone men in England shirts, walking slowly home looking very depressed. I felt disappointed, but not devastated. Once at home, though, I felt wired and in no mood for sleep. Brendan disagreed. He went straight to bed, straight to sleep.

Monday 12th July 2021.

Breaking News: Introducing the Lambda Variant. Even more lethal than Delta.

It's a dull day. I'm sure the nation will be low today after so much mounting excitement, so much tension, so much anticipation, so much anti-climax. I'm sure a lot of people have booked the day off and are probably wishing they'd gone in to work.

Breaking News: Since the pandemic began, there have been 5.1 million Covid cases reported in the UK and more than 128,000 deaths.

In the afternoon it was raining heavily. I sat on the settee next to Brendan and I watched the rain, against the backdrop of trees, listening to it hammering against the leaves. I always think when I see rain on TV, I'd love to sit inside and look out at the weather, but then I never do it because it seems such a waste of time, but today I did, because I could. So there.

Breaking News:Dr David Nabarro of the World Health Organisation has been critical of the British government's abandonment of masks and social distancing. "This dangerous virus hasn't gone away. Its variants are coming back and are threatening those who have already been vaccinated – we have to take it seriously."

And yet, it is today announced:

Breaking News: Despite huge global opposition, the Prime Minister confirms Freedom Day will go ahead on 19th July, bringing an end to masks and social distancing and the reopening of the final businesses, including night clubs.

Tuesday 13th July 2021.

It's overcast and breezy, dull and grey. I drive to the supermarket in town for my big monthly shop. On the way down I have the radio on, by accident actually, but it holds my attention because the two presenters are talking about Covid and Freedom Day.

"So, what do you think about the government proposals then?" one of the presenters asks cheerily.

"Well," comes the smooth reply, "The government advice is confusing. Surely, it's either masks or it's not masks... and leaving it to public choice is just being foolhardy."

They might be speaking in slightly cheesy, bright and breezy DJ tones, but I have to agree with their sentiment.

Breaking News: USA warn of a rare nerve syndrome linked to the Johnson and Johnson Covid vaccine.

Brendan waiting (in vain) for the pub to open.
Either that or he's using it as an excuse to have a sit down.

Thursday 15th July 2021.

Breaking News: Scientists accuse PM of "criminal" mass infection plan.

It's a cold day. A grey day. There is no sun at all, though a heatwave is promised for later. I had planned that we would go for a day out to Alderley Edge, but we both feel so tired. However, we shake ourselves out of our torpor and go anyway. We walk amongst the trees, Brendan sniffs at the ground and wees on everything. We're both feeling sluggish and I'm really cold. We end up sitting in the car, just to try and get warm.

In the afternoon, the heatwave arrives as promised. It's searingly hot when not in the shade. We sit under a tree for a very long time, with a view in the distance of the bare east Cheshire hills. Me and my dog, sitting together in the sunshine, enjoying the moment.

Breaking News: UK records highest daily Covid infection figures since January.

I watched the first episode of the 1970s TV series, *Survivors*, written by Terry "Daleks" Nation. It is painfully slow, there are long conversations of clunky, tedious exposition and everyone is so terribly-terribly middle-class and very unlikeable. If the pacing was doubled it could be classed as slow. I enjoy classic television from yesteryear, when they took time to build characters and set a scene, but I don't like this. The premise is simple enough; a virus has been released by the Chinese. (Typecasting, eh?) It wipes out huge numbers of people globally. It sounds eerily familiar. They say that truth is stranger than fiction, but actually truth *is* fiction. Or rather, fiction is the truth.

<u>Friday 16th July 2021.</u>

I take Brendan for a walk along the river. It's a pleasant, sunny morning and everything seems so quintessentially English. We sit in a field and the nearby church bells start ringing, not particularly tunefully and not particularly in time, but I assume it's a practice session. As the minutes pass, they become increasingly discordant and slightly frenzied.

We relax beneath a blue sky, surrounded by greenery, with the trees alive with birds, which – bizarrely – are mainly parakeets rather than sparrows and blackbirds, so it sounds more like a jungle and quintessentially *un*-English.

I don't know whether Brendan's picking up new habits, but there's a cigarette butt beside him and I'm sure it wasn't there a moment ago.

We carry on walking and meet a woman with a "no touch" dog. (Her expression, not mine.) Her dog approaches people to say hello and the woman bellows: "Don't touch him! He's a 'no touch' dog!" She says it's to protect her from Covid, because she's allergic to the vaccine. "From Monday, when lockdown ends, I'm resigned to a life of isolation... which isn't such a problem now, as I tend to like people less and less."

I heartily concur. She walks on and encounters other people. I repeatedly hear her yelling: "Don't touch him! He's a 'no touch' dog!"

I'm having quite a few disagreements with Brendan today. He's "got one on him" as my dad would say. He is doing the polar opposite of whatever I say. If I stand up, he sits down. If I sit down, he jogs on. It quickly becomes very annoying. But then I look at him, at his wise brown eyes and I feel guilty for being cross with him. I text Nicky and explain my exasperation. She texts back: "You feel GUILTY! What do you feel guilty for? For over-spoiling him?!" She's got a point.

When we get home, I check the weather station. At 4pm the temperature is 24.5 degrees outside. The heat remains fairly constant throughout the night and is unbearable. Not that sleep is easy to come by anyway.

Several neighbouring houses are having loud, raucous garden parties. At one, a group of children are singing pop hits from the past, including Abbas *Chiquitita.* Ah, angelic, you might think. But be warned, apparently, not all angels can sing. Sing a new song, chiquititas.

Midnight comes and goes. There are no signs of the parties coming to an end. As the hours wear on, they become more raucous and alcohol-fuelled. Brendan barks repeatedly. Presumably, these are pre-Freedom Day celebrations and are not technically legal until Monday.

Breaking News: Boris Johnson says worst of pandemic over but there are "difficult days ahead".

Saturday 17th July 2021.

Breaking News: England's chief medical officer, Professor Chris Whitty concedes that the number of people in hospital with Covid is doubling every three weeks. "We could get into trouble again surprisingly fast."

It's sunny and warm. Well, hot really. There have been weather warnings. At the field, the dog people and their dogs are all standing in the shade cast by the tall trees. The dogs lie down panting. So do some of the people. Neil from next door is lying on the grass, covered with sweat and complaining of his third hangover in three days. According to my maths, that averages out at one a day. He keeps getting them because he keeps drinking too much; it's not rocket science, though it might be rocket fuel.

Today, little Blossom is let off her lead for the first time. She wanders a bit, but never strays very far from her mum and dad. I wonder how Brendan will react to her now she's at liberty. He has a sniff then treats her like everyone else: he ignores her. As long as Blossom abides by his rules when accessing his field, there won't be any problem.

Breaking News: Police fear "Freedom Day" will bring a summer of "endless New Year's Eves".

I do a lateral flow test which comes back negative. Unlike Health Secretary, Sajid Javid, who has tested positive. Many people laugh when they mention this. Most people think it's some sort of Karmic justice.

Breaking News: 1,200 global scientists warn that Boris Johnson is pursuing a Covid policy of mass infection that poses "danger to the world" and is "unscientific and unethical".

Sunday 18th July 2021.

In the night I had a nightmare, something to do with an old church and ghosts or an evil presence. Brendan was there in spirit… maybe it was him haunting me… but not physically, but I knew he was close by. And he was in reality; he was hogging the bed. I was jolted from this nightmare, thankfully, by my laptop on my desk, suddenly playing music. The lid was down so it was in sleep mode, so this wasn't even possible, but at 1.30am a voice suddenly and tunefully asked me if I wanted to start a revolution. Well, although I think a revolution is in order, I won't be starting one at this time in the morning.

We're at the field before 8am and it was Brendan's idea. He's seen the weather report and knows it's going to be another unbearably hot day. At present, the air is clean and fresh, cool, not yet super-heated, as will happen before long. The field is covered with dew. And a detritus of bottles and cans.

Nobody comes to the field, because it's too early for the regulars. It makes me think about all the people who have disappeared, who no longer come here, like the young woman who liked cats, Sarah, who I used to bump into a lot, and Man With Old Alsatian, and Weird Jogger; he's a jogger and he's weird. There are a host of others, but I've already forgotten them. We'll probably never know what happened to them.

It keeps slipping my mind, but technically, this is the last day of lockdown. The very last day. Nicky texts over today's report from her Covid app. There are 2300 active cases in the local area, which is up 405 since last week. This doesn't seem such a good time to remove the last remaining Covid protocols.

Breaking News: Observer newspaper slates "incompetent" Prime Minister and "inexperienced" Health Secretary: "Johnson's rank unfitness for office is evident."

We sit in the gardens of Nicky's flats on Dad's

deckchairs. It's sunny and warm and the birds are singing. Brendan is being particularly contrary today. It's a shared garden, so he needs to sit close to us and we won't allow him to sit where he wants to, which is a short bus ride away, not under our watchful gazes. He is called back when he tries to slink off and is getting into a huffy mood. After much slinking and calling and huffing from everyone involved, Brendan selects the furthest possible place to station himself within the permitted area, which means he is sitting with his back to us, with his face against the ivy-covered garden fence. It looks peevish and ridiculous.

"God, look at him!" Nicky tuts and rolls her eyes. "You can tell he's *your* dog!"

Nicky has a call about her mum's friend, Pam, who is in hospital on a ventilator. It now seems her condition has deteriorated. The hospital has decided she isn't going to survive and the ventilator is going to be switched off, probably today. This is contrary to the last call, when they believed she was doing well. Nicky is very sad; it is another link with her mum coming to an end.

Breaking News: From nurses to shop staff, the public are *not* looking forward to restrictions being lifted.

While Nicky makes tea, I take Brendan for a short walk and we sit in the church yard near my dad's flat. This place has so many memories. I sit on the bench in the graveyard and Brendan sits on the grass beside me. We both seem to be in a melancholic mood, or rather, the air seems imbued with melancholy; I don't think it's actually coming from us. It's dusk, the light is fading and the darkness is drawing in over the trees, the church tower and the rooftops. In the distance, the sun sinks over central Manchester; it's a beautiful, golden spectacle, and yet there is so much sadness. The daylight and – I suddenly realise – the last hours of lockdown ebb away.

Breaking News: In 2019, 41% of the population owned a pet. Due to lockdown, in 2021 this figure has risen to 59%.

Monday 19th July 2021.

Breaking News: COVID WARNING: UK heading for the "biggest wave of infections ever seen".

It's Freedom Day. Ironically, I feel more imprisoned today than I have done since the pandemic started. I awoke after a nightmare. I get nightmares all the time now, and I never used to. I could actually remember this one and the feeling of terror it instilled. I was in a forest, but it was more like a studio set. The trees were just straight boughs, I wasn't aware of any canopy of leaves above. There were three people, I wasn't aware of their gender, I'm not sure whether I was one of them or just an observer. They were all dressed the same, in what looked like a red or purple uniform. They were clutching on to each other, as though in terror. There was a wind, but it was sudden, like the blast from a bomb. They looked into the distance, between the trees, and reacted in fear. A voice formed all around them, a whispered voice. "There's a storm ahead." Though the voice was calm, it was terrifying. I immediately awoke, covered in sweat, heart pounding. I felt tense and panicked. Even some time later, I was left feeling disturbed and unsettled.

Breaking News: UK records highest Covid cases in a single day since January.

This is the last (regular) day of my lockdown diary, because we are technically no longer in lockdown and besides, it's got to finish somewhere... it can't go on forever, even though the coronavirus is very likely to do just that.

When the pandemic started, I had some degree of faith in this government's handling of the affair. That faith has now completely and utterly ended. At this very moment – the Prime Minister is self-isolating because he has been in contact with a Covid-infected person, but he is *only* self-isolating under duress, because the nation erupted with criticism at his decision *not* to self-isolate. This fairly accurately sums up his entire attitude to the pandemic.

This morning, we're heading out at 7am, because Brendan is too hot. It's 25.5 degrees inside with the curtains shut and he's pacing and staring at me, tongue lolling out, panting. This first walk will possibly be the best thing about the day. It is certainly Brendan's favourite walk. He never wants it to end, or rather he never wants sitting down at the field to end.

Nicky texts to say she's on her way to Tesco. She says she's nervous, because she doesn't know how she'll feel now that masks have gone. She texts back a short while later, saying that every shopper is wearing a mask. It looks – fingers crossed – like the English people are taking it into their own hands to protect themselves and others, seeing as we are in the grip of a pandemic, something that the government has failed to grasp.

When we get home it's 26.5 degrees in the flat. It's so hot that Brendan stretches out on the bed and doesn't move. Oh wait, that's normal.

Breaking News: Supermarkets face backlash from shoppers: staff are failing to wear masks.

In the afternoon, I ask Brendan if he wants to go and sit at the field, but he's too hot to answer. I know he'd love to sit at the field, but only if I bring the field to him, so we sit in the garden instead. It's too hot, even in the shade of the apple tree. It's actually slightly cooler inside, because the curtains are closed, so after an hour we retreat back to our gloomily dark and still over-hot prison. We're no longer in lockdown, but we're still choosing – out of necessity – to stay inside.

All day the news features photographs of people in pubs and public places, crushed together, laughing, hugging, kissing. No wonder the virus is spreading.

Rosie's friend, Pam, died today in hospital after complications following Covid-19. Her daughter was with her at the time.

Rosie's friend, Pam

(19th July 2021)

Breaking News: Met Office issue first ever extreme heat warning amid scorching conditions across UK.

It's apparently been the hottest day of the year so far. At 8.30pm it's still 27.5 degrees outside, but it's gone dull and overcast; the sun is hidden behind clouds, so we head to the field. The grass smells like hay. We sit for nearly an hour and then head home. We pass a woman in the middle of the road; I can't see her face as she's bending down. She's trying to pick something up and she's talking to it. Even without seeing her face, I realise it's Sarah, the young woman who likes animals, who I haven't seen for over a year.

"Sarah?" I say tentatively.

She stands up and turns to me, surprised. For a moment she seems uncertain, then she smiles and says hello. She's picked up a bee from the road and is transporting it to safety.

"I thought you were dead!" I tell her. It's not my best opening line to a conversation.

"No." she says, quite unnecessarily. "I've just been really busy. I found a new place to volunteer with animals, so I've been out all the time."

We chat for a few minutes, until Brendan refuses to wait any more and sets off for home. We leave Sarah trying to find the perfect bush on which to install her bee friend.

Our day comes to an end. I go to bed, lying on the top of the duvet with my boy in our airless room. He keeps raising his head and looking at me accusingly, as though I'm in charge of the world's thermostat. But I'm not in control. On a wider scale, neither is anyone.

This is me signing off. This is Freedom Day ending. And this is our diary ending.

Breaking News: Nearly 40,000 new Covid cases recorded on so-called "Freedom day".

AFTERWORD/AFTERMATH/
EPILOGUE/EPITAPH

Once upon a time, the world was in a bit of a mess....
But then the coronavirus Covid-19 arrived and it got a
whole lot worse...

Since I stopped writing my diary a lot has changed.
The main thing is that after "Freedom Day" Covid
has stopped being a headline news story. Overnight,
it just... *stopped*. I don't mean Covid-19 itself abated,
because it certainly didn't, but suddenly – inexplicably
– the coronavirus was no longer big news. It just
dropped from the news radar. My online news feed has
gone from having perhaps twenty Covid headlines per
day, to having one occasionally, but usually there is no
mention of it at all. Either there is an intentional news
blackout on the subject, or the media and the public are
no longer interested in it.

Covid might have left the mainstream news, but it has
far from left the country or the planet. Infection figures
dipped and then rose again. They are currently still
rising. People are going about their business as normal,
fewer and fewer people are wearing masks, despite
the infection-rate still soaring, people are still being
hospitalised and people are still dying.

Studies have shown that the public respond to a
national crisis according to the urgency instilled in
them by the government. The UK government appear
to be trying to pretend that nothing is wrong, so
accordingly, people are assuming nothing is wrong.

Because Covid is no longer being widely reported – you really have to search for the information – most people probably think we're free of it. Fewer and fewer people are taking any precautions, so infections are climbing.

Breaking News: World Health Organisation: "Covid is a test and the world is failing".

The original intention of this account was to try and look for the small positives in every day, no matter how terrible things might be. That wasn't always possible, but I tried my best and I often succeeded. I wrote a lot every day; I wrote pages and pages. This diary is a considerably edited-down version, to give a flavour of our lockdown life and our routine. We packed a lot into every day, but after a while, we were packing a lot of exactly the same into every day. It's easy to fall into a routine. Brendan loves a routine; I claim that I don't, but there is something very reassuring in repetition. And sometimes, in times of great stress, upheaval and upset – of which we had plenty – you rely on a routine to keep you going.

Despite my plans, I didn't read any great books and I didn't watch many classic films. But I took up daily yoga, began making juice every day and I even gave up alcohol and haven't touched any since. I can't say I feel very much better for it, but I certainly don't feel any worse.

One of my main lockdown tasks was to try and train Brendan. I only require obedience for health and safety, to stop him getting lost, injured or killed. When there is no danger, he can be as wilful and expressive as he likes.

I soon gave up on my attempts at training and decided he was untrainable. That seems to be the point at which he decided he would, on occasion, become obedient. He's so contrary, but as I keep saying, I believe we all get the dog we deserve.

The day after my diary ended, tragically Remus died. He had an incurable liver problem and was put to sleep. Brendan loved Remus – in his own way. Remus was his most consistent canine friend. He is very much missed at the field. I don't think Brendan will ever have another friend quite like him.

Breaking News: Covid cases in England are 26 times higher than this time last year.

The Covid situation is currently worsening on a daily basis and there are rumours of a further lockdown. That in itself doesn't bother me, as lockdown life has – in many ways – come to feel normal, as though this is our real life now and what went before is actually the surreal part.

The first lockdown was a frightening time, no one knew what was going to happen or where it would end. And they still don't. I started out trying to look for the positive in every situation. Then our personal situation got immeasurablyworse. Still, I tried to cling desperately to anything good, or even slightly less terrible. We've had two funerals during this period; sometimes terrible is all there is.

If it wasn't for Brendan, some days I wouldn't have seen or spoken to a soul. Brendan lit up every day in some way, by running towards me at the field, by glancing at me and smiling, by looking at me with concern, or by making a heart-warming comment or telling a joke. His most important gift to me was just being here, by my side.

Breaking News: World Health Organisation warns "World faces going back to square one" as more Covid variants emerge.

Breaking News: Vaccines alone will not beat Covid.

Breaking News: End of July: after several days lull, UK Covid cases have again started to rise.

Breaking News: Britain's daily Covid cases rising exponentially.

Breaking News: Health leaders warn "NHS is as stretched now as it was at the height of the pandemic".

Breaking News: Daily cases rise above 28,000.

Breaking News: Scientists warn UK faces thousands of Covid deaths every year.

Breaking News: A survey suggests that 34,000 UK children are suffering from Long Covid.

Breaking News: Protection from Covid jab wanes within 6 months.

Breaking News: Covid returns to the Top 10 causes of death in England.

Breaking News: August: UK recording highest rates of Covid as Third Wave picks up pace.

Breaking News: Scientists warn UK "Worst is still to come"...

Breaking News: Omicron: New variant suspected of being immune to vaccine. Masks and social distancing to return.

Breaking News: Leaked! 10 Downing Street had a Christmas party last year amidst Covid restrictions.

Breaking News: Calls for Boris Johnson to resign.

Breaking News: Cases of Omicron doubling every 2 days.

Breaking News: Huge increase in Omicron cases threatens to overwhelm NHS.

Breaking News: Christmas 2021: UK reports more than 106,000 Covid cases in new daily record.

2023 AFTERWORD

It's not been easy reading and editing this account. This isn't a book I wanted to write... and it's the type of book I never want to have to write again. It was supposed to be a positive diary and it certainly starts in that vein, but then our world began collapsing around us and it had nothing to do with Covid, as terrible tragedies occurred in our lives.

Talking to people about the Covid pandemic, most tend to view lockdown as a demarcation point; there was Before Lockdown, During Lockdown and After Lockdown. Most people seem to feel they were robbed of three years. It was a very surreal experience. Looking back, with the amazing power of hindsight, virtually every protocol that was put in place was wrong, ineffective, pointless or just plain stupid. But nobody knew at the time.

Opinions about Covid and lockdown have changed dramatically over the past couple of years, as more data has come to light, more statistics have been revealed and more research has been collated. In a nutshell, most experts now believe there was no need for the hysteria, no need for lockdowns, no need for vaccinations – except in the case of the elderly or infirm – because the vaccines have ensured that the virus mutated and that's why it's still with us.

I have recently read several books about the pandemic and about lockdown with a view to writing an in-depth afterword to close this book, about what was done wrong, the disinformation and the cover-ups. In the end I decided it was a minefield and *Dog Days* didn't need it, as it is a personal account of the experience. The information is out there for anyone who cares to read about it.

Bringing us up to date, after this diary ended the Covid situation remained and indeed escalated, but as I've said, it was no longer headline news. It was like the world had been reconditioned in the night, because people stopped speaking about it, as though the coronavirus had gone, but it hadn't. Today, March 2023, Covid is alive and well and still killing people. A new variant is in circulation. It looks like Covid-19, as predicted by many, is like 'flu and is here to stay.

The country is currently in a mess. More pressing though, there is a full-scale war raging between the Ukraine and Russia, which constantly threatens to escalate into a nuclear exchange, so things are grim. As during lockdown, despite everything that's wrong with the country and indeed the world, when I'm walking with Brendan and watching him trotting along and sniffing with gusto, nothing seems all that bad.

THE END?

BREAKING NEWS: COVID FIGURES INCREASING... AVERAGE UK DEATHS 110 DAILY... COVID RATES IN YOUNG

ADULTS HIT RECORD LEVELS... 24TH AUGUST UK RECORDS 174 COVID DEATHS & OVER 30,000 NEW CASES... TOURISTS URGED TO AVOID CORNWALL AS CASES RISE ALARMINGLY... THE RE-OPENING OF SCHOOLS THIS WEEK LIKELY TO TRIGGER FURTHER COVID RISES... POSSIBLE RE-INTRODUCTION OF SOCIAL RESTRICTIONS... WARNING: COVID CONDITIONS WILL WORSEN OVER WINTER... UK RECORDS OVER 35,000 NEW CASES... 207 MORE UK COVID-RELATED DEATHS... 16/17-YEAR-OLDS TO BE OFFERED VACCINE... COVID CAUSING HAVOC WITH NHS... OVER 219 MILLION COVID CASES GLOBALLY... OVER 4,550,000 DEATHS WORLDWIDE... GOVERNMENT PUSHING FOR 12-15 YEAR OLDS TO BE JABBED, AGAINST EXPERT ADVICE... DEATH RATE CLIMBING: 668 UK COVID DEATHS THIS WEEK... TALK OF OCTOBER LOCKDOWN TO "PROTECT THE NHS"... COVID PATIENTS IN UK HOSPITALS CLIMB TO OVER 8000... UK COVID DEATH TOLL RISES 18% IN A WEEK... OVER 38,000 NEW UK CASES REGISTERED IN 24 HOURS... MORE LOCKDOWNS RUMOURED FOR AUTUMN & WINTER... BETA VARIANT CAN "ESCAPE" VACCINE... DEATHRATE STILL RISING... HOSPITALS INUNDATED... SHORTAGES... COVID CASES INCREASE... WORSE DAY SINCE... UNEMPLOYMENT... COVID VARIANTS... LOCKDOWN IMMINENT... RETURN OF SOCIAL DISTANCING... PM "DEAD SET" AGAINST FURTHER LOCKDOWNS... 158,000 COVID-RELATED DEATHS... ECONOMIC COLLAPSE... INCREASE IN HOSPITAL CASES... PM ADMITS THINGS NOW WORSE... ADVISORS WARN 2000-5000 PEOPLE A DAY COULD BE HOSPITALISED... FOOD SHORTAGES: EMPTY SHELVES... PLANS NEEDED TO PREVENT WINTER DISASTER... FUEL PRICES TO SKYROCKET... NO LORRY DRIVERS... PETROL SHORTAGE: PRICES TO SOAR... FUEL COMPANIES GOING BANKRUPT... SHORTAGE OF CARBON DIOXIDE AFFECTS FOOD PRODUCTION... SAFEGUARD WATER: RESERVOIRS DANGEROUSLY LOW... MID-SEPTEMBER: COVID DEATHS BREACH 1,000 PER WEEK... FOURTH DEADLY COVID WAVE FEARED... FOURTH COVID WAVE IS HERE... CHRONIC SHORTAGE OF LORRY & TANKER DRIVERS, AFFECTING UK LIFE... SCIENTISTS WARN UK "WORST IS STILL TO COME"... PM UNDER FIRE OVER DAMNING REPORT INTO THE GOVERNMENT'S HANDLING OF THE PANDEMIC... OCTOBER 2021: HUGE INCREASE IN COVID CASES AS WINTER GETS A HOLD... THE FUTURE LOOKS BLEAK... UK DAILY INFECTIONS

SURGE TO OVER 50,000... ARMY ASKED TO ASSIST DUE TO NHS STAFF SHORTAGES... SCIENTISTS URGE PUBLIC TO WORK FROM HOME... COVID CASES RISE.... FEWER WEARING MASKS... 50,000 NEW CASES... COVID IS BACK WITH A VENGEANCE... (TO BE CONTINUED...)

DEDICATION

This book is dedicated to the memory of
Brendan's granddad, known to me as Dad
and to Nicky's mum, Rosie
and to the beautiful Pixie.
And to all those who died during this time.

Acknowledgements

Gray and Brendan would like to thank our
remaining family, Nicky and Hector –

with all our love.

ALSO FROM GRAY FREEMAN

UNDERDOGS: how a man and a street dog form an unbreakable bond and a lifechanging friendship.

This is a book about a friendship between two people – except one of them is a dog. Together they were more than the sum of their parts. They embarked upon a journey of discovery around Britain: a life-changing tour which would ensure that they either stayed together forever... or never spoke again.

Underdogs is funny, light-hearted, sometimes poignant, often heart-warming. It is about a journey and about over-coming adversity.

It is about the challenges of adopting a damaged soul and the joys of spending every day with your best friend. Brendan crept into Gray's life when he most needed him, changed it around to suit himself and then had a nap.

ALSO FROM GRAY FREEMAN

underdogs III:
LIFE IN THE OLD DOG YET

TRAVELS WITH AN OLDER DOG

Gray Freeman
with Brendan Freedog

ONE MAN, ONE DOG, ONE VAN – NONE OF THEM AS YOUNG AS THEY USED TO BE.

Who doesn't love holidays?
Who doesn't love the English Lake District?
Who doesn't enjoy strolling around the countryside?
The answer to all these questions is BRENDAN.

THE UNDERDOGS EXPLORE THE LAKE DISTRICT AND LEAVE NO SCONE UNTURNED

The underdogs head north to the stunning Lake District and visit all 16 lakes – with their usual brand of hard-hitting investigative journalism and sitting down. They venture into the most remote valleys and the hidden corners... and have a rest.

Travelling with an older dog can be difficult and restricting. Travelling with a lazy dog who's missing his fix of daytime TV can be even more challenging. There are trials, there are tribulations, there is freak weather and there is lemon cake. It's fair to say that nothing goes according to plan, but ultimately, this is the story of two best friends enjoying their time together and trying to appreciate every moment, whilst being either scorched in a freak heatwave or battered by a cyclone.

ALSO FROM GRAY FREEMAN

the underdog

TRAVELS BEFORE BRENDAN
The Prequel to underdogs

THE RIVETINGLY EXCITING PREQUEL TO underdogs

Gray Freeman sets off in a van on a voyage of self-discovery - to fulfil a dream and travel around the coast of Britain. Without a dog! What was he thinking?

The plan was to see hidden corners of Britain and to explore remote coastlines, clifftops and forgotten byways, backwaters and other places that haven't yet been used to build shopping malls.

This was to be a life-changing experience, but not everything went according to plan.

The underdog is travel writing, but it is humorous and accessible, light-hearted and quirky. It is a celebration of travel, a love letter to the British coast.

This was to be the journey of a lifetime – and this is where it all began.

ALSO FROM GRAY FREEMAN

NOTHING IS AS IT SEEMS.

The Long Goodbye was a play. It was staged twice in Manchester. People laughed, people cried, people said how much they could relate to it. You will also be able to relate to it. It is funny, tragic and touching; it leaves a lasting impression.

YOU WAKE UP AND A WHOLE NEW LIFE HAS BEEN WRITTEN FOR YOU – A LIFE YOU KNOW MUST BE A LIE.

The Long Goodbye made a humorous, moving and memorable piece of theatre, and here it is presented as a "reading script" – between a script and a novel. It is accessible, at times laugh-out-loud funny and also deeply poignant. On the page it doesn't lose any of its humour or haunting impact.

EVERYTHING IS BIZARRE AND SURREAL, LIKE A 'SIXTIES TV SHOW. YOUR LIFE IS A PRISON; YOU ARE THE PRISONER.

Printed in Great Britain
by Amazon